D1247093

AMERICAN ARCHITECTS
AND THEIR BOOKS TO 1848

FRONTISPIECE Portrait of John Haviland by John Neagle, 1825. The Philadelphia architect holds a volume of James Stuart and Nicholas Revett's *Antiquities of Athens* (1762–1816). The Metropolitan Museum of Art, Alfred N. Punnett Fund, 1938 (38.82). All rights reserved, The Metropolitan Museum of Art.

AMERICAN ARCHITECTS
AND THEIR BOOKS TO 1848

Edited by Kenneth Hafertepe
and James F. O'Gorman

UNIVERSITY OF MASSACHUSETTS PRESS

Amherst

Copyright © 2001 by
University of Massachusetts Press
All rights reserved

Printed in the United States of America
LC 00-065569
ISBN 1-55849-282-8
Set in Adobe Caslon
Designed by Milenda Nan Ok Lee
Printed and bound by Sheridan Books, Inc.

Library of Congress Cataloging-in-Publication Data

American architects and their books to 1848 / edited by Kenneth Hafertepe and James F. O'Gorman.
p. cm. — (Studies in print culture and the history of the book)
Includes bibliographical references.
ISBN 1-55849-282-8 (cloth : alk. paper)
1. Architecture—United States. 2. Architecture, Modern—17th–18th centuries—United States.
3. Architecture, Modern—19th century—United States. 4. Architectural writing—United States—
History. 5. Communication in architecture—United States—History. I. Hafertepe, Kenneth, 1955–
II. O'Gorman, James F. III. Series.

NA707 .A47 2001
720′.973—dc21
00-065569

British Library Cataloguing in Publication data are available.

This book is published with the support and cooperation of the University of Massachusetts Boston and
with the financial assistance of Historic Deerfield, Inc., the Grace Slack McNeil Program in the History
of American Art at Wellesley College, and Williams College.

To
William H. Pierson Jr.,
dean of historians of American architecture
and
to the memory of
Robert L. Alexander,
who was to join us

CONTENTS

ILLUSTRATIONS

INTRODUCTION:

ARCHITECTS AND BOOKS

*Architectural ideas fly on literary wings. Since the Renaissance in Italy, books and, to a some-*what lesser extent, drawings have been primary vehicles of communication between architects and architects as well as architects and their public. This is true now, and it was especially true in this country's early years—during, that is, the period that forms the focus of the following essays.

John Neagle's 1825 portrait of John Haviland (frontispiece), which hangs in the Metropolitan Museum of Art, New York, records the fact. It shows the Philadelphia-based architect seated in front of a rendered perspective of his Medieval Revival Eastern State Penitentiary, holding one of the four volumes of James Stuart and Nicholas Revett's celebrated *Antiquities of Athens* (1762–1816), a publication accountable for the details of untold numbers of American buildings in the early nineteenth century. The portrait is a personal document, but it also pictures a then recently emerged type, the professional architect, and can be seen as an advertising display that shows off his skills as designer and draftsman and his credentials as a student of architectural history and classical theory. Haviland drew inspiration for buildings such as those he created in Philadelphia and elsewhere from books—such as Stuart and Revett's—which formed his own professional library or awaited his perusal in other collections. So did his peers.

It was during the late eighteenth and early nineteenth centuries that architects separated themselves from amateur designers, on the one hand, and from carpenters and masons, on the other. Among the attributes of this new professional class were the ability to draw—especially, eye-catching views of proposed buildings—and possession of or access to a substantial reference library that included the publications of the Italian, French, English, and—eventually—Anglo-American masters. In the period covered by these essays a client would have expected the architect to draw his designs from the precedent communicated by his books. In the eighteenth century, book learning acted as a mark of the gentleman designer; in the nineteenth, the library—like the present license of the lawyer, doctor, or architect displayed on an office wall—became one badge of the owner's qualification to undertake the work to be commissioned (figure INTR. 1).

It is the underlying assumption of the contributors to this volume—as it is of its editors, who were the conveners of the 1997 Deerfield-Wellesley Symposium on American Culture where these essays were first presented—that architects' books, including ones they own, ones they know of, and ones they write, are an integral part of the study of the history of building.

The following essays, then, are concerned with various aspects of the ownership, authorship, and usership of books by architects (and some others) during the period in which the profession emerged, and this gathering should prove valuable for historians of the book as well as of architecture. The authors of the present collection do not only consider books owned by or known to late eighteenth- and early nineteenth-century architectural designers. Nor are they principally concerned with cataloguing various examples of specific building details cribbed from specific pattern books, although that is a part of their work. The collective aim is larger. The authors have applied a broad definition to the category of architectural books, and they have studied not only books read but books written by early American architects. The 1997 Deerfield-Wellesley Symposium on American Culture, which this publication commemorates, coincided with the two-hundredth anniversary of the appearance at Greenfield, Massachusetts— just seven miles north of Deerfield—of Asher Benjamin's *Country Builder's Assistant,* the first book on architecture written by an Anglo-American. The papers there presented and here published range from studies of English books available in the colonies and early republic through the appearance of American architectural incunabula to the revolution in architectural publishing that occurred in the 1830s and 1840s.

These discussions of book collecting and book publishing demonstrate, as do other studies of this period, that the transition from colonial building practices to architectural professionalism was not a neatly chronological one. It began with the books and

FIG INTR. 1 Carpenter-turned-architect Aaron Morse (1806–49) of Concord, N.H., had himself daguerre-otyped in the 1840s with the signifiers of his new profession: drafting instruments and an open book. Courtesy of the Collection of William H. Skerritt; photo courtesy of the Society for the Preservation of New England Antiquities, Boston.

libraries available to eighteenth-century artisans and amateurs, craftsmen and gentle-men. Abbott Lowell Cummings summarizes his own half-century study of the archi-tectural publications available in New England, based on surviving libraries, probate inventories, documentary references, and books with inscribed owner's signatures, as well as the comparison of building details to published sources. He adds new titles and new insights to the existing standard references listed by Helen Park and Janice Schimmelman and points out that there is still much to be learned by further research.

Bennie Brown does the same for Virginia, although the well-known societal, economic, and other differences between the South and New England require him to take a separate approach. Drawing on wide documentary evidence, he reveals not only the variety of architectural and related books available in the colony but the clear distinction between the large handsome folios of design theory that graced the shelves of gentlemen's libraries and the smaller volumes of constructive information used by artisans on the job. Thus, the second William Byrd's Westover contained a large collection of Vitruvius, Scamozzi, Wotton, Felebien, Moxon, and others, as well as a few more practical works, but the architectural details of Westover itself cannot be traced to these tomes. Craftsmen's books, as Brown writes, apparently influenced the design of the house more than did Byrd's "largely academic" collection.

Two amateur designers, George Washington and Thomas Jefferson, hold prime positions in the history of Virginia architecture in the eighteenth century. Robert Dalzell focuses on Washington's Mount Vernon, remodeled at the beginning of the Revolution, as a "personal declaration of independence." Just as work on T. U. Walter's dome at the U.S. Capitol continued throughout the Civil War and thus became a symbol of federal unity, so Washington continued to fret about his dining room chimneypiece after assuming command of the Continental Army: the work at Mount Vernon provided a measure of stability during a disruptive time. But ironically, if understandably, the sources for the design of that chimneypiece, as for other details of the house, were English—either English architectural books or other American houses reflecting the same dependence on English sources. This fact reveals both the state of architecture in English North America at the time of the Revolution and the primarily English composition of the architectural libraries either owned by or accessible to the gentleman designer.

The most extensive eighteenth- and early nineteenth-century architectural library now known was that of Thomas Jefferson. This was, as Richard Guy Wilson writes, in fact a series of six libraries owned by Jefferson at various times or in various places, including his "library of the mind." Jefferson not only avidly collected books but catalogued his collection, listing volumes from those of antiquity to practical publications. Palladio, as is well known, was Jefferson's favorite author; well known too is the amateur designer's reliance on books, "out of which he fishes everything" according to Benjamin Henry Latrobe. In the twentieth century, imitation in architecture was long condemned, but standards in Jefferson's time were set by history. He relished his book-learned understanding of correct design and proudly noted the sources of motifs on his drawings. Monticello, Poplar Forest, the University of Virginia all show the marks of an architectural scholar. But Jefferson not only received; he gave forth. In his one book, *Notes on the State of Virginia,* he extended his vision beyond building, as Wilson says, to "passionate descriptions of America's natural scenery" and thereby helped "to establish an appreciation of landscape as a major motif" in American art and architecture.

Washington and Jefferson were gentlemen amateurs. With the coming of the new century the architectural profession emerged. Martha J. McNamara defines the Architectural Library of Boston, founded in 1809, as a semipublic "social library" set up to help promote the goals of architects "eager to define themselves as a profession." The initial catalogue listed fifty-five volumes on architecture and what used to be called its allied arts. Such a collection, housed in its own room, not only brought architects together but "gave both the books and the act of reading them a privileged aura." Like most of the social libraries founded in the early nineteenth century in Boston, it did not last beyond midcentury. (Could this have been because by then so many other, larger specialized libraries existed, or because by then the concept of architectural professionalism had been largely accepted?) In its heyday, however, the library represented "a body of knowledge to be mastered and a more elusive quality—taste—which would distinguish professional architects both from their clients and from other builders."

One of the users of Boston's social libraries was Charles Bulfinch. If Washington and Jefferson exemplify the eighteenth-century, book-collecting gentleman designer, Bulfinch represents a transitional period between the amateur and the professional architect. He sold his designs to others, but he also earned his keep as a public, political figure until his move to Washington at the age of fifty-four. James F. O'Gorman adds many titles to the list of Bulfinch's previously catalogued sources. We have long known of the volumes from his library which are housed at the Massachusetts Institute of Technology and listed in Harold Kirker's standard work. Using unstudied documentary evidence such as his book orders, his patronage of publications, his recommendation for volumes to be added to the Library of Congress, and notes on his drawings (like Jefferson, he proudly recorded his sources), O'Gorman broadens our knowledge of Bulfinch's professional perusal which, he suggests, points to a personality richer than we have heretofore been led to believe. He owned, used, or knew of works on Greek architecture, perspective, engineering, city planning, and landscape which must now be consulted by future scholars of Bulfinch's life.

Benjamin Henry Latrobe, who arrived in the United States in 1796, is often cited as

our first professional architect. As a draftsman he was head and shoulders above anyone else working in the country, and he is known from the researches of Jeffrey A.
Cohen and others to have possessed a fine book collection. This seems to have been
"one of the largest professional architectural libraries in this country" before Ithiel
Town's, so its dispersal is a major loss to history. Using collateral documents, however,
Cohen is able to reconstruct much of Latrobe's library by inference and so suggest the
range of his reading and his opinions of many books.

Latrobe's near contemporary and Bulfinch's principal New England follower was
Asher Benjamin. Although Jefferson's *Notes on the State of Virginia* contains some com-
mentary on the state of its buildings, Benjamin was the author of the first Anglo-
American architectural publication, *The Country Builder's Assistant* of 1797. Kenneth
Hafertepe puts that remarkable achievement (Benjamin was in his mid-twenties at the
time) into biographical, architectural, and literary context. The result is a vivid evoca-
tion of the laying of the cornerstone of American architectural publishing. Although
a work still aimed at the builder rather than the professional architect, Benjamin's little
picture book spawned the generic New England meetinghouse and influenced architecture as far as the Western Reserve. It also heralded a succession of other building
books, as Americans, no longer content to rely on their English and Continental forebears, began to produce their own works by adapting foreign designs to American conditions.

Owen Biddle's *Young Carpenter's Assistant* appeared in Philadelphia in 1805. As Michael J. Lewis points out, this was "the second work of architectural instruction written
and published in the United States." Biddle, like Benjamin, began his career as a house
carpenter. Their books, marking a change in the history of American architecture,
were milestones along the halting march leading to the professional class of architects
which emerged in the nineteenth century. Although Biddle—who died in his early
thirties, a year after the publication of his book—taught architectural drawing (as,
apparently, did Benjamin), he never fully abandoned the ranks of the builders, the
ranks from whom came his chief subscribers. As Lewis writes, he aimed to instruct
"men like himself: that is . . . Biddles rather than Latrobes—carpenters who could
devise serviceable designs, and could communicate them effectively by graphic means."
Benjamin's book showed finished designs; Biddle's showed how to draft a design; but
both addressed the builder. As Lewis observes, it is "remarkable how enduring and
adaptable the country's builder architects remained" in the face of the mounting professionalism introduced by Benjamin Henry Latrobe. Biddle's book continued to be
useful for a generation: John Haviland—whose own *Builder's Assistant* appeared in

1818–21—put out a new edition in 1833. Lewis concludes that Benjamin and Biddle's books were "nothing less than the beginning of a national architectural culture."

Damie Stillman surveys the first half of the nineteenth century in New York City, the period and place in which American architecture—or at least architectural publishing—came of age. Following John McComb Jr.—who, like Benjamin and Biddle, relied on English pattern books for his education and who catalogued his own library—came local architects such as Minard Lafever and Alexander Jackson Davis, who published their own influential books. Lafever produced five works in the second quarter of the century. They were derivative, but they were also popular and carried abroad that updated Neoclassical mode known broadly as the Greek Revival. Davis's *Rural Residences* adapted the English Picturesque cottage to the American landscape and greatly influenced the work of A. J. Downing, whose own books marked a revolution in American architectural publishing.

The last two essays describe works that signal a shift in the direction of early American architectural books and so bring our period to a close. Charles B. Wood III shifts from the book as a source of design ideas to "the American architectural book as object, as cultural icon." He compares Andrew Jackson Downing's *Treatise on the Theory and Practice of Landscape Gardening* of 1841 with Asher Benjamin's *Practical House Carpenter* in an edition of the same year to differentiate a "house pattern book" from a "builder's guide." A major distinction was one of readership: Downing addressed the client; Benjamin (and other earlier American authors), the builder. By thoroughly applying the methods of the emerging study of the history of the book, Wood demonstrates the differences in the production of the two works and emphasizes the revolutionary character of Downing's publication. Downing broadened the market for architectural publication at the same time that he changed the ground rules for architectural presentation. In all aspects Benjamin's work represented the past, Downing's the future, of architectural design and architectural communication. Architectural writers thenceforth would address consumers "from a growing middle class concerned with taste."

Although the gentlemen designers, master builders, and professional architects whose libraries and publications we explore were de facto historians in that they derived their rules from admired buildings of the past, it was only in 1848 that Louisa Tuthill produced the first American narrative of architectural history. Some authors had included brief histories, often cribbed from English or other sources, in the books they aimed at builders and designers, but Tuthill was the first to address a broader audience. Her book, like Downing's, marks a turning point in American architectural publishing. Tuthill was not herself an architect, but she had access to the most extensive architectural library remaining in private hands after Jefferson sold his books to the Library of Congress in 1815 and Latrobe's were dispersed after his death in 1820. By the end of the 1830s the architect Ithiel Town of New Haven and New York had amassed a renowned collection that approached 11,000 volumes, not to mention prints and antiquities, and it was easily available to the educated public. In Town's library, writes Sarah Allaback, "Louisa Tuthill found the 'history of architecture from the earliest times' and, with it, a path to good taste and ethical living." In her book, architecture assumed its nineteenth-century moralistic dimension, for like Downing, she aimed to make it a subject of importance far beyond the profession. Although women in general did not become architects until the next century, Tuthill at the end of the 1840s directed them to a subject worthy of their attention. From an arcane science of interest to gentlemen in the eighteenth century, architecture became in these writers' hands a subject of universal consequence.

The present collection not only suggests the richness of the subject but demonstrates the varieties of application possible from this kind of research. Although different essays treat related material, each author takes an independent approach. None of the essays is definitive: this is ongoing research. Our purpose will be fulfilled if the volume acts as stimulus and guide to future scholars of the history of architecture and the history of the book. The mid-nineteenth century saw the dawn of a new era in both building and books, one we may perhaps explore at another Deerfield-Wellesley symposium.

KENNETH HAFERTEPE
JAMES F. O'GORMAN
Deerfield, Massachusetts

AMERICAN ARCHITECTS
AND THEIR BOOKS TO 1848

I

THE AVAILABILITY OF
ARCHITECTURAL BOOKS IN
EIGHTEENTH-CENTURY NEW ENGLAND

Abbott Lowell Cummings

*The two most important American works of the last half-century which deal with the accessi-*bility of architectural books during the eighteenth century are Helen Park's *List of Architectural Books Available in America before the Revolution* and Janice Schimmelman's *Architectural Treatises and Building Handbooks Available in American Libraries and Bookstores through 1800.* Both authors used more or less the same set of sources—including institutional libraries, booksellers' catalogues, and newspaper advertisements—and covered much of the East Coast. Park found a total of 106 titles, and Schimmelman added 65 more. Concerning the earlier works, Park noted that "all but four booksellers' references, in newspapers and sales catalogues, and all except five references in institutional collections occur after 1750. References increase markedly about 1760."[1] And indeed, the first advertisement that antiquarian George Francis Dow found in the Boston press was in 1754.[2]

My own list of architectural books available in New England for the years before 1800 is based on a different set of sources, including probate inventories, scattered documentary references (in correspondence, building contracts, and so forth), and the books themselves which bear an owner's signature, the whole constituting a provenance file begun about 1950. In the compilation of her work, Park included the personal library of the eighteenth-century Boston mason Thomas Dawes, which is owned by the Boston Athenaeum, and that of gentleman architect Peter Harrison of Newport,

Rhode Island, and New Haven, Connecticut, known only from a probate inventory. To these I have added a small but significant number of collections associated with other individuals.[3]

With respect to eighteenth-century probate inventories, I have canvassed thoroughly those of Suffolk County, Massachusetts, and scanned the probate resources of Essex County, Massachusetts, and New Haven County, Connecticut. I am particularly grateful to William Hosley, director of the Antiquarian & Landmarks Society, Inc., of Connecticut, who has generously shared the results of his extensive survey of Connecticut River Valley probate inventories. These have revealed several builders' inventories with two or three architectural title references each for the Hartford area alone. Needless to say, much remains to be done with this category in other areas of New England for the period extending from the mid-eighteenth into the nineteenth century.

The most difficult problem with probate inventories is the inexplicit way in which the appraisers normally listed titles. Peter Harrison's inventory of 1775 is a good example. Despite the sanguine efforts of Harrison's biographer, Carl Bridenbaugh, to identify the brief, telegraphic descriptions found in that document, a fully cautious evaluation of the twenty-nine entries seems to permit positive identification of only six titles; for his assumptions with respect to nine additional items Bridenbaugh is probably on safe ground; but each of the remaining fourteen entries, including seven references to the writings of William Halfpenny, could refer to any one of several works.[4] For most inventories we must be content with such references as "Gibbs's Book of Architecture"—almost certainly *A Book of Architecture* (1728)—in the inventory of the estate of Joseph Brown of Providence, who died in 1786.[5] Brown had earlier been a member of the building committee for the Baptist Meetinghouse in Providence, and the reference to his ownership of Gibbs takes on added interest in light of the fact that James Gibbs's *Book of Architecture* is the earliest example I have found of a specific work whose use was reported in the press: when the meetinghouse was nearing completion in 1775, the *Providence Gazette* stated that the plan of the steeple "was taken from the middle Figure in the 30th Plate of Gibbs designs."[6]

My documentary references represent a variety of miscellaneous manuscripts. Examples are the agreement of 13 November 1794 between Oliver Phelps of Suffield, Connecticut, and his builder, Ashbel King, under the terms of which King was "to Rusticate Eight large Gate Posts in front of sd Phelps's new Dwelling House . . . agreeable to a plan or model in B[atty] Langleys Book of Artechitureship [*sic*], Letter E. plate 16"; the "Articles of agreement" dated 19 October 1803 for building the meetinghouse at Lenox, Massachusetts, which specified that "the steeple . . . [is] to be made conformable to the plan of a steeple laid down in plate No. 33 in Benjamin's Country Builders assistant"; and the often cited letter of gentleman architect Abraham Savage of Boston to Stephen Salisbury of Worcester, 13 August 1772, in which he notes that "Mr Safford [one of the builders] has [Edward] Hoppus's Book of Architecture."[7]

The books themselves, however, form the core of this study, and they are scattered far and wide in libraries, at historical societies, and in the hands of collectors or the original owners' descendants. The number of surviving libraries of individual eighteenth-century owners is miniscule. Still, to the library of Thomas Dawes of Boston we may add the fairly extensive library of Charles Bulfinch, which was begun in the eighteenth century and is now preserved at the Massachusetts Institute of Technology; architectural books owned by three generations of builders in the McIntire family of Salem, Massachusetts (of which I deal here only with those of eighteenth-century date); and the eighteenth-century beginnings of Asher Benjamin's library, which, as his life progressed, must have taken on impressive proportions. One should note also, in passing, that occasional nineteenth-century libraries, such as that of the Portland, Maine, architect John Calvin Stevens, contain a few works inherited from earlier generations—in this case, Stevens's Kimball family forebears, who began their building careers in Ipswich, Massachusetts, before migrating to Maine. Thus we find an undated edition of Abraham Swan's *British Architect* inscribed John Kimball, Ipswich, 1779, and *Pain's British Palladio* by William and James Pain in a 1797 edition, inscribed John Kimball Jr., Portland.[8]

In all categories of my provenance file, a total of 153 individual eighteenth-century books or references thereto have been found, and given the scope of the project, one may assume that many more will turn up in the course of time. Statistically, the breakdown of owners and users is as follows: fifty-four titles can be identified with "architects"; eighty-four titles are associated with master builders and building artisans; and fifteen titles were possessed by gentlemen or nonarchitectural professional persons.

For the group as a whole, the four most popular architectural authors in eighteenth-century New England (listed chronologically) appear to have been Batty Langley and Abraham Swan for the period before the Revolution, and William Pain and Asher Benjamin for the final quarter of the century. The Park list identified as "front-runners" the following works: William Salmon's *Palladio Londinensis* (1734), thirty-one references; Francis Price's *British Carpenter* (1733), twenty-seven; the *Builder's Jewel* (1741) by Batty and Thomas Langley, twenty-three, and the same number for Batty Langley's *Treasury of Designs* (1740), for a total of forty-six Langley references; Abraham Swan's *British Architect* (1745), twenty-two references; his *Collection of Designs* (1757), thirteen;

and *Designs in Carpentry* (1759) by the same author, six, for a total of forty-one Swan references.[9] Thus, Park's combined totals for the Langley and Swan titles show that our findings agree and confirm the architectural historians' long-standing impression that Langley's and Swan's were indeed the most used pattern books in New England before the Revolution.

My provenance file reveals the following breakdown with respect to Langley: five inscribed copies and two documentary references to *Treasury of Designs;* two inscribed copies and one documentary reference to *Builder's Jewel;* and five entries for other Langley items (including those imprecisely described) for a total of fifteen. Abraham Swan follows not far behind with a total of eleven entries: *Collection of Designs in Architecture,* one inscribed copy and three documentary references; *The British Architect,* two inscribed copies and one documentary reference; *Designs in Carpentry,* two inscribed copies and one documentary reference; and *Designs for Chimney Pieces* (1768), one inscribed copy.

For Park's two single front-runners, Salmon and Price, I have located only two copies of Salmon's *Palladio Londinensis, or, The London Art of Building:* a 1748 edition in the Boston Athenaeum, owned by Thomas Dawes of Boston; and a 1767 edition in the John Carter Brown Library, owned by the Providence, Rhode Island, builder, Martin Seamans. Three other references, however, can almost certainly be identified with William Salmon: "Sammon's Art of building" in Peter Harrison's inventory of 1775; the statement by Boston builder James Flagg to Robert Treat Paine of Taunton, Massachusetts, in a letter of 11 May 1772: "I now send you . . . the London Art of Building;" and the reference to "1 Salmons Art of Building" in the 1774 inventory of Joseph Gillander of Boston, "late of the Island of Dominica, Watchmaker."[10] I have found one copy only of Francis Price's *British Carpenter,* a 1765 edition owned by the McIntire family of Salem.

Following the Revolution, the works of William Pain comprise a total of fifteen items in my provenance file, including six references to the *Practical Builder* (first published in London in 1774, with a Boston reprint of 1792), and six also to the *Practical House Carpenter* (second edition published in London in 1788, with a Boston reprint of 1796). A single inscribed copy has been located for each of the three following works: *Builder's Companion* (in a 1762 edition), *Builders Pocket Treasure* (in a Boston 1794 edition), and *Carpenter's Pocket Directory* (in a Philadelphia 1797 edition). In addition there are three references to the *British Palladio* (1786) by James and William Pain; of (unrelated) James Paine's *Plans, Elevations and Sections* (1767), only a single copy has been found.

Finally, with respect to Asher Benjamin's *Country Builder's Assistant*—published first in Greenfield, Massachusetts, in 1797, with subsequent editions in 1798, 1800, and 1805—two inscribed copies of the first, eleven of the second, and three of the third edition have been located, together with one possible reference in an 1816 inventory to the item "builder's assistant."[11]

For the many other works that appear in my file in single or very small numbers, a few observations are in order. Exotic or unusual items are extremely rare, for the most part turning up in architects' libraries (of which more shortly) or, as one might expect, in the libraries of eighteenth-century American "gentlemen." The Salem merchant Ezekiel Hersey Derby, for example, owned a copy of William Wright's *Grotesque Architecture, or Rural Amusement* (London, 1790). Hersey's contemporary, the Salem lexicographer John Pickering, owned B. Seeley's *Stowe: A Description* in a London 1766 edition, and someone in or around Boston owned and donated to the Boston Architectural Library, as indicated in its 1809 catalogue, Joshua Kirby's *Perspective of Architecture* (1761).[12] It was somewhat puzzling, however, to find in the 1774 inventory of the Boston housewright John Ruggles, under the heading "Books of Architecture," the item "Horton House," valued at £4.[13] If this was the *Plans . . . of Houghton in Norfolk* by Isaac Ware, William Kent, and Thomas Ripley (1735), one would scarcely expect to find such a formal work in the hands of an artisan.

As for really early material, Park's sources revealed no references to Joseph Moxon's *Mechanick Exercises,* published serially in England beginning in 1678, but my provenance file contains at least two: "Moxon's Monthly Exercises" appears in a Boston list of books ordered from London in September 1683; and the 1727 estate inventory of the Saybrook, Connecticut, joiner Charles Gillam, lists "a book of Mechanical Exercise."[14]

Individual libraries, as noted earlier, have been of particular interest. Harrison's library is well known through his biographer, Carl Bridenbaugh, and the individual volumes owned by Thomas Dawes of Boston appear in Park's *List of Architectural Books.* One further item rounds out the list of thirteen architectural works presented to the Boston Athenaeum in 1809 by a son of Thomas Dawes, following his father's death: the Bulfinch library at the Massachusetts Institute of Technology contains volume 2 of the *Builder's Dictionary* (1734) with Dawes's signature and the date 1751. This volume contains also the bookplate of the 1809 Boston Architectural Library, but it wound up, somehow, among the books owned by Bulfinch!

Perhaps the most provocative item in the Dawes collection at the Boston Athenaeum is the London 1700 edition of Godfrey Richards's *First Book of Architecture, by Andrea Palladio.* This item was noted by Park but with no reference to provenance. It bears the signature "William Plowman His Book Octo ye 15th 1705." Considerable genealogical research has failed to place Plowman in New England, as one might wish, and unfortunately, this is one of the few Dawes items that do not bear his own signature and date of acquisition. Having been born in 1731, however, he could scarcely have come to own the item before midcentury, and one is left with little more than pure conjecture as to how and when this early work, first owned presumably in England, found its way to the New World.

For the three-generational building firm of McIntires in Salem, Massachusetts, we begin with the founder, Joseph McIntire, whose inventory of 1776 listed "5 books on Architecture."[15] The 1819 inventory of his more celebrated son, Samuel McIntire, lists "one Vol. Palladios' Architecture" at $10.00; "one [Volume] Ware's [Architecture]" at $8.00; "a Vol. of Architecture by Langley" at $2.00; "a [Volume of Architecture] by Paine" at $2.00 (McIntire's biographer, Fiske Kimball, suggests on the basis of usage that this may well have been Pain's *Practical House Carpenter*); "Dictionary of Arts & Sciences 1 Vol. folio" at $6.00; and "2 Vol. French Architecture" at $4.00.[16]

In 1852, at the administrator's sale of the estate of Joseph McIntire Jr., Samuel's nephew, "about 25 volumes of Architectural Books, some of them rare and valuable," were advertised. Identification of any of these works is an interesting exercise. Nothing has turned up so far with the signature of Joseph McIntire Sr., but two works signed Joseph McIntire (in the hand of the third member of the family to bear that name, born in 1779) are sufficiently early to have been owned by the first Joseph: Michael Hoare, *The Builder's Pocket-Companion* (London 1747 edition), and Francis Price, *The British Carpenter* (London 1765 edition). Both are now owned by the Peabody Essex Museum in Salem. Of Samuel's named books, the Langley could easily have been his father's, but speculation is useless. The two most interesting references are those to "2 Vol. French Architecture" (for which, again, we can only speculate), and the "one Vol. Palladios' Architecture," his most valuable book, appraised at $10.00. It was offered for sale after his death as "Paladia Architecture, best kind."[17] The long-established Salem Athenaeum has a maddeningly uninformative catalogue entry for a single early volume of Palladio, but the volume itself has been missing from their collections for many years.

The relatively large and impressive library of Charles Bulfinch at the Massachusetts Institute of Technology indicates that his active collecting of architectural books began well before 1800 and had earlier family foundations. A copy of Sebastien Le Clerc's *Treatise of Architecture*, writes the architect's granddaughter, Ellen Bulfinch, was not given to MIT by the family, so we do not know the date of the edition; however, it bears the signature of Bulfinch's uncle, the gentleman Charles Ward Apthorp, and the date 1759.[18] The Bulfinch library at Cambridge includes also a 1759 edition of John Miller's *Andrea Palladio's Elements of Architecture* which bears no signature. Nor can we be certain when or how Bulfinch acquired a 1638 Amsterdam edition of Jean Vredman's *L'Architecture contenant La Toscane, Dorique, Ionique, Corinthique et Composee, faict par Henri Hondius* . . .

The balance of titles published before 1800 are varied and, for the most part, progressive. I suggest two categories of acquisition: first, those titles probably acquired when Bulfinch was abroad between June 1785 and January 1787. These would include N. Wallis, *Complete Modern Joiner* (London 1783 edition); William Thomas, *Original Designs in Architecture* (London 1783 edition); *La Vignole Moderne* (Paris 1784 edition), purchased, perhaps, when he visited that city; and John Crunden, *Convenient and Ornamental Architecture* (London 1785 edition). Then, following his return, he continued to accumulate books: John Soane, *Plans, Elevations & Sections* (London 1788 edition); Soane's *Sketches in Architecture* (which Ellen Bulfinch states that her grandfather owned, though the copy is not now at MIT); John Miller, *Country Gentleman's Architect* (London 1789 edition); John Plaw, *Ferme Ornée or Rural Improvements* (London 1795 edition), and Plaw's *Rural Architecture*, which Ellen Bulfinch also says that he owned;[19] and Thomas Warton et al., *Essays on Gothic Architecture* (London 1800 edition). Additional items of architectural significance are the *New Copper Plate Magazine, or Monthly Cabinet of Picturesque Engravings* (published in London in 1792); James Malton's *Views of Dublin* (1792–95); and *Views of Bath and Bristol* (1794).

Books acquired or consulted by Asher Benjamin are of course a prime focus, though they extend my overview beyond 1800 to about 1815. The important question arises at the outset as to just when Benjamin began to build up a library (as opposed to consulting books). The evidence is clear that the influence of books on his career became profound while he was still in his early twenties. For his own *Country Builder's Assistant* of 1797, as I verified several years ago, some text was taken verbatim and details from plates taken bodily from William Pain's *Practical House Carpenter* (of which the Boston edition of 1796 was then readily available), and at least one plate was borrowed and its text copied almost verbatim from Pain's *Carpenter's Pocket Directory* (1781).[20] Pain's *Practical Builder* may have been used as well; it was, in any event, heavily relied upon in Benjamin's second work, *The American Builder's Companion* (Boston 1806).

The most unusual work Benjamin owned or consulted during his earliest years, however, was *The Carpenter's New Guide* (London 1793) by the English architectural engineer Peter Nicholson. Later in life Benjamin wrote, "In the year 1795 I made the drawings, and superintended the erection of a circular staircase in the State House, at Hartford, Connecticut; which, I believe, was the first circular rail that was ever made in New England." And he adds, "To the ingenious Peter Nicholson, of London, we are all indebted for this method. It was invented by him, and published in the year 1792."[21] Though penned at a much later period, this is the earliest date I have found referring to the presence of this Nicholson work in New England; Schimmelman found one or two references to it which might have dated as early as 1797.[22] But Nicholson was clearly not one of the popular authors among the New England building profession, and how the *Carpenter's New Guide* first came to Benjamin's attention in the upper Connecticut River Valley remains a mystery.

With respect to other books consulted by Benjamin, as revealed through his own publications, he wrote in the preface to the 1814 edition of his *American Builder's Companion,* "I am principally indebted to Sir William Chambers's incomparable Treatise on Civil Architecture" and stated further his indebtedness to "P. Nicholson's excellent books" on the subject of stairs. One important fact concerning Nicholson's works was happily uncovered in 1977 by a Boston University student of mine, Martha Coons: while Benjamin continued to lift material from the 1793 edition of Nicholson's *Carpenter's New Guide* in compiling the 1806 edition of *The American Builder's Companion*— for example, rendering of the orders, diminishing columns, and constructing groin ceilings—for the all-important section on stair building he utilized a new and updated version of that subject which Nicholson had just published in an 1805 revised edition of his *Carpenter's New Guide.*

One further reference to earlier architectural works appears in Benjamin's 1806 preface to *The American Builder's Companion:* "Old fashioned workmen, who have for many years followed the footsteps of Palladio and Langley, will, no doubt, leave their old path with great reluctance." With the mention of Langley, we come to the subject of Benjamin's own library. A few items that have been identified and appear in the provenance file raise the question of just when they were acquired. For whatever reason, they seem consistently to have been acquired later than the concrete indications of (or his stated references to) their use in his early work or published writings. A copy of the 1750 edition of Batty Langley's *Treasury of Designs,* for example, owned by the Boston Architectural Center, bears the signature of the Boston housewright Braddock Loring, the date 1799, and then the signature "A. Benjamin" and the date 1807. The most important work in this category, however, is a privately owned copy of the London 1794 edition of William Pain's *Practical House Carpenter,* the single most important influence in Benjamin's compilation of *The Country Builder's Assistant* in 1797. But the signature "A. Benjamin" and the price of $7.00 inscribed in the 1794 Pain item are unmistakably in a distinctive handwriting that Benjamin adopted about 1802. Still a third item, an undated edition of Abraham Swan's *British Architect*, recently acquired by the Peabody Essex Museum in Salem, also bears the distinctive post-1802 signature of Benjamin, as well as the stamp of the 1809 Boston Architectural Library. One might add that *The British Architect* is a work that has not been associated in any way with Benjamin's own architectural writings.

One final means of identifying the use or existence of eighteenth-century published architectural works in early New England—although this method has not figured in the compilation of my provenance file—involves those surviving architectural features which reveal unmistakably that they were copied from imported English books. One could compile a fairly extensive catalogue of examples, but in only a very few instances can the name of a known builder be associated with the English publication he undoubtedly possessed or used. The parlor chimneypiece of the Jeremiah Lee House in Marblehead, Massachusetts (figure 1.1), built during the late 1760s, is a classic example, revealing as it does the unquestioned use of plate 51 in Abraham Swan's *British Architect* (figure 1.2). Here we may come close to identification of the builder in the statement of a descendant that Jeremiah Lee's brother Samuel Lee (1714–79) "followed the business of his father [who had died in 1753], that is, he was a builder of houses and a merchant. He built the famous 'Lee mansion' at Marblehead."[23] Unsubstantiated by contemporary records, this reference to Samuel Lee's potential involvement remains little more than an interesting speculation, and regrettably, the inventory of his estate in 1780 mentions only "44 Books of Diffarant kind[s]."[24]

An equally interesting example of the use of architectural books can be found in the Piscataqua region of New Hampshire where in the mid-eighteenth-century Benning Wentworth Mansion at Little Harbor there is clear evidence again of a specific English architectural work (figure 1.3)—in this case plate 56 of Edward Hoppus's *Gentleman's and Builder's Repository*, first published about 1737 (figure 1.4). The design itself had appeared earlier as plate 64 of William Kent's *Designs of Inigo Jones* (1727), but for the period before the Revolution that highly formal and expensive work has been found only in Harrison's library. Architectural historian Rudolf Wittkower calls Hoppus an unscrupulous pirate, and the Hoppus plate would indeed seem to represent a much more logical source for the American work.[25]

James Garvin, architectural historian with the New Hampshire Division of Historical Resources at Concord, has identified nearly every builder in the Piscataqua region for the eighteenth and early nineteenth centuries. From his work we learn of several

FIG 1.1 Parlor chimneypiece, Jeremiah Lee House, Marblehead, Mass. Photo by Arthur Haskell. Courtesy of the Society for the Preservation of New England Antiquities, Boston.
FIG 1.2 (*right*) Detail from Abraham Swan, *The British Architect* (1758), plate 51.

artisans employed on Governor John Langdon's mansion, built in Portsmouth during the 1780s. One of these men clearly employed the lower portion of plate 48 of Swan's *British Architect* in his execution of the chimneypiece of the north parlor. Garvin has also shown the intertwined family relationships of these artisans: the books obviously got passed around. The 1764 inventory of William Lewis (1722–64), a Portsmouth carver, contained the item "Book Relating to the Carver Business," appraised at "£22 Old Tenor," and one would like to think, given all the circumstances, that this was Swan's *British Architect*.[26]

Yet, as noted, the unambiguous use of specific English architectural books throughout the eighteenth century seldom coincides with identifiable personalities. For example, in the late eighteenth-century Salem Town House of 1796 (built originally at Charlton but now relocated to Old Sturbridge Village) the model for the chim-

FIG 1.3 Council Chamber chimneypiece, Gov. Benning Wentworth House, Portsmouth (Little Harbor), N.H. Photo by Douglas Armsden. Courtesy of the New Hampshire Division of Historical Resources, Concord.

FIG 1.4 (*right*) Edward Hoppus, *The Gentleman's and Builder's Repository* (1737), plate 56.

neypiece of the best parlor (figure 1.5) was clearly plate 40 of William Pain's *Practical Builder* (figure 1.6), for which a Boston edition of 1792 was available. The master builder, however, remains unknown, though we have interesting evidence of the way the selective process worked as his eye (and perhaps also that of the client) moved back and forth across the median line, choosing those elements most favored for the final composition.

Finally, there is the important question of what has *not* been found, and why. An interesting case in point occurs in the work of Isaac Fitch, a Lebanon, Connecticut, builder of whom Governor Jonathan Trumbull wrote in 1785, "Mr. Fitch is the best Architect within the compass of my acquaintance . . . he is well acquainted with books of architecture. His genious is extraordinary."[27] When Fitch died in 1791, an inventory of his estate listed the three following items: "Gibbs Architecture" at twenty-four

FIG 1.5 Parlor chimneypiece, Salem Town House, originally in Charlton, Mass. Photo courtesy of Old Sturbridge Village.
FIG 1.6 (*right*) William Pain, *The Practical Builder or Workman's General Assistant* (1789), plate 40. Courtesy of the Society for the Preservation of New England Antiquities, Boston.

shillings; "1 Lectures on Architecture" at one shilling, sixpence (probably Robert Morris's *Lectures on Architecture*, second edition 1759; and "1 Book on [architecture]" at three shillings.[28] The exact nature of the last puts the question into context. Between 1784 and 1786, Fitch had built the New London courthouse, which reveals one provocative architectural surprise: an early use of the Palladian window, in which the tops of the flanking sidelights have been given a segmental profile (figure 1.7)—a concept that can be found in earlier European work.[29] But I have been able to identify an exact source for this idiosyncratic feature not in any of the usual works that circulated in New England throughout the eighteenth century but only in a single architectural work for which Park found no listing and Schimmelman found but one reference in a New York bookseller's list of 1800.[30] This is Thomas Rawlins, *Familiar Architecture* (London, 1768), a London 1795 edition of which can at least be found in the 1809 catalogue of the Boston Architectural Library.[31] The specific reference is to plate 6, a design for a house in which the treatment is confined to the frontispiece (figure 1.8). Even a casual perusal of Rawlins's work will discover at once that the content is thoroughly in character with any of a number of the eighteenth-century publications in vogue throughout New England and *ought* to have been here (though that argument admittedly carries very little weight). This final example, however, serves forcibly to illustrate the complexities of the study at large, of which, as noted earlier in connection with the provenance file, only the surface has been scratched.

NOTES

1. Helen Park, *A List of Architectural Books Available in America before the Revolution* (Los Angeles: Hennessey & Ingalls, 1973), 11; Janice Schimmelman, *Architectural Treatises and Building Handbooks Available in American Libraries and Bookstores through 1800* (Worcester, Mass.: American Antiquarian Society, 1986).

2. George Francis Dow, *The Arts and Crafts in New England, 1704–1775* (Topsfield, Mass.: Wayside Press, 1927), 221.

3. My Architectural Publications Provenance card file, which includes information on edition, ownership, and location of the individual items, will ultimately become part of the library collections of the Society for the Preservation of New England Antiquities in Boston. The society currently maintains a similar provenance file that covers primarily the period 1800 to 1900.

4. Carl Bridenbaugh, *Peter Harrison, First American Architect* (Chapel Hill: University of North Carolina Press, 1949), 168–70.

5. Providence, R. I., Probate Records, Will Book 7:12–13.

6. Quoted in Norman M. Isham, *The Meeting House of the First Baptist Church in Providence: A History of the Fabric* (Providence, R.I.: First Baptist Church, 1925), 11.

7. Phelps and Gorham Papers, box 93, New York State Library, Albany; original MS, Community Church, Lenox, Mass.; Charles H. Sawyer and Louisa Dresser, "The Salisbury Houses," *Worcester Art Museum Annual* 5 (1946): 86.

8. The entire Stevens library is now owned by the Maine Historical Society, Portland.

9. Park, *Architectural Books*, 39.

10. Bridenbaugh, *Peter Harrison*, 169; MS, Robert Treat Paine Papers, Massachusetts Historical Society, Boston; Suffolk County Probate Records, 74:229, Massachusetts State Archives, Columbia Point, Boston.

11. Luther Seymour estate, Connecticut Probate Records, Farmington District, file 2453, Connecticut State Library, Hartford.

12. The first of these three items is owned by the Boston Architectural Center, the other two by the Society for the Preservation of New England Antiquities, which also owns a rare copy of the Boston Architectural Library's constitution and catalogue, published in 1809.

13. Suffolk County Probate Records, 74:208.

14. Worthington Chauncey Ford, *The Boston Book Market, 1679–1700* (Boston: Club of Odd Volumes, 1917), 102; Ethel Hall Bjerkoe, *The Cabinetmakers of America* (Garden City, N.Y.: Doubleday, 1957), 102.

15. Essex County Probate Records, file 18108, County Courthouse, Salem, Mass.

16. Fiske Kimball, *Mr. Samuel McIntire, Carver: The Architect of Salem* (Portland, Maine: Southworth-Anthoensen Press, 1940), 23.

FIG 1.7 Courthouse, New London, Conn. Stereographic view, ca. 1870s, by Edward T. Avery's Photograph Rooms, 22 State Street, New London. Courtesy of the Society for the Preservation of New England Antiquities, Boston.

FIG 1.8 (*opposite*) Thomas Rawlins, *Familiar Architecture* (1768), plate 6.

17. Ibid., 26.

18. Ellen Susan Bulfinch, *The Life and Letters of Charles Bulfinch, Architect* (Boston: Houghton Mifflin, 1896), 83–84.

19. Ibid., 83.

20. See Abbott Lowell Cummings, "An Investigation of the Sources, Stylistic Evolution, and Influence of Asher Benjamin's Builders' Guides" (Ph.D. diss., Ohio State University, 1950).

21. Asher Benjamin, *Practice of Architecture . . .* (Boston: Benjamin B. Mussey, 1839), 93.

22. Schimmelman, *Architectural Treatises,* 399–400.

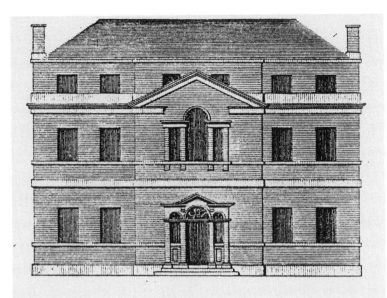

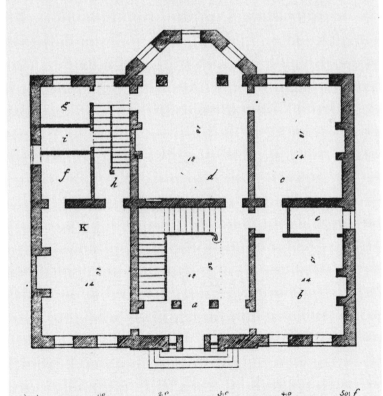

23. Thomas Amory Lee, "The Lee Family of Marblehead," *Essex Institute Historical Collections* 52 (1916): 231.

24. Essex County Probate Records, file 16650.

25. Rudolf Wittkower, *Palladio and English Palladianism* (London: Thames & Hudson, 1974), 88.

26. See James Leo Garvin, "Academic Architecture and the Building Trades in the Piscataqua Region of New Hampshire and Maine, 1715–1815" (Ph.D. diss., Boston University, 1983), esp. figs. 75–76 and p. 145.

27. Quoted in William L. Warren, *Isaac Fitch of Lebanon, Connecticut, Master Joiner, 1734–1791* (Hartford: Antiquarian & Landmarks Society, 1978), 1.

28. Connecticut Probate Records, Windham District, file 1369.

29. See, e.g., Adolf K. Placzek, James S. Ackerman, and Myra Nan Rosenfeld, *Sebastian Serlio on Domestic Architecture* (Cambridge, Mass.: MIT Press, 1978), plate 66 (palace of the French governor).

30. Schimmelman, *Architectural Treatises,* pp. 431–32.

31. *The Constitution of the Proprietors of the Architectural Library of Boston. Instituted 15th November, 1809* (Boston: T. Kennard, 1809). The Rawlins item is number twenty of a catalogue that includes fifty-five entries.

II

THE OWNERSHIP OF
ARCHITECTURE BOOKS IN COLONIAL VIRGINIA

Bennie Brown

In Virginia's first centuries, a large selection of architecture and other art-related books were present and being used. Preliminary research has identified more than one hundred titles that were available by the end of the eighteenth century, and an additional one hundred titles up to 1840.[1] The books I cite here are found in several kinds of primary sources: estate inventories and catalogues; correspondence and business ledgers; advertisements in newspapers and almanacs; and those original volumes that have survived in various collections. With so much material at hand, this essay focuses on the ownership of the architecture-based books in Virginia to the end of the eighteenth century, largely excluding Jefferson's and Washington's collections (which are presented in this collection).

In the formative days of the colony, books were quite rare and concerned more with practical than aesthetic matters. Even among the gentry, building echoed vernacular traditions of pre-Renaissance England, inflected by the frustrations and limitations of frontier life. William Fitzhugh of Stafford County filled his house with the most fashionable interior appointments, including tapestries hung from walls and a matching set of tapestry-covered chairs. Yet on the subject of architecture he asserted the precedence of practical needs in a new colony where craftsmen were scarce and had to be imported at great expense: "If you design this land to settle . . . you would build a very good house . . . the best methods to be pursued therein is, to get a Carpenter &

Bricklayer Servants, & send them to serve 4 or five years, in which time of their Service, they might reasonably build a substantial good house, at least, if not brick walls & well plaistered."[2] It should not surprise us, then, that evidence of architectural books during the colony's early days is seldom encountered.

Even eighteenth-century Virginians who invoked the name of a published architect did not necessarily own the book. A good example is Landon Carter of Sabine Hall in Richmond County, who cited Caesar's bridge over the Rhine (attributed to Vitruvius) as his source for a bridge he designed in 1770. A careful examination of Clement Edmund's translation of Caesar's *Commentaries* reveals that on the basis of unfounded tradition, Edmund attributed the design of the bridge to Vitruvius. Therefore, Landon Carter was citing the tradition that Vitruvius was architect for this project rather than owning and citing from an edition of Vitruvius's work. The largely preserved Sabine Hall library contains only one reference to an architectural book: Antoine Joseph Loriot's *Practical Essay on Cement and Artificial Stone* (1774), a title that reflects Carter's practical concerns in building.[3]

The earliest documented architectural books in the colony were adaptations and abridgments from popular European works that had been published in the decades following the Great Fire of London in 1666. A prime example is the very cryptic reference *Joachym Scughim of Architecture*. This turns out to be Vincenzo Scamozzi's *Mirror of Architecture* (1669) as translated by William Fisher from the abridged Dutch edition by Joachim Schuym. It is listed in the estate inventory of John Carter of Lancaster County in 1690 and thus has the honor of being the earliest architecture book on record in Virginia.[4] John, secretary to the colony and an important man in his own right, was the elder brother of the great Robert Carter, who was styled "King" because of his great wealth and power in Virginia politics. Robert inherited a large portion of his brother's library, which may have included this architectural volume. Unfortunately, Robert Carter's library and estate were destroyed in the fire that consumed his plantation house, Corotoman, in 1723. Scamozzi's book, if he did inherit it, seems to have been destroyed, since it does not appear in his estate inventory in 1732.[5]

Another major architectural title found in early Virginia was an edition of Palladio listed in the 1717 estate of carpenter Richard Brown, also of Lancaster County—the sole book he owned. The early date of the inventory, combined with the citation "To Andre Polados [*sic*] book of Architect . . . 11.0 [shellings]," indicates that he owned the earliest English translation of Palladio, first compiled by Godfrey Richards in 1663.[6]

In 1738 another John Carter (a son of Robert), in a letter to his brother Charles of

Cleve Plantation in King George County, made the earliest reference in the colony to the *Builder's Dictionary* of 1734. Both brothers were busily creating plantation compounds, at Cleve and at Shirley in Charles City County. At this time they were administering the estate of Mann Page for their widowed sister, Judith Carter Page, whose massive new house, Rosewell, was under construction in Gloucester County. Their interest was in gauging workmen's charges for completed work, a necessity for patrons to judge accuracy and honesty. John wrote, "If the Builder's Dictionary is at all to the purpose of your charge to the painter it makes Against you, Since in the cases Supposed the oyl [*sic*] & colours are found by the Workmen, and how much so ever You may rely on the Authority of this or the other Author . . ."[7] This reference leads one to believe that Carter was quoting not only from the 1734 *Builder's Dictionary* but also from Richard Neve's competitive *Builder's Dictionary*, the third edition of which was published in 1736.

Among various eighteenth-century estate inventories, only a handful of architectural titles have been identified, mostly practical works. Rarely would a library contain more than one title. Colonel Maximilian Boush of Princess Anne County owned a copy of William Leybourn's *Platform for Purchasers, Guide for Builders* (1668), which was listed in his estate inventory in 1728.[8] Dr. Nicholas Flood of Westmoreland County owned a copy of Neve's *Builder's Dictionary* in his extensive collection in 1776.[9] A York County resident, William Moss, listed a "Book of Architecture" in his 1772 inventory which—given its valuation at £2, was probably James Gibbs's *Book of Architecture* (1728)—a text that was both practical and aesthetic.[10] Local Williamsburg cabinetmaker, John Dickinson, owned Thomas Chippendale's *Gentleman and Cabinet-Maker's Director* (1754) as his only professional book in 1778—another book both practical and aesthetic.[11] John Parke Custis, son of Martha Custis Washington, owned a three-volume set of Colen Campbell's *Vitruvius Britannicus* (1715–25) by 1782, a major aesthetic work.[12] David Stewart of Fairfax County owned Edward Hoppus's *Practical Measuring* (1736) in 1782,[13] one of the most practical of builder's books. Other possible sources for architecture books in the colony can only be conjectured through obscure references in estate inventories such as that of another Williamsburg carpenter, Richard King, which cites the earliest examples in 1728 of "Books of Architecture" but offers no way to identify them.[14]

Several actual architectural volumes with Virginia provenance, acquired by the end of the eighteenth century, have survived. John Barloe of Haymarket in Caroline County owned Thomas Newton's English translation of Vitruvius, first published in

1771. In 1798, John Mason, merchant in Alexandria and Georgetown and son of George Mason of Gunston Hall, purchased the second edition of *Rudiments of Ancient Architecture* (1794).[15]

Advertisements in the Williamsburg-based *Virginia Gazette* for the years 1736 to 1780 mention several architectural titles. Regular advertisements for "just arrived" books in 1751 list Isaac Ware's translation of Palladio's *Four Books of Architecture* (1738), William Salmon's *Palladio Londinensis* (1734), and *Harmonic Architecture* (1741)—which may be a very obscure publication by J. Shortess.[16] Later listings advertise the *Builder's Dictionary* of 1734; *Critical Observations on the Buildings and Improvement of London* (1771); John Crunden's *Joyner and Cabinet-Maker's Darling* (1765); John Hamilton's *Stereography, or Complete Body of Perspective* (1738); William Hawney's *Compleat Measurer* (1717); Edward Noble's *Elements of Linear Perspective* (1771); James Smith's *Carpenter's Companion* (1733); and Abraham Swan's *Designs in Carpentry* (1759).[17]

Recorded sales of architecture books through the *Virginia Gazette* printing offices in Williamsburg are limited to a few titles. William Hunter sold two copies of Salmon's *Palladio Londinensis* in 1751 and also a single copy of Batty Langley's *Builder's Jewel* (1741).[18] Joseph Royle's daybook records a cryptic title, "System of Architecture £1.2.6 Sayer's Prints." This turns out to be a composite work coauthored by William and John Halfpenny, Robert Morris, and Thomas Lightoler, titled *The Modern Builder's Assistant: or System of Architecture*, which was published by Robert Sayer in 1757.[19] Among other buyers who patronized the *Virginia Gazette* printing office of John Dixon was Thomas Jefferson, who in 1778 purchased both Gibbs's *Book of Architecture* and William Kent's *Designs of Inigo Jones* (1727).[20]

George Wythe, tutor to the young Jefferson and then his law mentor, was known for his extensive legal and classical collection. His library, willed to Jefferson in 1806, was either incorporated into Jefferson's own collection or, in the case of duplicates, distributed to family members; none of Wythe's architecture books have been identified in the surviving Jefferson collection at the Library of Congress or in Jefferson's later collections. We do know that Wythe was interested in possessing a copy of Vitruvius and that Jefferson was seeking it for him in 1787 in Europe, but it seems that he was unsuccessful in finding the specific work: "The best edition of Vitruvius, which is with the commentaries by Ficinus, is not to be got here."[21] Since no such edition of Vitruvius can be identified, whatever edition Jefferson may have acquired for his mentor must have been one of the documented editions already recorded in the Jefferson library.[22]

A major source of architecture books in Virginia would have been the royal governors sent from England to administer the colony for the crown. Those who were patrons of the arts no doubt displayed the latest taste from Britain in their residential furnishings and in their private libraries. Unfortunately, the libraries that would be of importance in this study, such as that of Francis Nicholson (who designed the cities of Williamsburg and Annapolis), were rarely documented in their own time.[23]

The governor who seems to have made the most significant impact on Virginia architecture was Alexander Spotswood. The Governor's Palace in Williamsburg was completed during his tenure in 1720, and he remained in Virginia to establish Germanna, a major plantation in Orange County, near present-day Fredericksburg. He also patronized the College of William and Mary and assisted in the redesign of the main building, which had been destroyed by fire in 1705. His interest in architecture extended also to the design of the octagonal powder magazine in the center of town, and the new cruciform-plan Bruton Parish church.[24] At his death in 1740 he willed his vast library to the college. Unfortunately, a fire in 1859 destroyed most of the college collection. Only one Spotswood title survived: Jean Aimar Piganol de la Force's *Description des chateaux et parcs de Versailles* (1715).[25] Although Spotswood was reportedly more interested in the geometrical aspects of architecture than in design, his involvement extended to interior appointments and landscape gardening as expressed in de la Force's guidebook to Versailles.

Governor Francis Fauquier, who arrived in 1758, was a man of polite learning and academic pursuits whose education and interests were a major influence on the young Jefferson, then a student at William and Mary. When Fauquier died at the palace in 1768, a terse inventory lumped his library in a single entry.[26] He had been a member of the Society of the Dilettanti in London, an organization responsible for the publication of James Stuart and Nicholas Revett's *Antiquities of Athens* (1762–67); however, his name is not on the subscribers' pages. The few surviving books known to be from his library shed no light upon his artistic interests.[27]

The next governor, whose estate was recorded in 1770, was Norborne Berkeley, Baron de Botetourt. As far as we can determine, the modest library he brought to the colony did not include any significant architecture or art books. Other books he may have owned in England seem to have been few, even though he was a subscriber to Joseph Spence's *Polymetis* (1747) and Stuart and Revett's *Antiquities of Athens* (1762).[28] In addition, Lord Botetourt, along with his sister, the Duchess of Beaufort, was a patron and subscriber to a rare two-volume architectural work by Thomas Wright titled *Universal Architecture* (1755–58). This esoteric series of garden arbor and grotto designs, may have been among the "3 Books of Prints & Drawings in paste board" listed in Botetourt's palace inventory.[29]

The last royal governor, John Murray, Earl of Dunmore, administered Virginia in its final days as a royal colony, from 1771 to 1775. He brought with him (by his own estimation) a valuable estate, including a library of about 1,300 volumes.[30] Unfortunately, following his sudden departure from Williamsburg in 1775 and eventual departure from Virginia a year later, his personal estate, including the library, was sold at auction by the revolutionary government, and there is no known record of the contents. The remnants of his library that have surfaced in various private and public repositories indicate that Dunmore's evaluation of his library was accurate.[31] Through patronage by his father and himself as subscribers, he owned at least four major architectural volumes: Gibbs's *Book of Architecture* (1728); a first edition of Sir William Chambers's *Treatise on Civil Architecture* (1759); Robert Adam's *Ruins of the Palace of the Emperor Diocletian* (1764); and Batty Langley's *Ancient Architecture* (1742).[32] Whether he had them with him in Williamsburg can only be conjectured.

Several members of the local gentry had major pre-Revolution collections that merit further study. Aside from Jefferson's important library, largely acquired following the Revolution, the best architectural collections were owned by the Byrds at Westover, in Charles City County; Robert Carter of Nomini Hall, in Westmoreland County; and John Mercer of Marlborough, in Stafford County.

The largest of these was the Byrd library, which was primarily collected by the second William Byrd before 1744. In 1777, when it was advertised for sale, it numbered about 4,000 volumes.[33] William Byrd II was educated in England and spent many years there cultivating friends among the aristocrats at court. He was a member of the Royal Society and keenly interested in all forms of learning. He accompanied Sir John Percival on a tour of England as a precursor to his own later tour of the Continent; in France he visited Paris and Versailles.[34]

Byrd's wide-ranging experiences inculcated in him a European perspective on culture, remote from the stark realities of Virginia, and most of his library reflected this European viewpoint. Among some twenty-three architectural titles reflecting his English and Continental taste for the latest fashion were a series of plate books and theoretical treatises: Campbell's *Vitruvius Britannicus;* at least three editions of Palladio (especially those by Richards and Giacomo Leoni); Johannes Kip's *Britannia illustrata* (1708); Giacomo Leoni's translation of *The Architecture of Leon Battista Alberti* (1726); and Sir Henry Wotton's *Reliquiae Wottonianae; or, A Collection of Lives* (1651), which includes his *Elements of Architecture.* Byrd's French design sources included Sebastien Le Clerc's *Traité d'architecture* (1714), which is extant today; André Félibien's *Principes de l'architecture* (1676); Adam Perrelle's *Vues des belles maisons de France,* and Gabrielle Perrelle's *Vues de plus beaux endroit de Versailles,* both of seventeenth-century date; Vincenzo Scamozzi's *Cinq ordres d'architecture* (1655); and Claude Perrault's translation of Vitruvius, *Abrege des dix livres d'architecture* (1674). Italian works included Pietro Ferrerio's *Palazzi di Roma* (1655–78); Filippo de Rossi's *Ritratto di Roma Antica* (1654); Alessandro Donati's *Roma vetus ac recens* (1695), popularly called *Roma illustrata;* and Justus Lipsius's *Roma illustrata* (1645).

Byrd also owned several practical works, including two pattern books by William Halfpenny—*Practical Architecture* (1724) and *The Art of Sound Building* (1725)—as well as Nicholas Gauger's *Mechanism of Fire Made in Chimneys* (1715), Joseph Moxon's *Practical Perspective* (1677), and the only known copy of Moxon's *Mechanick Exercises* (1670) in Virginia.[35] The emphasis of Byrd's architectural collection was on illustrated books that served him as reminders of his English and European education and travels.

Westover, Byrd's mansion, was one of the most famous of the plantations in Virginia, and its layout reflected his developed tastes in architecture and furnishings. The extensive library was even housed in a separate flanking dependency. New research indicates that the present house was constructed about 1750 to replace an earlier house destroyed by fire.[36] Curiously, few details of the present house seem to have been influenced by the architecture books in Byrd's library; details that can be identified are related to architectural plates from books not in the Westover collection. Apparently the books of Byrd's craftsmen had more impact on the design of the house than his own largely academic volumes.

Robert Carter of Nomini Hall, grandson of King Carter, was a man of English upbringing and cultured tastes. His library, partially based upon his grandfather's collection, was second only to the Byrd library in size and elaboration. In 1774 its main portion, as catalogued by his plantation tutor Philip Fithian, numbered over 1,000 volumes; an additional 458 volumes were in Carter's Williamsburg house. By the end of the century, Carter had moved to Baltimore, Maryland, and at the time of his death in 1804 the library numbered about 3,000 volumes. Architectural titles included Langley's *City and Country Builder's and Workman's Treasury of Designs* (1740) and three others that survive today: Chambers's *Treatise on Civil Architecture* (third edition, 1768), Salmon's *Palladio Londinensis* (third edition, 1748), and Charles Perrault's *Parallèle des anciens et des modernes* (1688–97), whose fourth volume includes "L'Architecture, la sculpture et la peinture."[37] Carter had also acquired a copy of Chambers's *Civil*

Architecture in 1773 but must have kept it in Williamsburg, since it was not catalogued by Fithian.[38]

How Robert Carter may have utilized these volumes can only be conjectured, since Nomini Hall was destroyed in the mid-nineteenth century. Fithian left a clear record of its appearance in 1774, and Carter's letters reveal a major exterior renovation of the main house during the Revolution. Carter's son and heir, George Carter, left architectural renderings inside the Chambers volume outlining work for his own new house, Oatlands in Loudoun County, built about 1800.[39] These titles reveal more about George Carter's practical interest in architecture than that of his father.

In Stafford County, John Mercer of Marlborough compiled a vast collection of books, divided between his personal library and sale stock, of more than 1,800 volumes, most of which were sold after his death in 1768.[40] He owned a copy of Andrea Pozzo's *Rules and Examples of Perspective* (1707), translated by John James; Johannes Kip's *Views of English Country Homes*, also known as *Britannia illustrata* (1708); and Wotton's *Lives*.[41] He also owned several major plate books, including Jacques Rigaud's *Fifteen Views of Stow* (1739) and possibly his *Recueil choisi de belles palais, Chateaux de maisons royales de Paris* (1729–52), which was purchased by his son James from the estate in 1769.[42] An unidentified set of perspective plates, also purchased by James, may have been Jean Dubreuil's *Practice of Perspective*—commonly referred to as *The Jesuit's Perspective*—which was listed in James's estate inventory in 1793.[43] John Mercer also purchased four pattern books for William Bromley, a local joiner who was building Mercer's new house in 1747. These titles were standard practical works most often found in the libraries of craftsmen: Salmon's *Palladio Londinensis*, Langley's *Builder's Treasury*, Hoppus's *Architecture Displayed* (1738), and an unknown quarto edition of Palladio—probably Godfrey Richards's edition.[44]

Among practitioners of the building and cabinetmaking trades in Virginia, few collections of books can be documented. All too often, these individuals went unrecorded or, at best, appear only rarely or incidentally in documents, leaving little trace of their careers. Few of their estates or libraries were recorded, and those that were documented often cited only "a parcel of books" or, at best, "a Book of Architecture," with no other details. But the historical record is not entirely silent on these matters.

Through Carter Burwell's papers we know that he employed the carpenter and joiner Richard Baylis to assist in creating the impressive interiors of Carter's Grove in about 1751 and that Burwell purchased of a copy of Salmon's *Palladio Londinensis* from the *Virginia Gazette* printing office in 1751.[45] But although historians have suggested that Salmon's book influenced the design of Carter's Grove, Burwell was probably interested in it primarily for practical building price information. Whatever influence the plates from this book may have had on Baylis's work seems to have been minimal; other books were apparently of greater relevance to the design of Carter's Grove.[46] Since we have no records of other books owned by Baylis or Burwell, however, those sources can be no more than conjecture.

Several other artisans did leave records concerning their ownership of architecture books. Mardun (or Maurice) Eventon was a cabinetmaker who worked mainly in the James River basin west of Williamsburg and had one of the two largest architectural collections owned by a craftsman in Virginia. Our knowledge of his library rests on several advertisements he published in the *Virginia Gazette* promoting his business in 1777: "I have an elegant Assortment of Tools and Books of Architecture, which I imported from London and Liverpool." He was, he said, "well acquainted with the Theory and Practice in any of the grand Branches of the five ancient Orders; viz. Ornamental Architects, gothick, chinese, and modern Taste, &c." A later advertisement in 1779, announcing the sale of his possessions in Richmond, listed "12 or 15 Books of Architecture," including unspecified works by Swan, Pain, Langley, and Halfpenny.[47]

Another cabinetmaker who worked in Williamsburg was George Hamilton, who in 1774 also advertised his talents and expertise in the *Virginia Gazette*, informing potential patrons that he could execute "Ornaments and decorations for gentlemens Houses, Chimney Pieces, Door and Window Cornices, Mouldings and Enrichments . . . after the new Palmyrian Taste." Hamilton may have owned of a copy of N. Wallis's *Book of Ornaments in the Palmyrene Taste*, published in 1771. In any case, his advertisement is one of the earliest references to the Neoclassical influence on architecture in Virginia.[48]

There is significantly more information about William Bernard Sears's activity as a joiner-carver than we know of most other craftsmen: his indenture to George Mason at Gunston Hall under William Buckland around 1755; commissions for work on the local church at Pohick, where he did the carving about 1772–74; work for George Washington on a dining room chimneypiece at Mount Vernon in 1775.[49] We have yet to find an inventory for his estate, but his access to Buckland's books can give us a glue to what he may have owned. He must have been familiar with Langley's *Treasury of Designs,* because it is cited in the Truro Parish vestry book as a design source for William Copein, a local stonemason who worked with Sears at the Pohick church: "William Copein having undertaken to make a stone Font for the church according to a Draught in the 150th plate in Langleys Design being the uppermost on the left hand for the price of six pounds, he finding himself everything—the Vestry agree to pay him that sum for—finishing the same."[50] Also, Sear's extant example of architectural carving on the mantle at Mount Vernon clearly shows the influence of Swan's *British Architect.*[51]

The best-documented craftsman in colonial Virginia was William Buckland (figure 2.1).[52] A record of his library and a relatively complete trail of his commissions in Virginia and Maryland allow us to study the work of an artisan through both the person and his books. His first commission, Gunston Hall, offers visual examples that correlate specific designs in the house with well-established architectural plates. Gunston Hall shows the work of the young journeyman and his reliance on his sources before he developed his mature style and artistic identity for later patrons.

Buckland's library was the most important and comprehensive collection of architectural books in Virginia; he owned works touching on almost every aspect of architecture and design. Among his fourteen architectural titles were design books such as James Gibbs's *Book of Architecture* (1728), and Abraham Swan's *Collection of Designs* (1757) and *British Architect* (1745); encyclopedic works such as Isaac Ware's *Complete Body of Architecture* (1756); books on mensuration and mathematical application such as William Salmon's *Palladio Londinensis* (1734), and Edward Hoppus's *Practical Measuring* (1736); pattern books such as Batty Langley's *City and Country Builder's and Workman's Treasury of Designs* (1740) and *Ancient Architecture* (1742), Robert Morris's *Architectural Remembrancer* (1751), Abraham Swan's *Designs in Carpentry* (1759), and Thomas Lightoler, William and John Halfpenny, and Robert Morris's *Modern Builder's Assistant; or, System of Architecture* (ca. 1757). Perspective was represented by John Joshua Kirby's *Practice of Perspective* (1761), and two cabinetmaker's books: Thomas Johnson's *One Hundred and Fifty Designs* (1761), and Thomas Chippendale's *Gentleman and Cabinet-Maker's Director* (1754).[53] This diversity, however, reflects the artisan's interests in practical application and details, for there are no books of theory.

Buckland came to America as an indentured servant to supervise the completion of George Mason's new house, Gunston Hall, between 1755 and 1759.[54] In that capacity he transformed a modest preexisting brick shell of local vernacular style into a sophisticated design incorporating the latest and most fashionable London ideas of taste and interior arrangement. In essence, he created a sample house utilizing all the latest fashionable styles. The Classically designed front porch (originally intended as a frontispiece to the brick wall and later extended into the present porch) and the front hall with its phalanx of pilasters and touches of rococo carving were inspired largely by Ware and Swan. The elaborately carved ornaments in the Palladian Room are derived from Langley's *Treasury* and Swan's *British Architect*. The most exotic interior, the Chi-

FIG 2.1 Portrait of William Buckland by Charles Willson Peale, ca. 1774. Courtesy of the Mabel Brady Garvan Collection, Yale University Art Gallery, New Haven, Conn.

nese Room, has unique Gothic and Chinese detailing derived mostly from Chippendale's *Director.* The simple bedchamber and its closets with their Gothic traceried-fantail transoms were inspired by Langley's *Ancient Architecture.* And finally, the semi-octagonal garden porch is a unique blend of Gothic elements (also inspired by Langley's *Ancient Architecture*) combined with Morris's Classical motifs.[55]

Buckland's talents were also tapped for the design of the new courthouse for Prince William County in the nearby town of Dumfries; Mason was a trustee of the port town and prevailed upon his journeyman to provide the plans. Hidden behind one of the elaborate window entablatures in the Palladian Room at Gunston Hall is a series of pencil sketches that proved upon examination to be an eighteenth-century evolution of design influences derived mainly from Robert Morris's pattern book—and archaeological investigations of the courthouse site revealed the influence of Buckland's sketches.[56] The young artisan had created a courthouse plan unlike any found in Virginia before this time.

Over the next fifteen years, Buckland established a major workshop of apprentices and London-trained craftsmen working on commissions throughout the Northern Neck of Virginia. Among his known projects were the completion of Mount Airy in Richmond County and unidentified work at nearby Sabine Hall. He went where he could find the work, whether on local county projects, minor structures, drafts of houses for clients, or furniture. In 1771 he even solicited (unsuccessfully) a commission from Robert Carter of Nomini Hall, who already was considering remodeling his plantation house.[57]

In 1772, Buckland moved to Annapolis, Maryland, where he completed the Chase-Lloyd House and designed the Hammond-Hardwood House, his last commission, which was still under construction at his death.[58] His influence on houses and interiors in Virginia and Maryland was profound, for he brought to architectural design a certain level of English professionalism not often seen in Virginia architecture. He can be regarded as the first professional architect in America, for his career was based solely on designing, constructing, and installing architectural components and their furniture.

Yet even though we know a good deal about Buckland's life and professional projects, there are still many gaps in our knowledge of his work, which, of course, open the door to conjecture. With so much recent research into the technical production of architectural carving that is now attributed to specific craftsmen who worked under Buckland, a "Buckland school" of cabinetmaking and carving has emerged in the literature. And since he could have contributed to design renderings without being directly involved in their implementation (he often prepared "plans for a house"), it is impossible to measure the full range of his impact.[59]

The progression of the architecture book in Virginia follows two parallel streams. The first is the evolution of the architecture book in England and its relationship to the development of English architecture through the seventeenth century and explosion in the eighteenth. The second stream is the development of Virginia society as it progressed from unstable frontier in the seventeenth century to established colony in the eighteenth. Along both streams the accumulation of books and cultural refinements mirror these changes. The scarcity of books in the seventeenth-century colony reflects the practicality and starkness of frontier life. As plantations developed and flourished, however, the planters established themselves economically and socially by collecting around them the fine appointments of civility; their ownership of books was part of this plan. The only true architectural treatise available in the seventeenth-century colony, Scamozzi's *Mirror of Architecture,* was a composite of prevailing knowledge abridged from French, Italian, and English authors and dealing more with exterior treatment than with interior substance; it was typical of the architecture books found in London after the Great Fire. As the colonial planters' lifestyle stabilized and flourished in the eighteenth century, their libraries grew as well, and they began to collect more books on architecture and building practices. Large collections such as that of Landon Carter, however, emphasized practical knowledge related to measuring and pricing more than than proportions, style, or design.

Next, we begin to see the great collectors, with their grand houses and Continental education. William Byrd—who compiled a major library with an array of theory and design books, but also books to remind him of his English and European origins—collected more for academic value (theory, aesthetics, and fashion) than for function. These patrons of the arts set the tone of what was important, yet for the plans and details of their houses they seem to have relied more on the craftsmen they commissioned than on their own libraries. Even William Byrd's collection shows little relationship between his books and the design of his house.

By the end of the century, large libraries among the gentry of Virginia had become more prevalent, paralleled by an influx of luxury goods. But now even major collections such as those of the Carters and Mercers displayed architectural books more for function than for design. Where the titles of their books can be documented, one finds practical books such as Salmon's *Palladio Londinensis,* Langley's *Builder's Treasury,*

Hoppus's *Architecture Displayed* (books more relevant to the craftsman) as the primary architectural works in Virginia libraries.

The artisans themselves, the practitioners of the craft, were also concerned with the practical application of books to their work. Their own collections focused on functional pattern books and texts on other pragmatic matters such as mensuration. The design books they added to their collections, the better to attract patrons, reflected the sophisticated taste inherent in the established cultural strata of the colony. In essence, knowledge of the books at their disposal would be more helpful to the study of the use of architecture books in Virginia than those of the patrons. Knowing what they owned would enable a better perspective on the relationship of the building as constructed and the book as utilized in its plan. With the exception of Buckland's well-documented and comprehensive collection, however, few records of their books have survived.

Still, we have only begun to plumb the depths of the documentation to be found. Newly discovered inventories, letterbooks, and account books add more titles to the existing catalogue. And each new piece of information expands our knowledge of the place of books in the overall picture of Virginia architecture.

NOTES

1. The list uses a catholic definition of arts which includes architecture, perspective, archaeological studies, fine arts, technical works, cabinetmaking, engineering, and art aesthetics. Additional categories are landscaping, gardening, farming, botanical studies, crafts and industries, and travel accounts. This essay features the relevant books in the first set of categories.

2. William Fitzhugh, *William Fitzhugh and His Chesapeake World, 1676–1701: The Fitzhugh Letters and Other Documents,* ed. Richard Beale Davis (Chapel Hill: University of North Carolina Press for the Virginia Historical Society, 1963), 141–42, 175–76, 202–3.

3. Landon Carter, *The Diary of Landon Carter of Sabine Hall, 1752–1778,* ed. Jack P. Greene (Charlottesville: University Press of Virginia, 1965), 2:1135, 958; Gaius Julius Caesar, *The Commentaries of C. Julius Caesar,* ed. Clement Edmund ([London]: In the Savoy, 1677), 81. (Dates given for publications are those of the first editions unless there is documentation to the contrary for a specific work.)

4. John Carter, "Library of Col. John Carter of Lancaster County," *William and Mary Quarterly,* ser. 1, 8, no. 1 (1900): 18; Eileen Harris, *British Architectural Books and Writers, 1556–1785* (Cambridge: Cambridge University Press, 1990), 409–10.

5. Louis B. Wright, "'The Gentleman's Library' in Early Virginia: The Literary Interests of the First Carters," *Huntington Library Quarterly* 1, no. 1 (1937): 45–61.

6. Richard Brown Inventory, Lancaster County, Va., Wills, etc., no. 10, pt. 1 (1709–27), May 13, 1717, p. 221; Carl Lounsbury, *An Illustrated Glossary of Early Southern Architecture and Landscape* (New York: Oxford University Press, 1994), 11.

7. John Carter to Charles Carter, 26 August 1738, Plumner-Carter Letterbook, Alderman Library, University of Virginia, Charlottesville.

8. "Libraries in Colonial Virginia," *William and Mary Quarterly,* ser. 1, 4, no. 2 (1895): 95.

9. Nicholas Flood Inventory. Richmond Company, Va., Will Book 7 (1767–87), 1 June 1776, p. 266, Gunston Hall Archives, Lorton, Va.

10. William Moss Inventory, York County, Va., Wills & Inventories no. 22 (1771–83), 17 August 1772, p. 131.

11. Wallace B. Gusler, *Furniture of Williamsburg and Eastern Virginia, 1710–1790* (Richmond: Virginia Museum, 1979), 182.

12. "The Library of John Parke Custis, Esq. Of Fairfax County, Va.," *Tyler's Quarterly Magazine* 9, no. 1 (1927): 98.

13. James Stewart Inventory, Fairfax County, Va., Will Book D-1, 17 June 1782, p. 437, Gunston Hall Archives.

14. Marcus Whiffen, *The Eighteenth-Century Houses of Williamsburg* (Williamsburg, Va.: Colonial Williamsburg Foundation, 1984), 59–60.

15. These volumes are at present in, respectively, the library of the Virginia Historical Society, Richmond, and the Earl Gregg Swem Library of the College of William and Mary, Williamsburg, Va.

16. Whiffen, *Eighteenth-Century Houses,* 60–61.

17. By the 1760s there were two or three different printers of the *Virginia Gazette* publishing in Williamsburg at the same time, among them William Hunter (1750–61), Alexander Purdie and John Dixon (1766–75), and (note 33) Dixon and his later partner William Hunter Jr. (1775–78). See *Virginia Gazette:* (Hunter), 1 August 1755; (Purdie and Dixon) 17 and 24 September 1772; (Hunter) 24 and 31 May, 6 June 1751; (Hunter) 1 August 1755; Purdie and Dixon, 17 and 24 September 1772, 10 June 1773; Purdie and Dixon, 29 November, 13 December 1770; Purdie and Dixon, 18 July, 24 September 1772. Microfilm, Gunston Hall Library, Lorton, Va.

18. William Hunter, *Virginia Gazette* Day Book, 14 December and 2 September 1751, 11 June 1752, Alderman Library, University of Virginia, Charlottesville.

19. Joseph Royle, *Virginia Gazette* Day Book, 16 June 1764, Alderman Library, University of Virginia, Charlottesville.

20. Whiffen, *Eighteenth-Century Houses,* 63.

21. Thomas Jefferson, *The Papers of Thomas Jefferson,* ed. Julian P. Boyd, vol. 12 (Princeton: Princeton University Press, 1955), 127.

22. William B. O'Neal, *Jefferson's Fine Arts Library: His Selections for the University of Virginia Together with His Own Architectural Books* (Charlottesville: University Press of Virginia, 1976), 367–70.

23. See Bruce T. McCully, "Governor Francis Nicholson, Patron Par Excellence of Religion and Learning in Colonial America," *William and Mary Quarterly,* ser. 3, 39, no. 2 (1982): 310–33; John M. Jennings, "Notes on the Original Library of the College of William and Mary," *Papers of the Bibliographical Society of America* 41 (1947): 258–67.

24. Marcus Whiffen, *The Public Buildings of Williamsburg* (Williamsburg, Va.: Colonial Williamsburg, 1958), 67–103.

25. John M. Jennings, *The Library of the College of William and Mary in Virginia, 1693–1793* (Charlottesville: University Press of Virginia, 1968), 48.

26. Burke Davis, *A Williamsburg Galaxy* (Williamsburg, Va.: Colonial Williamsburg, 1968), 71–83; Graham Hood, *The Governor's Palace in Williamsburg: A Cultural Study* (Williamsburg, Va.: Colonial Williamsburg Foundation, 1991), 279.

27. George H. Reese, "Books in the Palace: The Libraries of Three Virginia Governors," *Virginia Cavalcade* 18, no. 1 (1968): 20–27.

28. The subscribers' pages in both Spence (1747) and Stuart and Revett, vol. 1 (1762), list "Norborne Berkeley, Esq."

29. Harris, *British Architecture Books,* 509; Hood, *The Governor's Palace,* 294. The subscribers page lists "Norborne Berkeley, Baron de Botetourt."

30. Hood, *The Governor's Palace,* 298.

31. Reese, "Books in the Palace," 30–31.

32. The subscribers page to Gibbs (1728) lists "Earl of Dunmore"; to Chambers (1759 ed.), "the Right Honourable Lord Dunmore"; to Adam (1764 ed.), "the Right Honourable William [*sic*], Earl of Dunmore"; to Langley (1742 ed.), "Lord Dunmore."

33. *Virginia Gazette* (Dixon and Hunter), 18 April 1777, 5, original in Gunston Hall Library, Lorton Va.

34. See John Percival, *The English Travels of Sir John Percival and William Byrd II: The Percival Diary of 1701,* ed. Mark R. Wenger (Columbia: University of Missouri Press, 1989).

35. See Kevin J. Hayes, *The Library of William Byrd of Westover* (Madison, Wis.: Madison House, 1997); Edwin Wolf II, *More Books from the Library of the Byrds of Westover* (Worcester, Mass.: American Antiquarian Society, 1978), 73–74.

36. Mark R. Wenger, "Westover: William Byrd's Mansion Reconsidered" (master's thesis, University of Virginia, 1981), 136 (Thomas Shippen to Dr. William Shippen, 30 December 1783, description of Westover), 42–60.

37. Philip Vickers Fithian, *The Journal and Letters of Philip Vickers Fithian, 1773–1776,* ed. Hunter D. Farish (Williamsburg, Va.: Colonial Williamsburg, 1957), 119, 84–85; John R. Barden, "Reflections of a Singular Mind: The Library of Robert Carter of Nomony Hall," *Virginia Magazine of History and Biography* 96, no. 1 (1988): 84–85; Brinton Sherwood, "Oatlands," *Historic Preservation* 18, no. 2 (1966): 52. The Chambers and Salmon volumes are at Oatlands in Loudoun County, Va., and the surviving volumes of the Perrault are at the Virginia Historical Society Library, Richmond.

38. Robert Carter, "Invoice to be bought & Shipped by Messrs. Edrd. Hunt & sons," 25 January 1771, pp. 11–14, in Letterbook, Robert Carter Papers, 1760–1815, Virginia Historical Society, Richmond.

39. Fithian, *Journal and Letters,* 80–82; R. Carter to Mr. Boulton, 17 January 1778, p. 3, in Letterbook, 1775–80, Duke University, Durham, N.C.; Sherwood, "Oatlands," 54.

40. Leo Le May, "John Mercer and the Stamp Act in Virginia, 1764–1765," *Virginia Magazine of History and Biography* 91, no. 1 (1983): 37.

41. John Mercer, Ledger Book G, leaves 35 and 141, in Bucks County Historical Society and Mercer Museum, Doylestown, Pa.

42. James Mercer, "Library of J[oh]n Mercer of Marlboro" (manuscript copy by William R. Mercer, 1879, of lost original), 4, in Brock Collection, Henry E. Huntington Library and Garden, San Marino, Calif.

43. James Mercer, "Account of Sales of Household Furniture pr. belonging to Estate of Judge [James] Mercer deceased," Spotsylvania County, Va., 6 April 1795, Will Book E (1772–98), p. 1591.

44. John Mercer, Ledger Book G, leaf 203.

45. Whiffen, *Eighteenth-Century Houses,* 266; Hunter, *Virginia Gazette* Day Book, 14 December 1751.

46. Mark R. Wenger, conversation with the author, 25 November 1999. I want to acknowledge the major contributions of Mark Wenger to this essay. Many times he kept me from venturing into dangerous waters of speculation and clarified many points in the new research into Virginia architecture.

47. Quoted in Whiffen, *Eighteenth-Century Houses,* 59; Gusler, *Furniture,* 162–63.

48. Whiffen, *Eighteenth-Century Houses,* 64.

49. Luke Beckerdite, "William Buckland and William Bernard Sears: The Designer and the Carver," *Journal of Early Southern Decorative Arts* 8, no. 2 (1982): 7–40; Truro Parish, *Minutes of the Vestry, 1732–85* (Lorton, Va.: privately printed by Pohick Church, 1974), 133–35; George Washington, *The Papers of George Washington: The Revolutionary War Series,* ed. Philander D. Chase (Charlottesville: University Press of Virginia, 1983), 1:337.

50. Truro Parish, Minutes, 129.

51. Thomas T. Waterman, *Mansions of Virginia: 1706 to 1776* (Chapel Hill: University of North Carolina Press, 1945), 288–90.

52. See Beckerdite, "William Buckland and William Bernard Sears," 7–41; Luke Beckerdite, "William Buckland Reconsidered: Architectural Carving in Chesapeake Maryland, 1771–1774," *Journal of Early Southern Decorative Arts* 8, no. 2 (1982): 43–88; [Bennie Brown], *Buckland: Master Builder of the 18th Century* (Lorton, Va.: Board of Regents of Gunston Hall, 1978).

53. For the most comprehensive analysis of Buckland's library see [Brown], "The Library of William Buckland," in *Buckland*, 27–40.

54. William Buckland, "Indenture of Service to Thomson Mason," 4 August 1755 (printed document with manuscript endorsement from George Mason, 1759), Gunston Hall Archives.

55. [Brown], *Buckland*, 29–38.

56. Carl R. Lounsbury, "An Elegant and Commodious Building: William Buckland and the Design of the Prince William County Court House," *Journal of the Society of Architectural Historians* 46, no. 3 (1987): 229–31.

57. Carter, Diary, 1:328, 428; [Brown], *Buckland*, 10.

58. Beckerdite, "Buckland Reconsidered," 43–84.

59. Robert Wormeley Carter, "The Daybook of Robert Wormeley Carter of Sabine Hall, 1766," ed. Louis Morton, *Virginia Magazine of History and Biography* 68, no. 3 (1960): 305.

III

GEORGE WASHINGTON, MOUNT VERNON, AND THE PATTERN BOOKS

Robert F. Dalzell Jr.

In August 1775, George Washington wrote to Lund Washington, his kinsman, friend, and manager at Mount Vernon: "I wish you would quicken Lamphere and Sears about the Dining Room Chimney Piece (to be executed as mentioned in one of my last Letters) as I could wish to have that end of the House completely finished when I return."[1]

Washington had arrived in Cambridge, Massachusetts, barely a month earlier to take command of the Continental Army. Whatever the future might hold, England and the colonies were at war, and the difficulties involved in molding the ragtag collection of patriot troops camped around Boston into an effective fighting force would have made a far more sanguine individual than Washington quake with fear. Indeed, it was an assignment he earnestly claimed he had not wanted, did not want. But despite all the problems he faced, there he was, writing home about the work he wanted done on his "mansion house," which had been under renovation for the preceding sixteen months.

That Washington could, at such a moment, concern himself so intently with a dining room chimneypiece underlines what anyone who knew him at all well understood: Mount Vernon was far more than simply his home. It was an extension of the man himself, a tangible emblem of his character, his personality, his hopes, his dreams. For more than four decades he served as its chief planner and architect, a task he shared with no one, not even Martha Washington. Signature and self-portrait, it reflected at every turn his sense of himself and his place in the larger world, and to this day it remains the most personal—the most intimate—expression of those things we have from his own hand.

So, of course, having begun to rebuild the house, he would want to see it finished as quickly as possible, come hell or high water—*or* revolution. But there was also a significant irony here. For at the very moment Washington was marshaling his forces to conduct what had become an all-out struggle to secure American independence from Great Britain, the dining room chimneypiece he was fretting over was being crafted—at his express instruction—to duplicate a plate in Abraham Swan's *British Architect,* an English architectural pattern book (figures 3.1, 3.2).

Washington's role as Mount Vernon's architect is now generally accepted as fact, but that has not always been so. Of the various alternatives, the most fully developed was proposed some fifty years ago by Thomas Waterman in his *Mansions of Virginia.* Waterman argued that an architect named John Ariss was responsible for planning most of the changes made at Mount Vernon over the years, and that he took his designs from William Adam's *Vitruvius Scotius.*[2] Neither of these contentions stands up to scrutiny. A "John Oriss" did advertise his services as an architect in the *Maryland Gazette* in 1751, mentioning that he used "Gibbs' Architect" in his work, and a "John Ariss" rented land from Washington at one point. Yet there is no evidence in Washington's papers that Ariss, or Oriss, ever worked on Mount Vernon in any capacity, and the various elevations of the house bear little if any resemblance to the plates in *Vitruvius Scotius.*[3]

Nor is Ariss/Oriss necessarily the most plausible person to have served as architect of Mount Vernon, if Washington himself did not do the work. A much likelier candidate, though no one to date seems to have argued the case, is William Buckland. British by birth, Buckland had begun his career in America by designing and executing the interior woodwork at Gunston Hall, the home of Washington's friend and neighbor George Mason. From there he went on to work as an independent artisan in the vicinity of Richmond and finally settled in Annapolis, where among other things he served as architect—in the full, modern sense—of the Hammond-Harwood house (figure 3.3).[4] Annapolis was a lively place during those years, and the Washingtons were in the habit of visiting the city at least twice a year. They knew and were entertained by all of Buckland's major patrons, and there were to be clear similarities between some of the more prominent flourishes on Buckland's houses and corresponding details at Mount Vernon as it emerged from the rebuilding that began just prior to the Revolu-

FIG 3.1 Design selected by George Washington from Abraham Swan's *British Architect* (1745) for the dining room chimneypiece at Mount Vernon. Courtesy of the Mount Vernon Ladies' Association.
FIG 3.2 (*right*) The dining room chimneypiece at Mount Vernon as completed in 1775. The paint shown in the photograph is lighter than the finish currently used in the room, but the lighter tone shows details of the carving more clearly. Courtesy of the Mount Vernon Ladies' Association.

tion.[5] Again, however, there is nothing in Washington's papers to indicate that he ever employed Buckland. Nor does Mount Vernon exhibit the extraordinary deftness that was the hallmark of Buckland's work and that made him, unquestionably, the most talented American architect of his day.

The absence of evidence linking any known architect, other than Washington, to Mount Vernon is reinforced both by what we know of traditions and practices in his society and by indisputable evidence that he felt perfectly comfortable designing complex buildings of several different kinds. Architecture, as a recognized profession,

FIG 3.3 The Hammond-Harwood House, Annapolis, Md., William Buckland, architect, ca. 1774. Photo by William H. Pierson.

barely existed in America before the Revolution; Buckland was paid as a craftsman and construction supervisor. Indeed, not until Charles Bulfinch began working in Boston in the 1790s would any American succeed in earning a living simply by designing buildings. In Virginia before the Revolution the typical pattern was for owners and artisans to work together in planning buildings, with the relative weight of the contribution of each varying from case to case.[6] Washington's contribution was decisive. We have plans in his hand for a pair of houses he had built in Washington, D.C., toward the end of his life; for the greenhouse and its accompanying slave quarters at Mount Vernon; for a highly innovative, sixteen-sided threshing barn, also at Mount Vernon; and for several smaller structures. His only surviving drawing of the mansion house at Mount Vernon is an elevation of the west front as it was rebuilt beginning in 1774 (figure 3.4), which shows clearly and strongly the features that were added at the time: the elongated profile of the structure, the hip roof with its stylish central pediment,

FIG 3.4 Drawing by George Washington of the west front of Mount Vernon, 1773. The drawing corrects the asymmetry of the facade, which in reality could not be done. Courtesy of the Mount Vernon Ladies' Association.

and rising over the whole the memorable—and notably unstylish—cupola. The drawing also depicts an essentially symmetrical placement of doors and windows, something that in practice was never achieved.

Work on Mount Vernon went on virtually without interruption from the time Washington took it over at the age of twenty-two until his death in 1799, and the resulting house reveals this history. It is not a great monument of architectural style but rather a medley of different styles, a kind of sampler of eighteenth-century taste. Nor do its various parts cohere particularly well. It is no Monticello; it has none of the bravura and little of the finesse of Jefferson's masterpiece. Yet the place still manages to convey—and powerfully—a sense of will, of focused, purposeful action. There is nothing casual or haphazard about Mount Vernon. Plainly, choices were made; alternatives were considered and rejected. What we see is what we were meant to see.

Though work on the house was continual, the major changes Washington made tended to cluster at two points. In 1758 and beginning again in 1774 he effectively doubled the size of the main building and added elaborate finishes inside and out. In the first instance the story-and-a-half house that had come to him from his half-brother Lawrence was raised by an additional full story, and several of the ground floor rooms were embellished with paneling replete with eye-catching, Classical details (figure 3.5). The stairway in the central passage was also reworked and enlarged (figure 3.6), causing the asymmetrical arrangement of windows on the west front of the house (figure 3.7). At this time, too, the exterior walls were covered with boards that were cut, beveled, and painted to look like rusticated stone (figure 3.8).[7]

In the second rebuilding of the house, substantial blocks were added to both ends of the structure, one containing a large room for entertaining, the other a new master bedchamber and below it a study for Washington. The two private rooms were relatively plain in finish, but the entertaining room was eventually adorned with a carved marble chimneypiece and applied plaster decoration in the style made popular in England by Robert Adam. Also, as part of the second rebuilding, the pediment and cupola were added, as well as new outbuildings on either side of the house, the nearest of which were connected to it by curved arcades, completing the basic, five-part composition that Lord Burlington and his circle of neo-Palladian enthusiasts had done so much to embed in the canon of eighteenth-century British architectural taste. The most striking feature added to Mount Vernon at this time, however, was the great piazza stretching across the entire east front of the main house. Covered by a flat extension of the roof supported by eight slender pillars rising a full two stories, it gives that side of the building—particularly when viewed from the Potomac River, which it faces—an airy, almost magical quality.[8]

The second rebuilding of Mount Vernon arguably did more to alter the house than the first, yet each in its own way expanded in a figurative as well as a literal sense the shadow the place cast in the world. The two renovations shared other similarities as well. Both occurred while Washington was absent from home much or all of the time—a great boon to scholars, since it means that the work is abundantly documented in his correspondence. Both building campaigns also coincided with critical points in Washington's life, a fact that played a significant part in determining what was done in each case.

The first rebuilding was planned in 1757, while he was commanding the Virginia Regiment in its efforts to secure the colony's western frontier against French and Indian attacks. Within a year, however, he would resign his command. He had long hoped to win a commission in the regular British army; having failed to do so, and with the war effort increasingly shifting to other theaters, he had little to gain from further military service. A chapter in his life was closing, and rather less gloriously than he had hoped. In effect, his decision to renovate Mount Vernon both marked that point and gave notice of how he proposed to manage the next chapter. In the future he would take his chances as a Virginia planter—if not necessarily of the first rank, at least not far from it, as his plans for the house indicated. But the work at Mount Vernon also promised to take almost all the money he had made from his command, and apart from that he had nothing more to fall back on than a very modest inheritance. As it turned out, the problem of how he was to support himself in a style commensurate with his greatly improved house was solved by his singularly advantageous marriage to the wealthy Widow Custis. Yet when he planned the work at Mount Vernon, he had not even begun to woo Martha Custis, whose first husband at that point was still alive and well. So it was a risky game Washington was playing, but as it so often did, luck favored him.[9]

Fifteen years later, by contrast, his financial situation and his position within the Virginia elite were in every way secure. For more than a decade he had been serving as a member of the House of Burgesses. Huge tracts of western land had come to him as a belated reward for his military service during the French and Indian War. At the death of his stepdaughter, Patsy Custis, he had even managed to clear a growing debt to his London agent, caused by low tobacco returns and excessively extravagant purchases of imported finery. He had also completely restructured the agricultural enterprise at Mount Vernon and was raising wheat as his primary crop instead of tobacco. As a result, in 1774—the year the carpenters and brickmasons returned to work at Mount Vernon—he stood before the world an independent gentleman, free of any claim that might have been pressed against him. Or at any rate that would have been his position had it not been for the policies of the British government—policies which, in the very month the work began anew at Mount Vernon, he was predicting "shall make us as tame and abject slaves, as the blacks we rule over with such arbitrary sway."[10]

In remarks like these, Washington made it clear that for him the issue at the heart of the deepening quarrel between England and America was personal autonomy—in a word, independence. Was he, then, choosing that moment to embark on a fresh remodeling of Mount Vernon as a way of asserting, symbolically, his determination to maintain control over his own life? Can houses substitute for rebellions, or become extensions of them? It is a fact that the family at Mount Vernon had no pressing need for the extra space that this latest renovation would create. Even more telling was Washington's steadfast commitment to continuing the work throughout the Revolution.

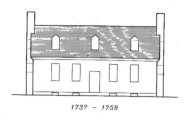

173? – 1759

1759 – 1774

FIG 3.5 Conjectural drawing of Mount Vernon as it came to George Washington and as he rebuilt it in 1758–59. Drawing by Jeffery F. Dalzell.

FIG 3.6 (*bottom*) The central passage and stairway, Mount Vernon. Courtesy of the Mount Vernon Ladies' Association.

FIG 3.7 (*opposite, top*) The west front, Mount Vernon. Courtesy of the Mount Vernon Ladies' Association.

FIG 3.8 (*opposite, bottom*) *Mount Vernon in Virginia,* aquatint by Francis Jukes after Alexander Robertson, 1800. Courtesy of the Chapin Library of Rare Books, Williams College, Williamstown, Mass.

The difficulties involved were vast, but he was adamant, as his instructions to Lund Washington about that dining room chimneypiece in the summer of 1775 indicate.

Mount Vernon rebuilt: George Washington's personal declaration of independence. It is an appealing notion, certainly. Yet there is also a notable problem with it, as that same dining room chimneypiece illustrates all too clearly. For its design—borrowed, as noted, from Abraham Swan's *British Architect*—clearly seems to point to Washington's continuing dependence on English cultural sources. And thanks to the skill of the artisan he hired to do the work, he got what he wanted. Like Buckland, William Bernard Sears had come from England to George Mason's Gunston Hall as an indentured servant, and both there and at Mount Vernon his work stands as a superb example of the woodcarver's art—but it is also, in design and conception, a thoroughly British example of that art.[11]

The same thing was true of scores of other details at Mount Vernon. If the five-part configuration of the main house and its flanking outbuildings echoed the taste of the English neo-Palladians, the oval window in the pediment, the "Venetian" window at the north end of the house, and the pilasters and pediments that framed the doorways in the central passage and west parlor—to mention only some of the more prominent examples—were all copied directly from English pattern books, the chief source being Batty Langley's *City and Country Builder's and Workman's Treasury of Designs*.[12]

At such points Washington seems to have been determined to make Mount Vernon as "correct" as he could, with correctness defined as whatever would most accurately duplicate accepted models of British taste. For that purpose the pattern books, with their precise proportions and crisply detailed engravings, were invaluable. But it is also possible to exaggerate the influence of pattern books at Mount Vernon. Like the frosting on a cake, the details taken from them tended to spread over the surfaces of the building without ever really engaging its structure. The Venetian window, for example, lacks the entire bottom portion of Langley's design, including its principal supporting elements; hence, it seems to float, unanchored, against the rusticated weatherboarding around it (figures 3.9, 3.10).

Nor, for all the use he made of them, did Washington seem particularly interested in owning pattern books. His orders for English goods never mentioned them, and the inventory of his estate listed only a handful of titles having anything at all to do with building. For practical information, there was Francis Price's *British Carpenter*. Langley was represented only by a book on gardening. A small volume by W. Watts, *The Seats of the Nobility and Gentry*, contained a collection of views, largely picturesque,

FIG 3.9 Design for a Venetian window from Batty Langley's *City and Country Builder's and Workman's Treasury of Designs* (1750). Courtesy of the Mount Vernon Ladies' Association.
FIG 3.10 (*right*) The Venetian window, Mount Vernon. Courtesy of the Mount Vernon Ladies' Association.

which revealed little about design. The only other relevant title was "Middleton's Architecture," which presumably referred to Charles Middleton's *Picturesque and Architectural Views for Cottages, Farm Houses, and Country Villas*. This important publication, in full folio, presented designs for houses modest in size but still quite modishly detailed. Part pattern book and part architectural treatise, it was the closest thing to either in Washington's library; however, it was not published until 1793—long after it could have had any impact on the several rebuildings of Mount Vernon.[13]

Since Washington did not own the architectural books he needed to plan the changes at Mount Vernon, he must have borrowed them, which would have been easy enough to do. He also had ready access—through buildings he had actually seen and liked—to information on architectural style, and in truth his most important borrowings were from those buildings rather than published sources. Since, too, he had never left the continent of North America except for a brief trip to Barbados, the buildings in question were all American. The great houses of tidewater Virginia and others that he admired on his travels across the Potomac to Maryland and northward to Philadelphia and New York and on beyond to New England: those were the chief architectural models he used at Mount Vernon.

To say this and nothing more, however, would be to ignore the fact that the American models Washington relied on—like the pattern books—tended to be distinctly British in conception and detail. The idea of covering the main house with beveled, sand-painted boards to imitate dressed stone, for example, probably came from Peter Harrison's work in Newport and Boston, but Harrison owed an enormous debt to British sources, including the pattern books.[14] The same was true of William Buckland. Moreover, in the broadest sense, virtually all the buildings Washington saw were products of a culture still fundamentally British, and the influence of British taste on American houses and house furnishing had, if anything, grown stronger over the eighteenth century, a circumstance that the growing use of pattern books both facilitated and demonstrates.[15]

In sum, to see Mount Vernon—as infused with British influences as it was—as an expression of independence seems problematic. Yet surely the same difficulty arises when one turns to the whole tangled process of cultural transmission, metropolitan influence, and provincial emulation which shaped the political principles fueling the patriot cause that brought Washington to Cambridge that summer. Using the cadences, the imagery, and the rhetoric of British opposition ideology, he and his associates were crafting a rebellion that they had come to identify as a struggle for American independence. That process has been described often enough, and its equivalent in house building has also been much studied. But one avenue of inquiry that remains relatively unexplored is comparative analysis. England too had its provincial emulators, and some of them built houses that also illustrate, in interesting ways, how the process of cultural transmission worked.

A case in point is Saltram, a substantial country house in Devonshire much embellished in the latter half of the eighteenth century by an ambitious family named Parker. In contrast to the great monuments of British country-house architecture—places such as Blenheim Palace and Houghton Hall, built for individuals at the pinnacle of national power, from designs provided by leading architects—Saltram seldom receives more than the briefest of mentions in architectural histories of the period. But the facts of its construction are revealing—and there are some notable similarities between Saltram and Mount Vernon.

As Washington did, the Parkers started with an existing house and over a period of several decades radically altered it. Working outward from a Tudor core onto which, at the end of the seventeenth century, had been grafted a large three-story block, the family's original architect (whose name is unknown) developed the east, south, and west facades of the building and added a line of rooms behind each. Two of the facades were wholly new, and the third consisted of the seventeenth-century block augmented by a pair of low wings leading to taller pavilions. At the time, some of the added rooms were probably left unfinished, for ten years later Robert Adam was called in to design a series of interiors, including a "great room" or "saloon," on the south side of the house. And as that work neared completion, the grounds were extensively relandscaped in the naturalistic, Capability Brown manner.

Standing in its remade setting with its walls smoothly stuccoed and painted, the transformed Saltram made a fetching picture, as many a visitor testified. Everything had been done in the latest taste. The symmetry of the new facades was flawless, and their careful detailing emphatically bespoke Palladian influence, as did the lavish interiors of the house. Yet for all its appeal, Saltram in the end fails, at least as a total composition. On close examination, the three new facades bear little relation to one another and none at all to the basic structure of the building. As the author of the National Trust's guidebook for Saltram remarks: "Evidently it was beyond the architect-builder to integrate the new work in three dimensions; viewed from the angles, all three facades of Saltram begin to look like elevations cut from a pattern book and wrapped around the Tudor building like a sash" (figure 3.11).[16]

Did it matter to the Parkers that their architect had failed them in this respect? Possibly, but chances are it did not. At least two designs survive for far more grandiose, more aesthetically satisfying remodelings of the house, but evidently the family preferred to limit the scope of the project. Indeed, the "architect-builder" in question may well have been Lady Catherine Parker herself, who seems to have commissioned the work. As the daughter of the first Earl of Poulett, she doubtless had a well-developed sense of what it took for a family to rise in the England of her day. Insofar as houses mattered—and plainly she thought they did—they ought to be fashionable and imposing, but it would have been foolish to overburden the family financially in laying that particular wager. The point was to avoid both undue scrimping and unnecessary extravagance, and apparently Catherine Parker's calculations came close enough to the mark: in 1785 her son, John Parker, was created Baron Bovingdon, and a generation later his son, another John Parker, became the first Earl of Morely.

FIG 3.11 The west front of Saltram House, Devon, Eng., showing the Parker family's additions with bits of the original Tudor building peeking out from behind. Courtesy of the National Trust Photographic Library, London / Nick Meers.

So Saltram, along with whatever else the Parkers brought to the table, served its purpose. A charming and comfortable house, it was also a credible country seat for an earl. If it was not a particularly good example of architectural style, the Parkers themselves did not always fulfill the idealized picture of country life sketched by Palladio and his admirers. At one point the Duchess of Devonshire wrote with affection of finding her friend John Parker, the one who later became Baron Bovingdon, "as dirty, as comical and talking as bad English as ever."[17] Yet the same John Parker had the good sense to hire Robert Adam to decorate his rooms and to let Sir Joshua Reynolds, whom he counted among his close friends, choose the pictures for Saltram's walls. Like the several facades of his house, Parker's personal qualities may have sat oddly together, but in the great game the family was playing, the purer forms of style were not required. Taste was enough.

As for comparing Saltram to Mount Vernon, there are at least three ways in which the two houses resemble one another. Both mix construction from different periods; both work hard at incorporating the high tide of Georgian fashion in architecture and decoration; and both succeed finally more in detail than as integrated wholes. At the root of these similarities, too, one senses the same kinds of complex calculations: the same determination to impress, balanced by the same careful adjustment of means to ends. At both Saltram and Mount Vernon, for example, the desired effect would have been easier to achieve had the existing buildings been removed from the site, but that would have raised costs as well.

Judicious economizing also had its limits at both houses, however. Where they produce their grandest flourishes, they do so without stinting, and in each case the grandest interior flourish comes in the form of a single, large room: the one at the north end of Mount Vernon, and Saltram's "saloon" (figures 3.12, 3.13). The two rooms even have certain features in common. Both are a full two stories high with deep cove ceilings; both are rectangular in shape with outsized Venetian windows centered on one long wall and fireplaces on the other; both have ceilings, walls, and woodwork decorated with geometric shapes, swags, and garlands, molded in low relief in plaster, in the best Adamesque manner.

The difference was that the Parkers could commission Robert Adam himself to create their room and to provide, in the bargain, designs for the carpet, the looking glasses, and even such minutiae as door handles, whereas for Washington such an arrangement was clearly out of the question. It was a matter of simple arithmetic. As provincials eager to appropriate metropolitan taste, he and the Parkers may have shared a common goal, but they were closer to London by several thousand miles than he was, and that made an enormous difference in how they played the game.

Yet the game in question was also the only one the Parkers were interested in playing, and therein lies a far more significant difference between the two houses. There is nothing at Saltram analogous to Mount Vernon's cupola or its piazza. Each was a marked departure from the standard taste of the day, which was something that the Parkers chose not to risk. Relentlessly, uncompromisingly correct, Saltram followed the approved rules to the letter; Mount Vernon did not. And that is what remains most striking and memorable about it.

FIG 3.12 The saloon at Saltram House, Robert Adam, architect. Courtesy of the National Trust Photographic Library, London.

What led Washington to stray where he did from the path of architectural correctness? Certainly he knew enough to stick to the rules if he had wanted to. The same pattern books from which he copied windows and chimneypieces contained a variety of standard roof designs without cupolas, and the east front of Mount Vernon, minus the piazza, was a reasonably acceptable example of a Classically composed facade. If the

FIG 3.13 The north room at Mount Vernon. Courtesy of the Mount Vernon Ladies' Association.

rules were broken at Mount Vernon, it was because Washington made a conscious decision to break them.

It is possible to imagine a variety of reasons why he made the choices he did. Several of the unorthodox elements he added to the house noticeably improved its appearance. For example, since extending the main structure to the north and south during the second rebuilding tended to make it look too long relative to its rather modest height, the piazza and the cupola can be seen as providing a pair of strong vertical thrusts to help counter that effect. The cupola also drew attention away from the asymmetry of the west front.

Unorthodoxy had other uses as well. Much of what Washington did to Mount Vernon had the effect of distinguishing more precisely, in fairly conventional ways, between the public and private spaces of the house. In adding a full second story in the first rebuilding, he doubled the amount of private space and set it off crisply from the public rooms below. In the second rebuilding, by adding both a large space for entertaining and a separate set of rooms solely for his and Martha's use, he granted strict parity to the two sides of the public/private division. At other points, however, the changes he made tended to blur, if not eliminate altogether, that same division, and again the piazza provides the most striking example.

Porches—front, rear, and side but invariably called "piazzas"—had just begun to appear in America. By 1770 Washington could have seen them on vernacular as well as high-style houses, particularly in the middle colonies, and there may even have been an earlier, smaller version of one at Mount Vernon. No doubt, too, he had seen porches in Barbados during the time he spent there with his brother Lawrence.[18]

Yet none of those examples would have had the dimensions of Mount Vernon's new piazza. In its great height and broad sweep along the entire length of the building, Washington's creation was truly original. In designing it as he did, he also dispensed with the tightly controlled patterns of access typically found in Georgian houses of the period. People were free to approach the piazza from outdoors or, through any one of three doors, from inside the house. There were no barriers or prescribed patterns of circulation. Considered in these terms, indeed, the piazza becomes more than just a departure from orthodox taste; it is directly at odds with that taste. Its primary function was to provide a sheltered space from which to enjoy the magnificent view of the Potomac that was Mount Vernon's greatest single asset. It was no Classically inspired, columned portico framing a grand entrance. In their simplicity, its pillars echoed the Tuscan order, but the proportions Washington chose for them stretched far beyond those mandated in the pattern books, which would have produced much thicker, heavier pillars, thereby impeding the view.[19]

Similarly, in using quadrant arms to connect the main house with the outbuildings on either side of it—a standard Palladian device—Washington boldly broke with established practice by not closing them in. The effect was lighter; it also gave visitors arriving at the west front a tantalizing hint of the delights that lay in store for them on the other side of the house.

In a word, pleasure: that seems to have been the standard Washington followed in such instances, making Mount Vernon a very different kind of place from Saltram, a house designed to impress which spoke unambiguously the language of power. Washington too hoped to impress, but he meant to please himself in the bargain and others as well, if he could. The result was a house that mixed orthodoxy and innovation, combined power and pleasure, in a way that made it difficult to characterize even then.

In the midst of the Revolution, Bryan Fairfax, a longtime friend and neighbor, wrote Washington: "I was yesterday at Mt. Vernon, where I hope it will please God to return you in time, & I like the House because it is uncommon for there has always appeared too great a Sameness in our Buildings."[20] But the "uncommon" house Bryan Fairfax admired left Baron Friedrich von Steuben—the man who did so much to transform Washington's army into a properly drilled, European-style fighting force—singularly unimpressed. "If . . . Washington were not a better general than he was an architect the affairs of America would be in a very bad condition," he confided to a friend after seeing Mount Vernon.[21]

Presumably, von Steuben's salvo never reached his commander's ears, and Washington's papers contain no record of his reaction to Fairfax's comment. Nor did he ever have much to say about architecture in general terms. But happily, his silence was not absolute. In a series of letters written toward the end of his life he did hazard a number of highly revealing remarks on the subject.

The letters related to the pair of rental houses he eventually had built in "the Federal City," as he continued to call the place that would soon become the nation's capital and bear his name. Half investment and half patriotic gesture, the project turned out to be more troublesome than he had expected, but it did have one pleasant consequence: it enabled him to pursue his acquaintance with Dr. William Thornton, who generously offered to supervise construction of the houses. Washington had first encountered Thornton through the doctor's design for the National Capitol, which the judges had chosen—with Washington's enthusiastic support—as the best of those submitted. A native of Tortola in the West Indies, Thornton had earned his medical degree in Scotland and, in addition to busying himself as an amateur architect, was an inveterate tinkerer as well as a gifted painter and writer.[22] In accepting his help, Washington wanted no misunderstanding about his own architectural abilities: he knew what he liked and nothing more. What he neglected to add was that in his own mind such knowledge counted for a good deal.

By the time Thornton became involved in the project, Washington had already drawn up a neat, workmanlike floor plan for the two houses. They were to be joined in a single structure with their principal doorways side by side in the center. Apparently there were no elevation drawings, but in a letter to Thornton, Washington did propose placing a pediment in the center of the roof, with a dormer window on either side of it. In Philadelphia he had seen double houses with pediments, which, as he said, "pleased me." Thornton did not like the idea of a pediment, however, arguing that it would not add "any beauty" and taking it to be, as he wrote, "a Desideratum in

Architecture to hide as much as possible the Roof." In London, parapets often served that purpose, and that was the solution he recommended.[23]

In framing his reply, Washington seemed a bit stung by Thornton's reaction to the pediment scheme (after all, Mount Vernon had a pediment!) and in a roundabout way tried to justify his original suggestion. He knew that "rules of Architecture" existed "to give Symmetry, and just proportion to all the Orders, and parts of building in order to please the eye," and being ignorant of those rules, he had probably violated them. Still, he felt that "small departures" from the rules would be noticed "only by the skilful Architects, or by the eye of criticism." The great majority of people could just as easily be pleased "with things not quite orthodox."[24] In short, the rules were there to be broken.

Thomas Jefferson could well have said the same thing. At Monticello he broke or bent at least as many rules as he followed, beginning with the site of the house high atop his beloved "Little Mountain." Pleasure was a vital part of his architectural vision, and as Washington did with the piazza at Mount Vernon, he too seemed eager to move beyond the standard configuration of spaces in Georgian-style houses to something less preoccupied with power and control. Witness his total elimination of the grand ceremonial staircase as a design feature at Monticello.[25]

Yet one suspects that in the end Monticello would have seemed *too* eccentric for Washington's taste, too completely centered on its creator and his pleasure. By temperament he was too moderate, too measured in all things, to travel where Jefferson did in his loftier flights. Ultimately, what he hoped to achieve—what he must have hoped he had achieved at Mount Vernon—was some sort of balance between contradictory imperatives, between what struck his fancy and what the pattern books prescribed, between pleasure and power. Such a balance, after all, was the stuff of which virtue was made, at least as Washington understood it.

And in 1774, the year that began the rebuilding of Mount Vernon which would include the piazza, virtue had become a singularly important concept. In its name, Washington and scores of other colonial leaders were seeking to define the ground on which they stood in their continuing quarrel with Great Britain. Their goal, they said, was simply to preserve rights and liberties that Americans had enjoyed since the earliest days of settlement. This they were doing, moreover, not for any selfish reason of their own but for all Americans confronting the exactions of a government locked in the hands of corrupt, overbearing officials.

Balance, then—pleasure and power, freedom and restraint—that is how Washington seems to have seen Mount Vernon as he planned his second major rebuilding of the house. Surely, too, the work begun in 1774 represented a pledge to a future beyond resistance—beyond America's deepening conflict with Great Britain. For there the house would stand, greeting the world with its formal, highly Anglicized entrance front, while on the river side, with the piazza, it became something totally different: open, informal, bare of unnecessary ornament, its soaring structure breaking free of Classical restraints, thanks to Washington's ingenious design. Two worlds, with a clear progression laid out from one to the other: an American political primer in wood.

There as well, presiding over it all, would be that unfashionable cupola—unfashionable but also intriguingly evocative. For though houses with cupolas were rare in America, one that Washington unquestionably knew was the Governor's Palace in Williamsburg, and finding himself locked in conflict with the authority that structure represented, what could have been more logical than to appropriate its details for his own use? A single, imperial source of power was unacceptable in America; a cupola was simply a bit of decoration anyone could have who wanted one. To be sure, none of this may have been on Washington's mind, but he was a person who hardly ever acted without reflection. He also had a superb feel for gesture, as he would demonstrate time and again in the crowded years ahead. Through all those years, too, he would remain committed to independence—and to building his "uncommon," his singularly original, house.

NOTES

Following the Deerfield Symposium, parts of this essay were published in the author's *George Washington's Mount Vernon: At Home in Revolutionary America* (New York: Oxford University Press, 1998), a book co-written by Lee Baldwin Dalzell.

1. George Washington (hereafter GW) to Lund Washington, 20 August 1775, in *The Papers of George Washington*, ed. William W. Abbot and Dorothy Twohig (Charlottesville: University Press of Virginia, 1983–), rev. ser., 1:335.

2. Thomas T. Waterman, *The Mansions of Virginia: 1706 to 1776* (Chapel Hill: University of North Carolina Press, 1945), 268–98.

3. *Maryland Gazette*, 22 May 1751. The pattern book in question—William Adam, *Vitruvius Scotius; Being a Collection of Plans, Elevations, and Sections of Public Buildings, Noblemens and Gentlemen's Houses in Scotland: Principally from the designs of the Late William Adam, Esq. Architect* (Edinburgh: Messrs. A. & C. Black, n.d.)—does not appear in Helen Park, *A List of Architectural Books Available in America before the Revolution* (Los Angeles: Hennessey & Ingalls, 1973). Among the other houses Waterman attributes to Ariss, based on similarities to plates in *Vitruvius Scotius*, are Mount Airy in Richmond County and John Carlyle's house in Alexandria. In tracing Ariss's ancestry, Waterman surmises that he was the great-grandson of Nicholas Spencer, who purchased, with John Washington (the great-grandfather of George Washington), the land on which Mount Vernon was eventually built.

For a brief discussion of the architectural planning process at Mount Vernon that stresses the variety of sources Washington relied on and the importance of the role he himself played, see Walter M. Macomber, "Mount Vernon's Architect," *Historical Society of Fairfax County, Virginia* 10 (1969): 1–10.

4. The most complete account of Buckland's life and career is Rosamond Randall Beirne and John H. Scarff, *William Buckland, 1734–1774: Architect of Virginia and Maryland* (1958; reprint, Baltimore: Maryland Historical Society, 1970). See also William H. Pierson Jr., *American Buildings and Their Architects: The Colonial and Neo-Classical Styles* (Garden City, N.Y.: Anchor Press, 1970), 150–56; and on Maryland architecture in general, including Buckland's work, Mills Lane, *Architecture of the Old South: Maryland* (New York: Abbeville Press, 1991), 12–73.

5. The details of one of Washington's trips to Annapolis, including the names of the people who entertained him, can be found in *The Diaries of George Washington,* ed. Donald Jackson and Dorothy Twohig, 6 vols. (Charlottesville: University Press of Virginia, 1976–79), 3:136–37. On the growth and decline of trade and the merchant class during this period, see Edward C. Papenfuse, *In Pursuit of Profit: The Annapolis Merchants in the Era of the American Revolution* (Baltimore: Johns Hopkins University Press, 1975).

6. Pierson, in *American Buildings,* 141, goes so far as to assert that "most colonial buildings were not designed at all, but were simply built by local craftsmen who worked with available materials and skills in the established tradition." In contrast, Dell Upton, in *Holy Things and Profane: Anglican Parish Churches in Colonial Virginia* (Cambridge, Mass.: MIT Press, 1986), 28, emphasizes the precision of the planning process—at least in the case of parish churches—and its complexity: "The responsibilities that we customarily assign to the professional architect . . . were handled by a bewildering variety of people . . . If we cannot conceive of traditional craftsmen reeducated by cultivated gentlemen, we cannot locate design entirely in the builder to the exclusion of his client either. Who designed the churches? They all did. The fracture of high style and vernacular, of design and execution, along clear class or craft lines is impossible."

7. Pierson, *American Buildings,* 174–75, 186–87. A recent analysis of the structural changes made at Mount Vernon over the years is contained in the excellent, highly detailed "Historic Structure Report" prepared in 1993 for the Mount Vernon Ladies' Association (and now among the manuscripts in its library) by Mesick, Cohen, Waite, Architects. See also Dennis J. Pogue's fine overview of the development of the plantation during GW's proprietorship, "Mount Vernon: Transformation of an Eighteenth-Century Plantation System," in *Historical Archaeology of the Chesapeake,* ed. Paul A. Shackel and Barbara J. Little, (Washington, D.C.: Smithsonian Institution Press, 1994), 101–14.

8. In addition to the sources cited in the preceding note, Charles C. Wall, *George Washington, Citizen Soldier* (Charlottesville: University Press of Virginia, 1980), contains useful information about GW's second rebuilding of Mount Vernon.

9. The most complete biography of GW remains Douglas Southall Freeman's magisterial *George Washington: A Biography* (New York: Scribner, 1948). Less encyclopedic but still solidly reliable and considerably more lively is James T. Flexner's four-volume study, of which the relevant volume here is the first, *George Washington: The Forge of Experience (1732–1775)* (Boston: Little, Brown, 1965). Two other biographies particularly helpful for this period are John E. Ferling, *The First of Men: A Life of George Washington* (Knoxville: University of Tennessee Press, 1988), and Paul K. Longmore, *The Invention of George Washington* (Berkeley: University of California Press, 1988).

10. GW to Bryan Fairfax, 24 August 1774, in Washington, *Papers,* col. ser., 10:154–56.

11. Sears's work with Buckland at Gunston Hall—including the distinctive features of his carving—is analyzed in detail in Luke Beckerdite, "William Buckland and William Bernard Sears: The Designer and the Carver," *Journal of Early Southern Decorative Arts* 8, no 2 (1982): 7–40.

12. See Batty Langley, *The City and Country Builder's and Workman's Treasury of Designs: Or the Art of Drawing and Working the Ornamental Parts of Architecture* (1740; reprint, New York: B. Blom, 1967), plates 51, 38, 54, 49, and 55. Mesick, Cohen, Waite, Architects "Historic Structure Report," 121–29, offers a brief but comprehensive analysis of the use of printed architectural sources at Mount Vernon.

13. *Inventory of the Contents of Mount Vernon, 1810, with a Prefatory Note by Worthington Chauncey Ford* (Cambridge, Mass., 1909); for the listing of books, see 14–40. Complete titles, arranged by subject, can be found in *A Catalogue of the Washington Collection in the Boston Athenaeum*, comp. and ann. Appleton P. C. Griffin (Boston: Boston Athenaeum, 1897), app., 482–565. For further identification and description of the relevant titles, see John Archer, *The Literature of British Domestic Architecture* (Cambridge, Mass.: MIT Press, 1990), and Park, *List of Architectural Books.*

14. Carl Bridenbaugh treats Harrison's life and work in *Peter Harrison, First American Architect* (Chapel Hill: University of North Carolina Press, 1949); on the Redwood Library, see 48–53. See also Pierson, *American Buildings,* 142–50.

15. Among the many studies that have emphasized this point are Henry Glassie, *Folk Housing in Middle Virginia: A Structural Analysis of Historic Artifacts* (Knoxville: University of Tennessee Press, 1975); James Deetz, *In Small Things Forgotten: The Archeology of Early American Life* (Garden City, N.Y.: Anchor Books Doubleday, 1977); Richard L. Bushmann, *The Refinement of America: Persons, Houses, Cities* (New York: Knopf, 1992); and Kevin M. Sweeney, "High-Style Vernacular: Lifestyles of the Colonial Elite," in *Of Consuming Interests: The Style of Life in the Eighteenth Century,* ed. Cary Carson, Ronald Hoffman, and Peter J. Albert (Charlottesville: University Press of Virginia, 1992).

16. National Trust, *Saltram, Devon* (N.p., 1986), 38. This guidebook contains a detailed description of the house as well as a history of its building and biographical information about the Parkers.

17. Quoted in ibid., 51.

18. Jack Crowley in "Inventing Comfort: The Piazza" (an unpublished essay that the author was good enough to share with me in 1994) provides a fine discussion of the initial appearance of and possible sources for porches on American houses. His view is that West Indian influences were less important than the "stoops" *(stoeps)* found on houses in areas settled by the Dutch. Crowley describes Mount Vernon's piazza as "innovative" and notes that Washington "intended it to be a social space, not a token of Palladian style."

19. Mesick, Cohen, Waite, Architects, "Historic Structure Report," 123. The source for the details of the pillars (though not of their proportions) was Langley's *Treasury of Designs,* plate 51, where they appear as part of the design used for the Venetian window at the north end of Mount Vernon.

For a more extensive discussion of the use of the Tuscan order at Mount Vernon, see Scott Campbell Owen, "George Washington's Mount Vernon as British Palladian Architecture" (master's Thesis, University of Virginia, 1991). James S. Ackerman, in "The Tuscan/Rustic Order: A Study in the Metaphorical Language of Architecture," *Journal of the Society of Architectural Historians* 42 (1983): 15–34, provides a provocative discussion of the symbolic connotations of the Tuscan order. Of such matters, however, GW was almost certainly ignorant.

20. Bryan Fairfax to GW, 29 March 1778, Washington MSS, Library of Congress.

21. Quoted in Peter Stephen DuPonceau to Anna L. Garasche, 9 September 1837, copy the Mount Vernon Ladies' Association Library. DuPonceau, who had served as von Steuben's secretary and aide-de-campe, was confiding his memories to his granddaughter in his old age.

22. The building of Washington's houses in "the federal city," along with their subsequent history, is described in John P. Riley, "George Washington's Capital Hill Townhouses," *Mount Vernon Ladies' Association Annual Report, 1990,* 31–35. On William Thornton's life and career, see *Dictionary of American Biography,* 18:504–7. GW's strong partiality to the "grandeur, simplicity and beauty" of Thornton's plan for the Capitol was conveyed in a pair of letters to the Federal City Commissioners written 31 January and 3 March 1793, in *The Writings of George Washington from the Original Manuscript Sources, 1745–1799,* ed. John C. Fitzpatrick, (Washington, D.C.: U.S. Government Printing Office, 1931–44), 32:325, 363.

23. GW to William Thornton, 20 December 1798, in ibid., 37:6; William Thornton to GW, 25 December 1798, copy in Papers of George Washington, Office, Alderman Library, University of Virginia, Charlottesville.

24. GW to William Thornton, 30 December 1798, Washington, *Writings,* 37:79.

25. The most complete account of Monticello and its building is Jack McLaughlin's excellent *Jefferson and Monticello: The Biography of a Builder* (New York: H. Holt, 1988). Though none of them provide as much detail as McLaughlin's book, other thoughtful treatments of the subject are Paul Wilstach, *Jefferson and Monticello* (Garden City, N.Y.: Doubleday, Page, 1925); Frederick Doveton Nichols and Ralph E. Griswold, *Thomas Jefferson, Landscape Architect* (Charlottesville: University Press of Virginia, 1978); William Howard Adams, *Jefferson's Monticello* (New York, 1983); Pierson, *American Buildings,* 287–316; Lane, *Architecture of the Old South,* 90–125; James S. Ackerman, *The Villa* (Princeton: Princeton University Press, 1990), 185–213; and Giles Worsley, *Classical Architecture in Britain: The Heroic Age* (New Haven: Yale University Press, 1994), 285–87. An earlier version of my comparison here between Mount Vernon and Monticello can be found in Robert F. Dalzell Jr., "Constructing Independence: Monticello, Mount Vernon, and the Men Who Built Them," *Eighteenth-Century Studies* 26 (1993): 543–80.

IV

THOMAS JEFFERSON'S "BIBLIOMANIE"
AND ARCHITECTURE

Richard Guy Wilson

Writing to John Adams in 1815, Thomas Jefferson rued the recent sale of his library to the United States Congress with the complaint "I cannot live without books." Four years later, to another friend, he claimed that books were "a necessary of life." These letters confirmed the long-standing passion that Jefferson had confessed to one of his London agents in 1789: "I labour grievously under the malady of Bibliomanie."[1]

The library of an intellectual—or, in eighteenth-century terminology, a man of letters—can provide insights into that individual's mind (though one should remember the caveat that owning a book does not mean one has read it), and Jefferson was not only one of the most prominent intellectuals among the founding fathers but also one of America's most important architects. He and his library and readings have been studied from almost every imaginable perspective. Scholars have traced the origins of his political ideas to various Scottish and English philosophers and examined his imaginative mind with reference to his reading of the bard Ossian.[2] Researchers have exhumed his book-collecting habits, sought to learn when and how he acquired the various volumes, and, in an extreme act of fidelity, published a catalogue of the nearly 7,000 books he sold to Congress.[3]

In particular, scholars have pored over the various volumes he owned or recommended from an architectural point of view in an effort to determine how these may have influenced the designs of his buildings. Fiske Kimball in the 1910s was the first architectural historian to try to relate Jefferson's architectural library to his designs, and William B. "Pete" O'Neal in 1976 provided a thorough catalogue of the architectural titles.[4] Searching Jefferson's books for what he drew from them—or, as the British term it, "motif mongering"—offers a key, but the libraries he assembled, how he conceived of and used them, and his own *Notes on the State of Virginia* are all central to understanding Jefferson's architecture.

Jefferson's books might be imagined as existing in six different libraries. The first, collected prior to 1770, contained about 400 books. The second, the most famous, was composed of the nearly 7,000 volumes Jefferson assembled between 1770 and 1815, when he sold it to Congress after the British had burned the Capitol. His third library consisted of the books he assembled thereafter (for he immediately began purchasing replacement copies of volumes he had sold) and until his death in 1826, when it was dispersed. Jefferson kept a fourth, his "petite format library" of some 600 volumes, at Poplar Forest, his retreat near Lynchburg, Virginia. A fifth library can be conceived of as the list of approximately 8,000 volumes which he recommended for the new University of Virginia in 1825. The final and sixth library might be identified as his library of the mind: it comprises the commonplace books and journals in which he copied passages and made notes from books all his life.

Jefferson's first 400 volumes were those he inherited from his father, Peter Jefferson, along with books he purchased in Williamsburg while attending the College of William and Mary and then studying law. They were kept at Shadwell, his father's house, which stood across the Rivanna River from the small hill where he later constructed Monticello. A fire on 1 February 1770 destroyed Shadwell and most of its library. Writing to a friend about his "late loss . . . of every paper I had in the world, and almost every book," Jefferson explained that the cost of the books burned was £200 sterling and lamented, "Would to god it had been the money; then had it never cost me a sigh!"[5]

Jefferson's second library had become by 1815 one of the largest individual book collections in the country. Reflecting his personal interests, it contained legal works, poetry, history, scientific treatises, and architectural books; he owned more books dealing with architecture than any other American during these years. He collected avidly. Between the fire in 1770 and 1773 his purchases averaged one book per day—phenomenal for someone living essentially on the western frontier. When Jefferson left for France in 1784, he estimated that his library had 2,640 volumes, and during his nearly five years abroad he added at least 2,000 more. He described the method of purchasing: "While residing in Paris, I devoted every afternoon I was disengaged, for a summer or two, in examining all the principal bookstores, turning over every book with my own hand, and putting by everything which related to America, and indeed whatever was rare and valuable in every science. Besides this, I had standing orders during the whole time I was in Europe, on its principal book-marts, particularly Amsterdam, Frankfort, Madrid and London, for such work relating to America as could not be found in Paris."[6]

Obviously, Jefferson's books reflected his interests: among the 6,707 books sold to Congress in 1815, he listed 1,336 as politics, and his law category contained 692 (after all, Jefferson read for the law and practiced that profession for many years, but ultimately he was a politician). The library contained 271 books catalogued as religion, which reveals his concern and wide reading in a subject on which his opinions have sometimes been castigated. There were 208 volumes of foreign modern history. He did not have a category of fiction, which he generally dismissed as a waste of time, but his language and literature classification contained 602.[7]

In organizing and classifying these books, Jefferson had avoided the common method of shelving volumes by size; instead, he created his own system based on Francis Bacon's *Advancement of Learning* (Bacon, John Locke, and Isaac Newton were his three "idols"). Jefferson converted Bacon's three categories of Memory, Reason and Imagination into History, Philosophy, and Fine Arts (figure 4.1). These he separated into further categories, concluding with what he called "chapters." For instance, chapter 1 was Ancient History. Within Fine Arts, chapter 31 was Gardening; chapter 32, Architecture; chapter 33, Sculpture. The last, chapter 46, he labeled "Polygraphical" and described its contents as "Authors who have written in Various branches" (figure 4.2).

Jefferson's architecture books were a small part of the 6,707 volumes sold to Congress: the official list contained 43 titles classified as architecture, and 25 more under gardening, painting, and sculpture.[8] Clearly, Jefferson had access to or knew of other architectural books, since the list he drew up for the University of Virginia included many more. (The list that O'Neal compiled for his *Jefferson's Fine Arts Library* (1976) contains 130 titles classified as architecture, and 19 more on painting, music, and sculpture. That total, however, included some books Jefferson ordered for the university but never owned, as well as books he classified elsewhere, such as surveying, guidebooks to cities, and naval architecture.) Yet even the 43 architectural titles sold to Congress in 1815 easily ranks as one of the most impressive private architecture libraries in the United States at the time.

Jefferson assigned his architecture books an order: both the list he sent to Congress and his list for the university began that chapter with volumes on ancient buildings,

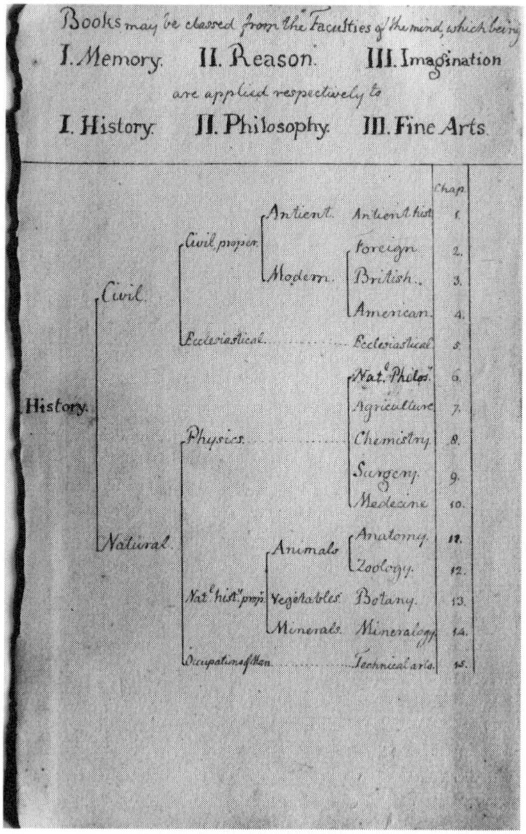

Books may be classed from the faculties of the mind, which being

I. Memory.   II. Reason.   III. Imagination

are applied respectively to

I. History.   II. Philosophy.   III. Fine Arts.

				Chap
History.	Civil.	Civil proper.	Antient.	Antient hist.	1
			Modern. Foreign	2.
			British.	3.
			American.	4.
		Ecclesiastical.	Ecclesiastical	5
	Natural.	Physics.	Nat. Philos.	6.
			Agriculture	7.
			Chemistry	8.
			Surgery	9.
			Medecine	10.
		Nat. hist. propr.	Animals Anatomy.	11.
			Zoology.	12.
		Vegetables Botany.	13.
		Minerals Mineralogy.	14.
	Occupations of Man.	Technical arts.	15.

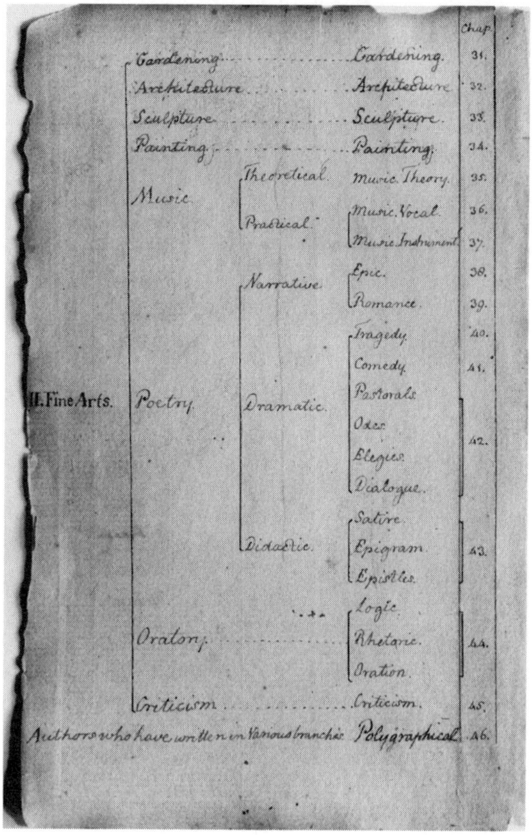

				Chap
		Gardening	Gardening.	31.
		Architecture	Architecture	32.
		Sculpture	Sculpture.	33.
		Painting	Painting.	34.
	Music	Theoretical.	Music. Theory.	35.
		Practical.	Music. Vocal.	36.
			Music. Instrument.	37.
		Narrative.	Epic.	38.
			Romance.	39.
II. Fine Arts.	Poetry	Dramatic.	Tragedy.	40.
			Comedy	41.
			Pastorals.	
			Odes	42.
			Elegies	
			Dialogue.	
		Didactic.	Satire.	
			Epigram	43.
			Epistles	
			Logic	
	Oratory		Rhetoric	44.
			Oration.	
	Criticism		Criticism.	45.
	Authors who have written in various branches		Polygraphical	46.

FIG 4.1 Thomas Jefferson's library catalogue, 1783. Courtesy of the Massachusetts Historical Society, Boston.
FIG 4.2 (*right*) Thomas Jefferson's library catalogue, 1783. Courtesy of the Massachusetts Historical Society, Boston.

such as Julien-David Le Roy's *Les ruines des plus beaux monuments de la Grèce* (1758). Next came the architecture of different countries, such as Johann Karl Krafft and Pierre Nicolas Ransonette's *Plans . . . des . . . maisons et des hôtels à Paris,* which was published in parts during 1801 and 1802. (Jefferson purchased his copy of the first part on 24 December 1804 for $40 and subsequently tried to buy further parts.)[9] Following the titles arranged by country came books that provided architectural models of what we might call "modern architecture"; to Jefferson this meant primarily the Classical revival during what we label today the Renaissance and its progeny. Jefferson's hero was Palladio, and over the years he owned at least seven editions of Palladio's books.

He preferred the English-language editions by Giacomo Leoni of Palladio's *Four Books,* published in 1715, 1721, and 1752, though he also obtained a French edition. (He never owned the Lord Burlington–sponsored Isaac Ware editions, which received the sanction and approval of the English Palladians.) From books on contemporary design models, Jefferson's architectural catalogue progressed to a natural conclusion: more technical books illustrating the actual processes of construction, such as Batty Langley's *Practical Geometry* (1729), the two-volume *Builder's Dictionary* (1731–34), Charles Plumier's *L'Art de tourner* (1701), and Philibert Delorme's *Nouvelles Inventions pour bien bastir* (1576). Delorme's book illustrated for Jefferson the method for wood-framed domes and is the source for the construction at Monticello.[10] He sold his copy to Congress in 1814 and hence had to borrow a copy when the university's rotunda was constructed.[11] This list that Jefferson drew up implied a deliberate order: history or the ancients came first, then nationalities, followed by modern design, and finally execution or technique. It was a carefully articulated and rational system.

Jefferson's reliance upon these books is well known. Benjamin Henry Latrobe backhandedly complimented Jefferson's talents to a correspondent: "Jefferson was an excellent architect out of books," and "I am cramped in this design by his [Jefferson's] prejudices in favor of the architecture of the old french books, out of which he fishes everything."[12] In many cases Jefferson clearly spelled out his sources; for instance, on the back of a drawing for the rotunda he wrote, "Rotunda, reduced to the proportions of the Pantheon and accommodated to the purposes of a Library of the University."[13] It was Latrobe who suggested a domed building (although Jefferson had earlier, in 1791, proposed one for the United States Capitol), and taking the suggestion, Jefferson turned to the Leoni edition of Palladio, but he misunderstood the concept of the sphere as the inner space and instead transcribed the sphere as the exterior skin (figure 4.3). For Jefferson, pure geometric forms such as cubes and spheres embodied perfection.[14]

Equally important, Jefferson made the rotunda the central structure of the academical village and altered its meaning: the dome, which had symbolized the cosmos to the Romans and then the heavens in Christian cathedrals, now became the symbol of enlightenment and rationality. It housed the library, figuratively and literally the mind of the university. It was one of Jefferson's many accomplishments to make the library the physical center of the modern university.

The theme of the library as the central feature can be found also in Jefferson's other buildings, including Monticello. Monticello I (the house designed and constructed between about 1769 and the early 1780s) owes a debt, as many scholars have indicated,

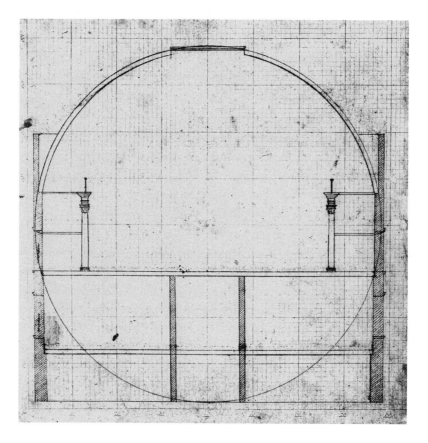

FIG 4.3 Thomas Jefferson, section of the university's Rotunda (library), ca. 1818–19. Pricking, iron-gall ink on laid paper engraved with coordinate lines, 8³/₄ × 8³/₄ in., N-239s. Thomas Jefferson Architectural Drawings, University Archives, Special Collections Department, University of Virginia Library.

to Robert Morris's *Select Architecture* (1755), Leoni's translation of Palladio, and several villas shown therein (figure 4.4). Monticello I's plan and organization can be read in many ways but the hierarchy is clear. Jefferson placed the house on top of the hill and submerged the services—cooking, larders, storage, stables—into the hillside in an outflung Palladian scheme. Above that, the ground floor of the central pavilion contained drawing room, dining room, bedroom, and a passage. On the upper or second floor Jefferson located one large room, that served as the library and opened on the upper portico. The highest elevation on the mountain, then, was the library—quite clearly the central hierarchical element.

About 1792 Jefferson began a redesign of Monticello that substantially altered the relationship of the library to the rest of the building. Construction began about 1796,

FIG 4.4 Thomas Jefferson, study for elevation of Monticello I, ca. 1771–72. Ink on laid paper, 18³/₄ × 13¹/₂ in., N-47. Thomas Jefferson Architecural Drawings, University Archives, Special Collections Department, University of Virginia Library.

and although it was substantially completed by 1809, Jefferson continued to make alterations until his death in 1826. In so doing he created the house that we know today and that graces the back of the nickel (figure 4.5). As with Monticello I, Jefferson's sources for the new Monticello's design included Leoni's Palladio and Morris's *Select Architecture* but also other books in his library as well as observations made during his travels abroad.

Among the major exterior changes was the dome capping the garden facade of the house and creating an image without parallel for its period in the United States. But the interior space of the dome apparently had no real function—a puzzling lack of purpose, since Jefferson normally had rational reasons for what he did. Perhaps he intended that space for the library but decided that the journey from his first-floor

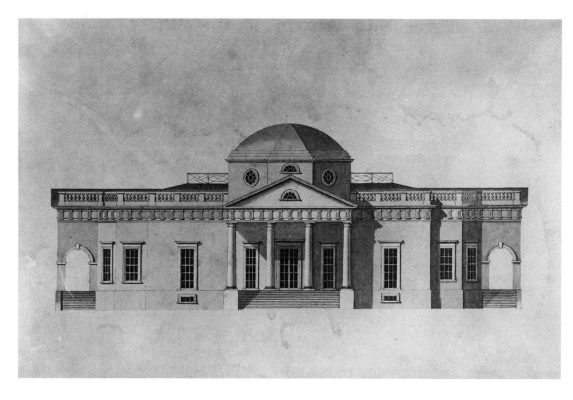

FIG 4.5 Monticello, west elevation, drawn by Robert Mills, ca. 1803. Ink and wash on paper, 16 × 20¹/4 in., N-154/K155. Thomas Jefferson Papers. Courtesy of the Massachusetts Historical Society, Boston.

bedroom to the dome was too lengthy? This is pure conjecture, but the unused space is surprising, given Jefferson's overwhelming desire in almost every endeavor to find utility. Strikingly, Jefferson's new Monticello made the library integral with his bedroom. He created one continuous space that united his bedchamber, cabinet (or study), and library (figure 4.6). One visitor, Margaret Bayard Smith, characterized it as his "sanctum sanitarium."[15]

The library that the visitor sees today at Monticello holds only about 1,200 books, but contemporary descriptions note that in Jefferson's own rooms, books were stacked on high tables and the floor. Isaac Jefferson, a slave, explained how Jefferson used them: "Old Master had abundance of books; sometimes would have twenty of 'em down on the floor at once—read fust one, then tother. Isaac has often wondered how Old Master came to have such a mighty head; read so many of them books; and when they go to him to ax him anything, he go right straight to the book and tell you all about it."[16]

Isaac Jefferson's words confirm what Jefferson's granddaughter Ellen Randolph

FIG 4.6 Monticello, view of the library from the cabinet. Photo courtesy of the Thomas Jefferson Memorial Foundation. Copyright © 1993 Robert C. Lautman / Monticello.

Coolidge—a companion and secretary during his later years—once observed: "Books were at all times his chosen companions"; he preferred them to the company of many individuals.[17] The picture one imagines finding—if one could have invaded the library-study-bedroom—is of shelves filled to overflowing, books piled up and spread out on the floor, Jefferson surrounded by books as in a dream realized, living among books, day and night, at the fingertips, to be read, looked at, touched, and caressed.

On the surface, Jefferson's contribution to American architectural writing appears minimal: he never wrote a book on architecture and indeed did not support—as far as we know—the early efforts of Asher Benjamin or Owen Biddle. Apparently, he never owned Benjamin's *Country Builder's Assistant* (1797) or Biddle's *Young Carpenter's Assistant* (1805), though he did own several American imprints such as William Birch's *City of Philadelphia* (1800), and he had access to the price books of the Carpenters' Company of Philadelphia. In his voluminous correspondence, however, Jefferson often mentioned building, especially his own projects, and for projects such as the design of universities, his advice was frequently sought.[18]

One finds Jefferson's real contribution as an architectural writer, though, in *Notes on the State of Virginia,* his only published book. In spite of the title, it covers more territory than just Virginia and comments on everything: military forces, climate, seaports, aborigines, and manufactures. Written in 1780–81 and revised over the next several years, *Notes* was originally published in French (in Paris) in 1785 and then in English (in London) in 1787. Writing partially in response to French queries and also to the assertion of the French naturalist Georges-Louis Leclerc, Comte de Buffon, that the American environment produced inferior species of animals (and, by extension, humans), Jefferson indulged in "American exceptionalism." Nevertheless, he wrote, "The genius of architecture seems to have shed its maledictions over this land," and "the first principles of the art are unknown." And of Williamsburg, he observed, "The College and Hospital are rude, misshapen piles, which, but that they have roofs, would be taken for brick-kilns."[19] Jefferson might be claimed as the originator of America's slash-and-burn school of architectural criticism.

Of much greater and future significance, however, are Jefferson's passionate descriptions of America's natural scenery. He wrote: "The passage of the Patowmac [*sic*] through the Blue ridge is perhaps one of the most stupendous scenes in nature," and then painted a picture in words: "You stand on a very high point of land. On your right comes up the Shenandoah having ranged along the foot of the mountain an hundred miles to seek a vent. On your left approaches the Patowmac, in quest of a passage also. In the moment of their junction they rush together against the mountain, rend it asunder . . . The piles of rock on each hand . . . [are] the evident marks of their disrupture and avulsion from their beds by the most powerful agents of nature."[20]

Over the years Jefferson acquired prints and paintings of many of the views he described in *Notes*. He considered Niagara Falls among America's natural wonders and displayed two prints of the "Cascade" in the Monticello dining room. He also hung there a painting of Virginia's Natural Bridge (figure 4.7), which coincidentally he owned and extolled as "the most sublime of Nature's works . . . The fissure, just at the bridge, is, by some admeasurements, 270 feet deep, by others only 205. It is about 45 feet wide at the bottom, and 90 feet at the top; this of course determines the length of the bridge . . . A part of [its] thickness is constituted by a coat of earth, which gives growth of many large trees . . . You involuntarily fall on your hands and feet, creep to the parapet and peep over it. Looking down from this height about a minute, gave me a violent headache. . . . It is impossible for the emotions, arising from the sublime, to be felt beyond what they are here: so beautiful and arch, so elevated, so light and springing as it were, up to heaven, the rapture of the Spectator is really indescribable!"[21]

Though written within the eighteenth-century convention of describing landscape, these statements have left as a legacy the importance of landscape to American art and architecture. Likewise, when later in the book he asserted, "Those who labour in the earth are the chosen people of God," he helped create the ethos of the countryside as the repository of American values. Jefferson's heirs include Thomas Cole, Ralph Waldo Emerson, John Muir, John Burroughs, and of course, in architecture, A. J. Downing, Gustav Stickley, and Frank Lloyd Wright. Certainly Jefferson was not the only writer to establish an appreciation of the landscape as a major motif in American design, but he was among the earliest. He conceived of buildings such as Monticello and those of the University of Virginia as both participants in the landscape and points from which to view that landscape.

All these themes—Jefferson's love of books, his libraries and their centrality in his architecture, his reliance upon books for design, and his appreciation of landscape—came together at Poplar Forest, the retreat he designed and built about 1806 to 1811 in Bedford County, outside of Lynchburg, Virginia. It was, he told Dr. Benjamin Rush, "a place, 90 miles from Monticello . . . which I visit three or four times a year . . . I have fixed myself comfortably, keep some books here, bring others occasionally, am in the solitude of a hermit."[22]

Poplar Forest's plan, an octagonal outer shape that encloses a cube and other forms, probably owes its origin to a book, Wilhelm Gottlieb Becker's *Neue Garten- und Landschafts-Gebäude* (1798–99), which Jefferson purchased on 21 June 1805 at a cost of

FIG 4.7 J. C. Stadler, engraver, after William Roberts, *Natural Bridge*, 1808. Courtesy of the Thomas Jefferson Memorial Foundation.

$17, plus $2 for the binding. Plate 20b (figure 4.8), showing a garden temple, provides the clearest link with the plans Jefferson sketched in 1806 and subsequently built.[23] The sequence of spaces at Poplar Forest consist of an entry porch, a narrow hall, a cube-shaped dining room, and at the end of axis the library-parlor, overlooking the landscape beyond.

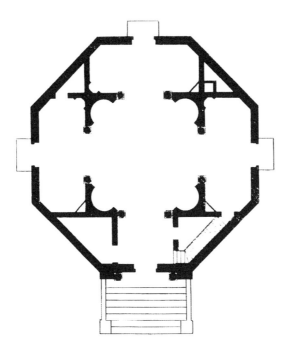

FIG 4.8 Wilhelm Gottlieb Becker, *Neue Garten- und Landschafts-Gebäude* (1798–99), plate 20b.

Here we can imagine Jefferson with his "petite format library" of over 600 volumes, indulging what he described as "a canine appetite for reading."[24] Here his granddaughters Ellen and Cornelia remembered him reading, sometimes aloud, his 108 volumes of British poets, or Buffon's *Histoire Naturelle,* or John Bell's edition of Shakespeare— or sitting deep in thought while gazing out on the landscape. As a youth Jefferson discovered the Roman poet Horace and copied into his commonplace book a passage that became part of his library of the mind: "O' rural home: when shall I behold you! When shall I be able, now with books of the ancients, now with sleep and idle hours, to quaff sweet forgetfulness of life's cares!"[25]

NOTES

1. Jefferson to Adams, 10 June 1815, in *The Writings of Thomas Jefferson,* ed. Andrew A. Liscomb and Albert Ellery Bergh (Washington, D.C.: Thomas Jefferson Memorial Association, 1905), 13:301; Jefferson to Richard Rush, 22 June 1819, in *The Works of Thomas Jefferson,* ed. Paul Leicester Ford (New York: Putnam, 1905), 12:127; Jefferson to Lucy Ludwell Paradise, 1 June 1789, in *The Papers of Thomas Jefferson,* ed. Julian P. Boyd (Princeton: Princeton University Press, 1958), 15:163.

2. See, e.g., Douglas L. Wilson, "Jefferson and the Republic of Letters," and Rhys Isaac, "The First Monticello," both in *Jefferson Legacies,* ed. Peter S. Onuf (Charlottesville: University Press of Virginia, 1993), 50–76, 77–108.

3. William Harwood Peden, "Thomas Jefferson: Book Collector" (Ph.D. diss., University of Virginia, 1942); Charles B. Sanford, *Thomas Jefferson and His Library* (Hamden, Conn.: Archon Books, 1977); Douglas L. Wilson, *Jefferson's Books* (Charlottesville, Va.: Thomas Jefferson Memorial Foundation, 1996); and E. Millicent Sowerby, comp., *Catalogue of the Library of Thomas Jefferson,* 5 vols. (Washington, D.C.: Library of Congress, 1952–59).

4. Fiske Kimball, *Thomas Jefferson, Architect* (Boston: privately printed, 1916); William Bainter O'Neal, *Jefferson's Fine Arts Library: His Selections for the University of Virginia Together with His Own Architectural Books* (Charlottesville: University Press of Virginia, 1976).

5. Jefferson to John Page, 20 February 1770, in Jefferson, *Papers,* 1:34–35.

6. Jefferson to Samuel H. Smith, 21 September 1814, in Jefferson, *Writings,* 14:191.

7. These figures are from Sanford, *Thomas Jefferson and His Library,* 94–95, 99.

8. Ibid., 94.

9. O'Neal, *Jefferson's Fine Arts Library,* 179.

10. Douglas James Harnsberger, " 'In Delorme's manner—': A Study of the Applications of Philibert Delorme's Dome Construction Method in Early 19th-Century American Architecture" (master's thesis, University of Virginia, 1981).

11. Jefferson to General Joseph Smith, 21 June 1825, University of Virginia Collection, Charlottesville.

12. Latrobe to John Lenthall, 3 May 1805, quoted in *The Correspondence and Miscellaneous Papers of Benjamin Henry Latrobe,* 3 vols., ed. John C. Van Horne et al. (New Haven: Yale University Press, 1984–88), 2:197 n. 1.

13. Jefferson, drawing N 331, University of Virginia Library Special Collections.

14. Joseph Lasala, "Comparative Analysis: Thomas Jefferson's Rotunda and the Pantheon in Rome," *Virginia Studio Record* 1 (fall 1988): 84–87; Jefferson, "An Account of the Capitol in Virginia," in Fiske Kimball, *The Capitol of Virginia: A Landmark of American Architecture,* rev. ed., ed Jon Kukla with Martha Vick and Sarah Shields Driggs (Richmond: Virginia State Library and Archives, 1988), 13.

15. Margaret Bayard Smith, *The First Forty Years of Washington Society,* ed. Gaillard Hunt (1906; reprint, New York: Frederick Ungar, 1965), 71.

16. Quoted in James A. Bear Jr., ed., *Jefferson at Monticello* (Charlottesville: University Press of Virginia, 1967), 12.

17. Quoted anonymously in Henry S. Randall, *Life of Thomas Jefferson* (New York: Derby & Jackson, 1858) 3:346.

18. Jefferson to L. W. Tazewell, 5 January 1805, Special Collections, University of Virginia; Jefferson to the Trustees for the Lottery of East Tennessee College, 6 May 1810, Library of Congress.

19. Thomas Jefferson, *Notes on the State of Virginia,* ed. William Peden (Chapel Hill: University of North Carolina Press, 1953), 153.

20. Ibid., 19.

21. Ibid., 24–25.

22. Jefferson to Benjamin Rush, 17 August 1811, Library of Congress.

23. S. Allen Chambers Jr., *Poplar Forest and Thomas Jefferson* (Forest, Va.: Corporation for Jefferson's Poplar Forest, 1993), 31, 33, identifies the Becker source.

24. Jefferson to John Adams, 17 May 1818, in *The Writings of Thomas Jefferson,* ed. Henry A. Washington (New York: Derby & Jackson, 1859), 7:104.

25. *Jefferson's Literary Commonplace Book,* ed. Douglas L. Wilson (Princeton: Princeton University Press, 1989), 83.

V

DEFINING THE PROFESSION:
BOOKS, LIBRARIES, AND ARCHITECTS

Martha J. McNamara

*In 1809 a group of builders founded the Architectural Library of Boston "for the encourage-*ment of the Sciences—Architecture, Painting and Sculpture; and for the mutual advantage of each other and our associates."[1] In its constitution, published the same year, the library's proprietors defined the scope of the collection, the terms of admittance, and the rules of book borrowing (figures 5.1, 5.2). With the constitution they also published a catalogue of the library's holdings: fifty-five volumes, primarily English pattern books and books on drawing and perspective. As the first public library in New England devoted exclusively to architecture and allied arts, the Architectural Library of Boston signaled the development of a professional self-consciousness emerging among architects during the early nineteenth century. Its founders used a new framework for reading, the semipublic "social library," to help promote their professional goals.

To understand the library's significance—its initial establishment, its activities, and, ultimately, its demise—we must place this innovative institution within the larger context of changing attitudes toward books, libraries, and reading in the early Republic. The early nineteenth century saw an explosion of printing, reading, and publishing. Not only were the numbers of books published in U.S. urban centers vastly outstripping eighteenth-century levels, but historians of the book also point out that publishing in this period was highly decentralized—a pattern underscored by the publication of Asher Benjamin's *Country Builder's Assistant* in Greenfield, Massachusetts.

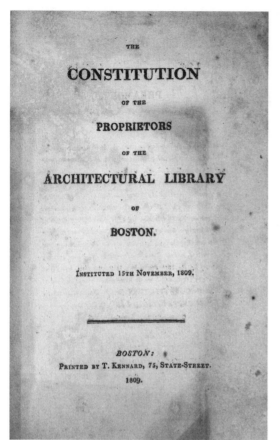
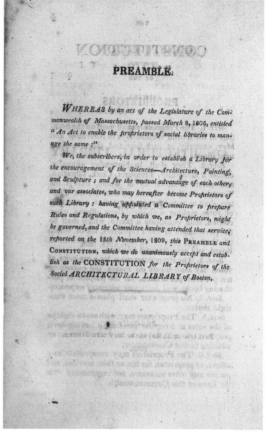

FIG 5.1 Title page of *The Constitution of the Proprietors of the Architectural Library of Boston* (1809). Courtesy of the Society for the Preservation of New England Antiquities, Boston.
FIG 5.2 (*right*) Preamble of *The Constitution of the Proprietors*. Courtesy of the Society for the Preservation of New England Antiquities, Boston.

Underlying these widespread changes were a number of transformations: a rapid increase in the rate of literacy, new print and papermaking technologies that reduced the price of books, improvements in marketing, and a general speeding up of communication.[2] Historians of architecture, for the most part, have not assessed the impact of reading and the spread of reading and publishing on architects or their clients.[3] But recognizing reading as a *process* and the role of architectural publications within that process is fundamental to an understanding of the profession of architecture in the United States in the early nineteenth century. In this context, the establishment of a library explicitly for the collection and dissemination of architectural texts to an exclusive group of designers eager to define themselves as a profession represents an important moment in the relationship between books and buildings.

Scholars who have touched on the founding of the Architectural Library of Boston have seen it primarily as a symptom or byproduct of architectural professionalization. Christopher Monkhouse's study of architect Alexander Parris's book collecting noted his donation of at least one book to the library's collection. Jack Quinan's work on the early architecture profession situated the library in relation to nascent architectural schools and professional organizations in Boston at about the same time and Edward Zimmer's dissertation on Alexander Parris explored Parris's active involvement with the library.[4] The primary focus of this scholarship has been on the library's holdings and their ultimate disposition. Missing, however, is an assessment of the Architectural Library of Boston as an example of one of the most popular and powerful cultural institutions emerging in the early nineteenth century: in short, as a *library*.

The Architectural Library's constitution and catalogue published in 1809 provides valuable information about the role of this institution in the professionalization of architecture.[5] Five members of the Boston building community instigated the library's organization: Ithiel Town and Solomon Willard (architects), Samuel Waldron and Nathaniel Critchet (housewrights), and John Gill (stucco worker).[6] It seems clear that of these founders, the moving force behind the library was Ithiel Town. Town's personal library amounted to 11,000 volumes when it was offered for sale in the 1840s, and he was also involved in establishing such organizations as the New York Academy of Fine Arts in 1835.[7] Solomon Willard, best known for his design of the Bunker Hill Monument, was a life subscriber to the Boston Athenaeum, an active member in the Massachusetts Charitable Mechanic Association, and vice president of the Boston Mechanics' Institution.[8] Samuel Waldron and John Gill were members of organizations catering to the building trades in Boston, including the Society of Associated Housewrights and the Massachusetts Charitable Mechanic Association (MCMA).[9] Except for Town's, very little is known about the possible scope of these builders' personal libraries or about their book-buying activities. Clearly, however, the founders of the library felt the need for easy access to printed works on architecture and fine arts. Perhaps they believed that this access would become more difficult as expensive books found their way to elite institutions. As an example, the death of colonial builder Thomas Dawes resulted in the donation of his valuable library to the Boston Athenaeum in January 1809.[10]

The organizational structure of the Architectural Library of Boston echoed that of eighteenth-century "social" or "subscription" libraries. It was a joint-stock or proprietary library in which individuals purchased shares in order to gain the privilege of borrowing books. Each proprietor could own up to eight shares, and each share gave the proprietor one vote at the library's monthly meetings. Although the initial cost of shares is unknown, by 1827 they were worth $5.60 apiece.[11] The borrowing terms were quite liberal. Every proprietor was allotted 26 percent per year of the value of the library "which he shall receive in the use of books only; but if he doesn't take the percentage allowed him in the use of books . . . he shall forfeit it to the funds and be charged the same as though he had received it."[12] The total value of the library as printed in the 1809 catalogue was about $500, 26 percent of which is $130. To borrow a book, a proprietor was assessed percent of the value of the book as determined by the library's governing board. To borrow, therefore, one of the most highly valued books in the collection, Antony [sic] Desgodetz, The Ancient Buildings of Rome, cost only thirty-three cents. One of the most inexpensive, Peter Nicholson's Student's Instructor, would cut into a proprietor's allocation by only two cents. It is this complicated borrowing policy that explains the careful valuation of each volume in the library's catalogue (figure 5.3).

The initial collection of fifty-five books, as indicated in the 1809 catalogue, represented a broad range of publications that would have been useful to ambitious builders who were looking to define architecture as a profession separate from that of builders and mechanics. English patternbooks included those of Batty Langley, Abraham Swan, and William Pain. Building and construction techniques were represented by such carpenters' guides as Asher Benjamin's American Builder's Companion and Owen Biddle's Young Carpenter's Assistant. Ten of the fifty-five books concerned drawing and perspective; five were devoted to painting.

Although the constitution indicated that future acquisitions would be made through purchase (three-quarters to be works on architecture and perspective and the rest on painting and sculpture), it seems likely that most of the initial collection was acquired through donation. In this way, the Architectural Library of Boston differed from other social libraries, whose proprietors usually ordered books as soon as enough library shares were purchased. One of the first actions of the Social Law Library founded in Boston six years earlier, for instance, was to order 1,000 law books from England. Moreover, booksellers, always on the lookout for new markets, often advertised special discounts for newly established social libraries.[13]

Surviving volumes from the Architectural Library show evidence of previous ownership and underscore the notion that the initial collection was pulled together from individual donations rather than acquired through planned purchasing.[14] Signatures in

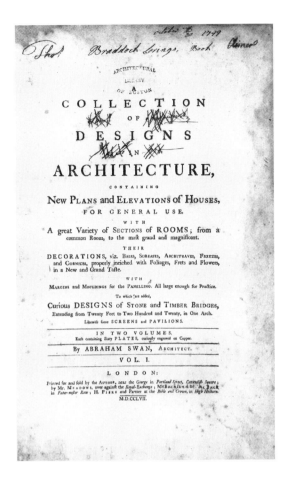

FIG 5.3 Catalogue of the Architectural Library of Boston showing the values assigned to each volume for borrowing purposes. Courtesy of the Society for the Preservation of New England Antiquities, Boston.
FIG 5.4 (*right*) Title page of Abraham Swan, *A Collection of Designs in Architecture* (1757), bearing the Architectural Library stamp and the signatures of three previous owners. Courtesy of the Society for the Preservation of New England Antiquities, Boston.

two volumes indicate that they had a similar provenance and, most significantly, had been owned by Boston housewright and Architectural Library shareholder Braddock Loring. The first, a copy of Abraham Swan's *Collection of Designs in Architecture* (London, 1757), has the library's red stamp on the title page and three inscriptions: "Samuel Sedgwick, Ma[r,y?] 1770"; a partially illegible signature, "Thos. [Aimes?]," which presumably came after Sedgwick's; and "Braddock Loring's Book, October 30, 1799" (figure 5.4).[15] Two of these inscriptions, "Thos. [Aimes?]" and the Loring signature and date, also appear in the 1750 edition of Batty Langley's *City and Country Builder's and Workman's Treasury of Designs;* a third inscription, however, "A. Benjamin 1807," indicates that perhaps Asher Benjamin donated the volume to the Architectural Library (figure 5.5). Benjamin's signature also appears on Abraham Swan's *British Architect,* along with the ink inscription "E. S." subsequently crossed out.[16]

Despite the fact that the proprietors probably did not hand-select the collection from booksellers' offerings, their decision to publish a catalogue and to print large, decorative bookplates testify to the care given to identifying the library as a cohesive, enduring institution and to a concern for systematically ordering the collection. Surviving volumes bearing Architectural Library of Boston bookplates, with Federal period swags and inked numbers corresponding to the published catalogue, indicate that the catalogue and bookplates were most likely produced at the same time (figures 5.6 and 5.3).

The bookplates found in four of the surviving volumes also provide valuable information about the collection's history; in particular, they confirm that the library continued acquiring books after the catalogue's initial publication. Although *The Builder's Dictionary: or Architect's Companion* (London, 1734) does not appear in the 1809 catalogue, a copy bearing an Architectural Library bookplate and the signature of the Boston builder Thomas Dawes survives among the volumes of the Bulfinch library at the Massachusetts Institute of Technology.[17] The bookplate number "62" indicates that it was acquired after the initial collection of fifty-five volumes, and its subsequent renumbering to "83" proves that at one time the library's collection numbered more than eighty volumes (figure 5.7). Two other surviving bookplates also have their initial numbers crossed out and a second number recorded in ink. These changes verify that the collection must have been reordered at some time after the catalogue's publication, perhaps to allow for later donations. *The History of Whitby Abbey,* by Lionel Charlton, for instance, appears in the published catalogue as number 40, whereas the bookplate number in the extant volume is "40" later corrected to "60" (figures 5.8, 5.9, and 5.10).[18] This volume also bears the pencil inscription "Parris donation" on the title page, which could indicate either the book's donation to the library by Alexander Parris in 1809 or its ultimate bequest to the Massachusetts Charitable Mechanic Association in 1850 with the rest of the library, which had been housed in Parris's office since 1837 (figure 5.11).[19]

The physical organization of the library also underscores the institution's importance to the professionalization of architecture. Although its initial location cannot be determined, after 1822 it occupied a room at 96 Court Street, close to Alexander Parris's office at 93 Court and steps away from Boston's commercial center. In that year the Architectural Library had come largely under the control of the Society of Associated

FIG 5.5 Title page of Batty Langley, *The City and Country Builder's and Workman's Treasury of Designs* (1750), bearing the Architectural Library stamp and the signatures of Braddock Loring and Asher Benjamin. Photo by the author.

FIG 5.6 (*right*) Bookplate in Joshua Kirby, *The Perspective of Architecture* (1761). Photo by the author.

Housewrights, founded in 1804, which worked to encourage fraternity among builders, provide relief for those in distress, and establish rules regarding apprentices. In 1826 the Associated Housewrights voted to hold a school in the "Library room" for "the instruction of Apprentices in Architectural Drawing." They paid the "Lybrarian" James McAllaster for "fixtures, chairs &c for Library Room and expences of School."[20] Housing the library in a dedicated space, appointing a librarian to care for the collection, and holding classes in architectural drawing helped to foster the cohesion of the emerging profession by establishing architecture as an exclusive activity requiring careful study and training. A library room, after all, furnished with chairs and tables to accommodate the readers, promoted a "communal reading performance" rather than

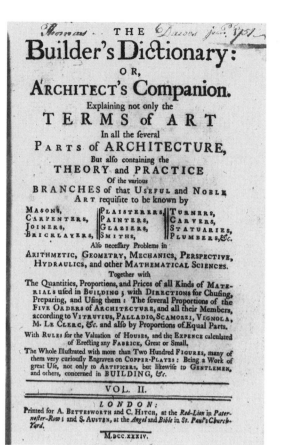

FIG 5.7 Title page of *The Builder's Dictionary: or, Architect's Companion* (1734), bearing the signature "Thomas Dawes junr. 1751." Courtesy of the Rotch Library of Architecture and Planning, Massachusetts Institute of Technology.

FIG 5.8 (*right*) Bookplate in *The Builder's Dictionary* indicating the renumbering of the Architectural Library's collections. Courtesy of the Rotch Library of Architecture and Planning, Massachusetts Institute of Technology.

FIG 5.9 (*opposite, top left*) Bookplate in Lionel Charlton, *The History of Whitby Abbey* (1779). Courtesy of the Society for the Preservation of New England Antiquities, Boston.

FIG 5.10 (*opposite, right*) Page from the catalogue of the Architectural Library showing the entry (no. 40) for *The History of Whitby Abbey*. Courtesy of the Society for the Preservation of New England Antiquities, Boston.

FIG 5.11 (*opposite, bottom left*) Title page of *The History of Whitby Abbey* with pencil inscription "Parris Donation" in upper right corner. Courtesy of the Society for the Preservation of New England Antiquities, Boston.

BOSTON
ARCHITECTURAL
LIBRARY.

No. 60

THE
HISTORY
OF
WHITBY,
AND OF
WHITBY ABBEY.

Collected from the original Records of the Abbey, and other authentic Memoirs,
never before made public.

CONTAINING,

Not only the History of Whitby and the Country adjacent, but also the Original and
Antiquity of many particular Families and Places in other Parts of Yorkshire.

DIVIDED INTO THREE BOOKS.

Book I. The History of Whitby, and of Whitby Abbey, before the Conquest.

Book II. The Continuation of that History to the Dissolution of the Monastery.

Book III. The further Continuation of that History to the End of the Year 1776,
with the present State of Whitby, &c. &c. &c.

Nescire quod antequam natus esses actum est, id semper esse puerum. CICERO.

By LIONEL CHARLTON,
Teacher of the Mathematics at Whitby.

YORK:

Printed by A. Ward; and sold in London by T. Cadell, in the Strand, and
G. Robinson, in Pater-noster-Row: As also by all the Booksellers in York; and
by J. Monkman, Bookseller in Whitby.

M, DCC, LXXIX.

27—Ferme Ornée, or Rural Improvements; a series of domestic and ornamental designs, suited to parks, plantations, rides, walks, &c. consisting of fences, pavillions, farm-yards, sporting boxes, single and double cottages, &c. By John Plaw; engraved in aquatinta, on 38 plates, with appropriate scenery, plans, and explanations. 9 00

28—The Practice of Perspective, by a Jesuit of Paris, with 150 plates.

29—A new collection of an hundred Views in Rome. 4 50

30—The Carpenter's Complete Instructor, in several hundred designs. By Abraham Swan. On 53 plates. 3 50

31—The Rudiments of Architecture, or the Young Workman's Instructor. With 50 plates. 3 00

32—Select Architecture, being regular designs of plans and elevations of Houses. By Robert Morris. 50 plates. 3 00

33—The American Builder's Companion, with 44 plates. By A. Benjamin. Boston, 1806. 6 00

34—The Carpenter's New Guide, being a complete book of Lines for Carpenters and Joiners, on 78 plates. By Peter Nicholson. 5 00

35—The Carpenter's and Joiner's Assistant, containing practical rules for making all kinds of joints for doors, shutters, &c. on 79 plates. By P. Nicholson. 5 00

36—The Practical Builder, or Workman's General Assistant, by William Pain. 5 00

37—The Young Carpenter's Assistant, on 44 plates. By Owen Biddle. Philadelphia, 1805. 4 50

38—The Principles of Geometry, Mechanics, Mensuration and Perspective, geometrically demonstrated, together with the orders of architecture, &c. on 38 plates. By B. Langley. London, 1730. 3 50

39—N. Willis' Designs for Chimney-pieces and Door-cases, 36 plates. 2 50

40—The History of Whitby Abbey. By Lionel Charlton. 2 00

41—The History of Thetford. By Thomas Martin. 2 00

OCTAVOS.

42—Ozanam's Mechanics and Perspective, 1712. 2 50

43—The Handmaid to the Arts, 2 vols. 4 00

44—The Student's Instructor in drawing and working the five orders of Architecture. By Peter Nicholson. 2 00 an isolated private activity. Moreover, the lodging of books devoted to architecture and the fine arts in a special room gave both the books and the act of reading them a privileged aura.[21] Drawing classes further established the exclusivity of the profession by defining a set of specific skills to be acquired through education.[22] The library and school, then, served to bolster the argument for architecture as a *profession* rather than merely an occupation.

The Associated Housewrights continued to acquire shares in the Architectural Library of Boston but ultimately did not have the financial wherewithal to support the institution. By 1827 the Associated Housewrights owned a controlling interest in the Library. That same year a committee of five—including Alexander Parris, Solomon Willard, and the "Lybrarian" James McAllaster—looked to merge the Architectural Library with the Boston Athenaeum. The merger fell through because of the Athenaeum's insistence upon maintaining complete control of the books and requiring the Associated Housewrights to pay for the room in which they were kept. By 1829, financial pressures caused the Housewrights to give up the room on Court Street, and the Architectural Library's holdings were transferred to the office of Alexander Parris, where presumably they stayed, despite occasional attempts of society members to revive interest in reopening a separate room. At last on 7 January 1850 the books were transferred to the Massachusetts Charitable Mechanic Association by James McAllaster.[23]

Thereafter, the trail of the books becomes murky. The records of the MCMA indicate that its own library had been a source of concern for some time, and in 1847 the members had discussed turning their books over to the Boston Public Library. Instead, however, when they moved into their new building, designed by William Gibbons Preston, library rooms were prepared on the first floor.[24] By 1850, then, the Architectural Library no longer functioned as an independent institution; instead, it became part of a much larger library belonging to the Massachusetts Charitable Mechanic Association.[25]

The early nineteenth century was an age of libraries. A recently published checklist of printed library catalogues from 1801 to 1875 lists 3,355 items—representing those libraries that went to the trouble and expense of printing guides to their collections.[26] These include circulating libraries, social libraries, and (of most interest to those studying the building trades) mechanics' and apprentices' libraries. In Boston, libraries proliferated—both popular and often ephemeral circulating libraries, run largely by booksellers as an added source of income and patronage, and elite institutions that survive today, such as the Boston Athenaeum and the American Academy of Arts and Sciences. Social or subscription libraries, as they were sometimes called, formed the largest group. The earliest one in America was the Library Company of Philadelphia, founded in 1731, but their real growth in numbers occurred in the early nineteenth century.[27]

The library historian Jesse Shera has argued that 1790 marks a turningpoint in the development of social libraries. Before that time, progress was slow and intermittent, whereas after 1790 there was a period of rapid expansion which he terms the "golden age" of social libraries. In Massachusetts alone their number rose from five in the years just following the Revolution to thirty-five in 1795 and continued at that level until about 1830, when the number began to decline.[28] The Boston Library Society (with Charles Bulfinch as an early member), founded in 1792 and housed after 1794 in the Tontine Crescent, is perhaps Boston's best example of an early social library. The Boston Athenaeum, however, founded in 1807, quickly eclipsed the Boston Library Society in both membership and holdings.

The collections of these early libraries can best be described as "general"—religious tracts, fiction, biographies, and travel accounts—although the Boston Athenaeum, from the start, probably included works on architecture and the fine arts. The Massachusetts General Court in 1805 had acknowledged the increased interest in subscription libraries by passing a statute allowing for their establishment and regulation. Any library founded by subscription was required to have the word "social" in the title, which explains why "Social Architectural Library" was the legal title for the Architectural Library of Boston in 1809.[29] This library represents a second phase of the social library movement: a shift toward collections that focused on a specialized aspect of reading and can essentially be seen as attempts to adapt the form and organization of the social library to a specific reading public.[30]

The Architectural Library of Boston should be viewed within this context of the establishment and growth of social libraries. Like that of the Architectural Library, the collections of most social libraries were small—over half had no more than one-hundred volumes—as were the original membership rolls: most ranged from twenty-five to forty-nine members, and often the membership over the life of a library did not exceed the numbers of the founding group. Additionally, as with the Architectural Library, the cost of membership was relatively low: for most, $1.00 to $4.00 per share; the price only occasionally rose as high as $25.[31]

Of the libraries with collections relating to architecture and design which emerged in Boston during this period, perhaps the best known is the Boston Athenaeum. Also a proprietary library, the Athenaeum attracted members of Boston's elite, specifically Boston's men of business. Among the initial proprietors, however, were Charles

Bulfinch, developer Uriah Cotting, and developer-builder Cornelius Coolidge.[32] Subsequent proprietors and life members included Alexander Parris and Solomon Willard. The Athenaeum collections, though strong in the fine arts, contained only a handful of architectural publications. The 1827 catalogue includes Palladio's *First Book of Architecture* and Batty Langley's *Builder's Treasury,* both probably part of the gift of Thomas Dawes's architectural library in 1809.[33] One volume, Joshua Kirby's *Perspective of Architecture,* bears the inscription "Presented to Boston Athenaeum by Mr. Ashur Benjamin this 1 March 1810," indicating an affiliation with the Athenaeum of architects who had not become members. Founded just two years after the Athenaeum, the Architectural Library of Boston clearly sought to provide a collection more closely focused on volumes of use to the professionalizing building trades.

In 1820, however, another venue for printed material relating to architecture emerged in Boston: the Mechanic Apprentices' Library. Institutions targeting mechanics had their origins in Great Britain: the first Mechanics' Institute was established in Birmingham in 1795, and by the 1820s a number of mechanics' institutes with associated libraries were thriving. In Connecticut the "Mechanic Library Society of New Haven" was established in 1793 and Jeffrey Cohen has written about early attempts of the Carpenters' Company of Philadelphia to establish a school of architecture and its attendant collecting of architectural books.[34]

Boston's first mechanics' organization, founded in 1795 as the Associated Mechanics of the Town of Boston and subsequently renamed the Massachusetts Charitable Mechanic Association, was dedicated to "promoting mutual good offices and fellowship; in assisting the necessitous;—encouraging the ingenious, and in rewarding fidelity."[35] In 1820, William Wood, a retired Boston merchant, approached the association with the idea of establishing a library of some 500 volumes which he had collected through donations "for the use of the mechanic and all needy apprentices."[36] The MCMA installed the Mechanic Apprentices' Library in the upper floors of a building at the corner of Cornhill and Franklin Streets and, after soliciting further donations, published a catalogue of its holdings, including a list of donors.[37] The list contains names from the very top of Boston society—Harrison Gray Otis, David Sears, Christopher Gore— plus a few names of architects and housewrights such as Asher Benjamin and Alexander Parris. Although the catalogue's 792 titles clearly catered to a wide range of reading tastes—they include novels, religious tracts, and travel accounts—sixteen can be identified as architectural treatises, including: "Benjamin's Builder's Assistant" and Thomas Rawlins, *Familiar Architecture* (1795). These titles are grouped with others relating to science, such as "A System of Chemistry" and "The Principles of Mechanics." In contrast to the Architectural Library's catalogue, however, this list has only one title related to the fine arts, "Fuseli's Lectures on Painting delivered at the Royal Academy," and no works on perspective.

The Mechanic Apprentices' Library in Boston was the first of a number of New England mechanics' libraries: Portland Apprentices' Library, also 1820; Salem Mechanic Library, 1821; and the Mechanics' and Apprentices' Library, Providence, 1821–23.[38]

Social libraries went into a slow but steady decline during the years 1815 to 1850. Shera notes that most did not survive their founders but were either absorbed into other libraries or merely disappeared, their collections dispersed to the membership. John Wight, reporting on public libraries to the Massachusetts legislature in 1854, described the demise of such institutions:

> For a few years after the formation of the library everything goes on well. Its books are read with avidity. New books are occasionally added. Those who have shares find it pleasant and improving to participate in its advantages. But before many years its prosperity begins to decline. Some of the proprietors have deceased. Others have removed from the town. Others have been unfortunate in business. The annual assessments cease to be paid. New publications are no longer purchased [and] the library gradually falls into disuse.[39]

This sad outline of the fate of many social libraries parallels that of the Architectural Library of Boston. Although it played an important role in the creation of a professional identity among architects in Boston, it ultimately lost its coherence as an institution when it was absorbed into the Massachusetts Charitable Mechanic Association Library.

The collection of the Architectural Library of Boston exemplifies the early stages of professionalization in its three-part emphasis: on traditional works of long-standing repute, on technical manuals stressing particular skills to be mastered, and on volumes cultivating taste through knowledge of the fine arts. Dell Upton's work on the professionalization of architecture in the early nineteenth century has pointed to the parallel tracks pursued by publishers of builder's guides and the first professional architects.[40] Upton argues that the intent of the builder's guides produced by Asher Benjamin and others was to render the builder independent of the client; at the same time, professional architects were trying to define architecture as a design process distinct from mere building construction. The first step for both groups was to assert that competent practice in architecture required mastery of a discrete body of knowledge. The establishment of specialized libraries was important to this process, and in this light the

Architectural Library of Boston can be seen as serving a very different purpose from that of the majority of social libraries.

In order to understand the relationship between a library and an emerging profession, we must look at the way occupational groups professionalize. Historically, a professional pursuit has been defined as a full-time occupation gained, in part, through demonstrated competence in a given field of knowledge—in short, a demonstration of expertise. Admission to a profession has meant membership in an exclusive organization and adherence to a code of conduct which makes service to the public paramount and enables the professional to adopt an impartial, dispassionate stance toward the client. We can think of professionalization, though, as essentially a marketing strategy rather than a standard of quality. Within that strategy, defining a specific body of knowledge is the first step because it gives a profession claims to expertise—and therefore something to market. As the sociologist Magali Larson has pointed out, early nineteenth-century professional groups depended on selling their time and knowledge rather than a product.[41] To do so successfully, they had to create consumer demand for something that was wholly intangible. They had to convince prospective clients that their occupational group's specific skills entitled them to a monopoly on a particular kind of work. The process or, as Larson calls it, the "project" of professionalization therefore actually creates a commodity—expertise—while also creating a market for that commodity.

For professions such as architecture the commodity created was the profession member. Standardized training and codes of conduct ensured that the profession would demonstrate coherence as a group while setting its members apart from others with claims to similar skills. Ultimately, this process allowed the exclusion of nonprofessionals, established legitimacy for the profession, and created an ideological commitment to the profession's services. The collection of the Architectural Library of Boston, therefore, served the needs of a professionalizing occupation by articulating a body of knowledge to be mastered and a more elusive quality—taste—which would distinguish professional architects both from their clients and from other builders. In this attempt to gain professional distinctiveness, the proprietors of the Architectural Library followed not just the legal profession and its establishment of the Social Law Library but also the medical doctors, who founded the Second Social or Boston Medical Library at about the same time.[42]

The Architectural Library of Boston, therefore, uniquely targeted the needs of architects who were attempting to establish themselves as a profession. While some elite libraries contained works related to the fine arts and to architecture, none included the range of materials available at the Architectural Library. Moreover, the mechanics' libraries, although offering a wide range of technical manuals related to building and engineering, did not as a general rule include architectural pattern books in their collections. The Architectural Library of Boston, though short-lived, can be seen as an important step in the professionalization of architecture. It signaled the growing professional self-consciousness of early nineteenth-century architects in their attempts to define their field of expertise and to give that expertise a physical reality.

NOTES

1. *The Constitution of the Proprietors of the Architectural Library of Boston Instituted 15th November, 1809* (Boston: T. Kennard, 1809).

2. David D. Hall, "The Uses of Literacy in New England, 1600–1850" in *Cultures of Print: Essays in the History of the Book*, ed. David D. Hall (Amherst: University of Massachusetts Press, 1996), 37. On the spread of reading and books throughout New England, see William J. Gilmore, *Reading Becomes a Necessity of Life: Material and Cultural Life in Rural New England, 1780–1835* (Knoxville: University of Tennessee Press, 1989).

3. An important exception is Dell Upton, "Pattern Books and Professionalism: Aspects of the Transformation of Domestic Architecture in America, 1800–1860," *Winterthur Portfolio* 16 (1984): 107–50.

4. Christopher Monkhouse, "Parris' Perusal," *Old-Time New England* 58 (October–December 1967): 51–59; Jack Quinan, "Some Aspects of the Development of the Architectural Profession in Boston between 1800 and 1830," *Old-Time New England* 68 (July–December 1977): 33; Edward Zimmer, "The Architectural Career of Alexander Parris" (Ph.D. diss., Boston University, 1987);

5. The *Constitution of the Proprietors* outlined the organization's mode of governance and rules for borrowing and included the only known catalogue of the library's holdings, but it did not provide a list of the proprietors.

6. Quinan, "Development of the Architectural Profession," 33.

7. R. W. Liscombe, "A 'New Era in My Life': Ithiel Town Abroad," *Journal of the Society of Architectural Historians* 50 (March 1991): 12.

8. On Willard's career, see William Wheildon, *Memoir of Solomon Willard, Architect and Superintendent of the Bunker Hill Monument* (Boston: Bunker Hill Monument Association, 1865); Zimmer, "Architectural Career of Alexander Parris," 284.

9. Nathaniel Critchett was listed in the Boston Directory as a housewright from 1809 to 1816 but does not appear to have been involved in other Boston builders' organizations. Information on Critchett, Waldron, and Gill is from Christopher Hail, *Boston Architects and Builders Compiled from the Boston Directory, 1789–1846* (Cambridge: Massachusetts Committee on the Preservation of Architectural Records, 1989), and Gerald W. R. Ward, "The Society of Associated Housewrights of the Town of Boston, 1804–37" (unpublished paper on deposit at the Library and Archives of the Society for the Preservation of New England Antiquities, 1973).

10. Helen Park, *A List of Architectural Books Available in America before the Revolution* (Los Angeles: Hennessey & Ingalls, 1973), 28–29.

11. In 1827 the Associated Housewrights of Boston owned twenty-five shares of the Architectural Library, which were valued together at $140. Ward, "Society of Associated Housewrights," 20–21.

12. *Constitution of the Proprietors,* art. 2.

13. Edgar J. Bellefontaine, "Social Law Library Report of the Librarian for the Year Ending Sept. 30 1968" (typescript on deposit at the Social Law Library, Boston); Jesse H. Shera, *Foundations of the Public Library* (Chicago: University of Chicago Press, 1949), 68–85.

14. Eight extant volumes from the Architectural Library of Boston have been identified: Joshua Kirby, *The Perspective of Architecture . . . from the Principles of Dr. Brook Taylor,* (London, 1761); Batty Langley, *The City and Country Builder's and Workman's Treasury of Designs . . .* (London, 1750), and John Soane, *Sketches in Architecture . . .* (London, 1798), are in Memorial Library, Boston Architectural Center, Boston; Lionel Charlton, *History of Whitby Abbey* (London, 1779), William Pain, *Pain's British Palladio: or the Builder's General Assistant* (London, 1790); and Abraham Swan, *A Collection of Designs in Architecture* (London, 1757), are in the Library and Archives of the Society for the Preservation of New England Antiquities, Boston; *The Builder's Dictionary; or, Architect's Companion,* vol. 2 (London, 1734), is in the Bulfinch Collection, Rotch Library of Architecture and Planning, Massachusetts Institute of Technology, Cambridge; and Abraham Swan, *The British Architect,* 2d French ed. [n.p., n.d.], is in the Phillips Library, Peabody Essex Museum, Salem, Mass. I would like to thank Abbott Lowell Cummings for drawing my attention to the titles in the Bulfinch collection and at the Peabody Essex Museum and the Langley volume at the Boston Architectural Center.

15. A share in the Architectural Library of Boston was donated to the Associated Housewrights Society by Braddock Loring's widow, Mary, in 1823. Ward, "Society of Associated Housewrights," 19.

16. I would like to thank William La Moy, librarian, the Phillips Library, Peabody Essex Museum, for verifying the inscriptions in the Swan volume.

17. The provenance of *The Builder's Dictionary* is murky. The inscription "Thomas Dawes, 1751" indicates that it was owned by Dawes early in his career, but it was not in the Dawes library donated to the Boston Athenaeum in 1809. How the book came to the Bulfinch collection after it had been acquired by the Architectural Library is also a mystery. I would like to thank Merrill Smith, librarian, Rotch Library of Architecture and Planning, Massachusetts Institute of Technology, for information about this and the Bulfinch collection in general.

18. The bookplate of Batty Langley's *City and Country Builder* (number 22 in the catalogue) was initially numbered "22" and later renumbered "38." One volume, Joshua Kirby, *The Perspective of Architecture . . .* (London, 1761), listed as number 6 in the catalogue, was incorrectly numbered "5" on its bookplate, corresponding to Kirby's *Dr. Brook Taylor's Method of Perspective Made Easy . . .* (London, 1768), and was never renumbered.

19. Monkhouse, "Parris' Perusal," 52; Ward, "Society of Associated Housewrights," 19–22; Zimmer, "Architectural Career of Alexander Parris," 278–80; Records of the Massachusetts Charitable Mechanic Association, Massachusetts Charitable Mechanic Association, Quincy (hereafter MCMA Records), 6: 259–60.

20. In 1822 the Associated Housewrights appointed a committee consisting of Ephraim Marsh, Alexander Parris, and Seth Copeland to purchase the majority of shares in the Architectural Library. They also voted that "the same Committee who was chosen to purchase shares in the Boston Architectural Library be authorized to pursue such Measures as they may think Expedient to organize said Library." It may have been this vote that prompted the renumbering of the books and, possibly, the marking of each book with the red "Architectural Library of Boston" stamp. See "Records of the Associated Housewrights in Boston"; box 12, MCMA Records; Ward, "Society of Associated Housewrights," 1–14, 19–20.

21. James Raven, "From Promotion to Proscription: Arrangements for Reading and Eighteenth-Century Libraries," in *The Practice and Representation of Reading in England,* ed. James Raven et al. (Cambridge: Cambridge University Press, 1996), 175–201.

22. My view of the school for "Architectural Drawing" differs slightly from that of Edward Zimmer ("Architectural Career of Alexander Parris," 278), who argues that the founders were not interested in turn-

ing apprentices into architects but merely wanted them to be able to read and work with architects' plans. No matter what the Associated Housewrights' aspirations for their students might have been, establishing such a school helped to define drawing as a requisite skill for the profession of architecture and therefore advanced the aspiring architects' "project of professionalization." On professionalization as a "project," see Magali Sarfatti Larson, *The Rise of Professionalism: A Sociological Analysis* (Berkeley: University of California Press, 1977).

23. Ward, "Society of Associated Housewrights," 20–22; Zimmer, "Architectural Career of Alexander Parris," 278–80; MCMA Records, vol. 6, 6 Jan. 1848–7 Jan. 1852, p. 231. See also Joseph T. Buckingham, *Annals of the Massachusetts Charitable Mechanic Association* (Boston: Crocker & Brewster, 1853), 99.

24. Preston's involvement in the design of Mechanics' Hall could explain how two volumes with bookplates of the Architectural Library came into Preston's possession: Joshua Kirby's *Perspective of Architecture* and Batty Langley's *City and Country Builder* also bear Preston's bookplate, and he subsequently donated them to the Boston Architectural Club, precursor to the Boston Architectural Center. A third volume from the collection of the Architectural Library now at the Boston Architectural Center, John Soane's *Sketches in Architecture,* may also have been donated by Preston. I would like to thank Susan Lewis, librarian, Boston Architectural Center, for her help with the provenance of these volumes.

25. The association's library was apparently destroyed in a warehouse fire during the 1960s. Conversation with Rick Purdy, Massachusetts Charitable Mechanic Association, September 1997.

26. Robert Singerman, *American Library Book Catalogues, 1801–1875: A National Bibliography* (Urbana: University of Illinois, 1996). For pre-1801 catalogues, see Robert B. Winans, *A Descriptive Checklist of Book Catalogues Separately Printed in America, 1693–1800* (Worcester, Mass.: American Antiquarian Society, 1981).

27. Shera, *Foundations of the Public Library,* 68–85; Raven, "From Promotion to Proscription," 175.

28. Shera, *Foundations of the Public Library,* 68–85.

29. Massachusetts Statutes 1805, chap. 72, sec. 3.

30. Shera, *Foundations of the Public Library,* 68–85.

31. Ibid.

32. Ronald Story, "Class and Culture in Boston: The Athenaeum, 1807–1860" *American Quarterly* 27 (May 1975): 178–99.

33. *Catalogue of Books in the Boston Atheneum* (Boston: W. L. Lewis, 1827).

34. Sidney Ditzion, "Mechanics and Mercantile Libraries," *Library Quarterly* 10 (1940): 197–99; Jeffrey A. Cohen, "Building a Discipline: Early Institutional Settings for Architectural Education in Philadelphia, 1804–1890," *Journal of the Society of Architectural Historians* 53 (June 1994): 140.

35. *Constitution of the Massachusetts Charitable Mechanic Association* (Boston: J. T. Buckingham, 1814), preamble.

36. *Report of the Committee on the Library in Relation to the Mechanic Apprentices' Library Association* (Boston: Printed at the Office of the Bunker Hill Aurora, 1859), 3–4.

37. Buckingham, Annals of the Massachusetts Charitable Mechanic Association, 164–67.

38. This compilation derives from the list of printed catalogues in Singerman, *American Library Book Catalogues.*

39. John B. Wight, "A Lecture on Public Libraries Delivered in Boston in the Hall of the House of Representatives, 1854," quoted in Shera, *Foundations of the Public Library,* 78.

40. Upton, "Pattern Books and Professionalism," 107–50.

41. Larson, *Rise of Professionalism,* esp. chap. 1.

42. Philip Cash, "The Professionalization of Boston Medicine, 1760–1803," in *Medicine in Colonial Massachusetts, 1620–1820,* Proceedings of the Colonial Society of Massachusetts, 57 (1980): 69–94.

VI

BULFINCH, BUILDINGS, AND BOOKS

James F. O'Gorman

Charles Bulfinch was a bookish man who came from a bookish family. His grandfather, the first Charles Apthorp, filled his house with publications, including volumes on architecture. Nor were these merely decorative. This was a family of readers. We get some inkling of that fact from letters written by the designer's mother, Hannah Apthorp Bulfinch, letters penned early in the second decade of the nineteenth century—when, that is, Bulfinch himself was middle-aged—but surely reflecting long-standing habits.

In the spring of 1810, Hannah Bulfinch wrote to her siblings in England, "We get many new publications here. As I have much leisure I devote my morning to serious reading, beginning with the scriptures, always most interesting; the latter part of the day my daughters are usually with me and we entertain ourselves with the most approv'd new and popular productions." And in the fall of that year she continued in the same vein to the same correspondents: "We have lately read those works you mention, except Clark's Travels, which have not yet reach'd this country. I shall probably be among the first to see them whenever they arrive, as my love for reading . . . induces my Children and friends to procure every work for me that is much approv'd."[1] In fact, the *Travels* of the antiquarian Edward Daniel Clarke would prove of interest not only to Hannah Bulfinch but to her son as well.

Books formed an integral part of Charles Bulfinch's life—especially, of course, books on architecture. His granddaughter Ellen Susan Bulfinch left a charming account of their prominence and impact upon her youth. In her *Life and Letters* of her grandfather, published in 1896, she remembered:

"In my childhood, my little sister and I were sometimes indulged with the privilege and delight of looking at our grandfather's English books on architecture, with numerous plates of plans and elevations of country seats, hunting lodges, farmhouses, etc., the 'house-books,' as we called them, which were piled upon the dining-table while we searched eagerly for the well-known engravings. [John] Soane's 'Sketches of Architecture' was one of the titles; but our favorite was [John] Plaw's 'Rural Architecture,' which contained the wonderful circular house 'on an island in the Lake of Winandermere, designed and built by the Author' . . . [Plaw's] frontispiece . . . showed an English landscape, with two female figures and represented Taste, accompanying Rural Simplicity, and pointing to the . . . round villa."[2]

Harold Kirker's well-known catalogue of Bulfinch's personal holdings lists both the Soane and the Plaw, although only the Plaw remains with what is left of the designer's books in the Rotch Library at the Massachusetts Institute of Technology. Kirker listed in all twenty-seven titles of books either at MIT or known from Ellen Bulfinch and other family sources to have been in Bulfinch's collection.[3] I have added several more volumes that I can demonstrate Bulfinch knew, although they were not necessarily located in his own library. To assess the impact of books on Bulfinch's career, one must look beyond those volumes "piled upon the dining-table," in Ellen Bulfinch's graphic memory, to consider his perusal in general: the books he knew and used and the books he wanted to acquire whether or not he did as well as the books he owned. My preliminary research provides a glimpse of Bulfinch's literary resources and, by association, his multifaceted learning. This inquiry has led me to suspect that the Bulfinch we now know is a two-dimensional shadow of the three-dimensional mind that emerges from a larger inventory of his reading.

Bulfinch's access to books was manifold. He not only had his own library but actively supported other collections as well. He was, for example, an organizer of the Boston Library Society in 1792, and a trustee in 1794, when he gave it the use of the splendid oval room behind the Palladian window in the center of his new Tontine Crescent.[4] Later, just before he left Boston for Washington, D.C., he held the position of librarian at the prestigious American Academy of Arts and Sciences.[5] These positions made available to him a wide spectrum of publications, including books in his profession. In 1802, as we learn from its printed catalogue, the academy owned William Salmon's *Palladio Londinensis: or, the London Art of Building* of 1734, as well as a volume of Vitruvius published in Paris in 1684. By 1815 the Boston Library Society owned the 1770 edition of Joseph Priestley's work on perspective, a title we know Bulfinch studied.[6] Books such as Priestley's are often excluded from discussions of architects' libraries, yet Bulfinch's study of perspective plausibly had an impact upon his work in urban design.

Two other potentially important sources of books for Bulfinch were the collections of the Boston Athenaeum, founded in 1807, and the Architectural Library of Boston, founded late in 1809.[7] We do not know whether he was a proprietor of the Architectural Library—given his financial straits, he perhaps could not afford to be—but it would be far fetched to think he did not know something of that social library's contents. The catalogue of 1809 lists fifty-five books on painting, architecture, and perspective—almost all, of course, English. Bulfinch's perusal went beyond even this large list of books, but he may have found some of his information in this collection or that of the Athenaeum.

Kirker relied largely on what is preserved at MIT to prepare his list of Bulfinch's architectural library, but like so many others he had no interest in Bulfinch's study of linear perspective. Nor did he delve very deeply into other kinds of documents for information about the designer's literary resources. But a richly suggestive lode of information lies in textual sources such as Bulfinch's orders for books from abroad, his patronage of at least one English publication, his recommendations for volumes to be added to the Library of Congress, correspondence related to the sale of some of his books after his death, and notes on his drawings now at the Library of Congress and elsewhere.

To reduce this mass of new information to some kind of preliminary order, I have integrated new and old knowledge under a series of arbitrary rubrics: Bulfinch's use of bookish inspiration in his (1) works of Roman-based Classicism, (2) works in Classical Greek style, (3) works in Gothic style, (4) structure, (5) perspective studies, and (6) urban planning. The mere range of these topics suggests that Bulfinch's was a more interesting and inquisitive mind than we have been led to believe.

We know Bulfinch chiefly as a follower of such English masters as William Chambers and Robert Adam—as an adherent, that is, of the Roman Classical tradition that had dominated Western architecture since the quattrocento. His Massachusetts State House is a pastiche of forms derived from Chambers, Adam, and James Wyatt. It needs to be observed, then, that no copy of either Chambers's *Treatise on Civil Architecture* (1759) or Adam's *Works in Architecture* (1773–79) is known to have been in Bulfinch's possession, nor were they in the Architectural Library of Boston. But perhaps we need not seek such literary sources for one who knew Somerset House and the Williams Wynn house first-hand from his trip abroad in 1785–87. From his return to Boston to the second decade of the nineteenth century, the architect turned habitually to Roman-based, Neoclassical inspiration as interpreted by his English peers.

This is the Bulfinch we know best. He may not have had Chambers or Adam in hand, but he could refresh his memory of their works from other books that he did own. Among his resources were such volumes as John Crunden's very popular *Convenient and Ornamental Architecture* (1785) and William Thomas's *Original Designs in Architecture* (1783). Of the latter, Eileen Harris has written that it was "clearly intended to emulate Adam's *Works*."[8]

But Bulfinch cast a broader bibliographical net. Within his own library there were works produced outside the circle of the Adams, and, casting our own net wider still, we will fish up examples of an even more catholic taste in source material.

Bulfinch's interest in Greek architecture has been largely overlooked because of his stature as a leading architect of New England Federalism, and because he left Boston just as the Greek Revival hit town. It must be admitted that his focus on things Greek was late in coming and minimal in impact upon his work. It nonetheless represents another dimension of his intellectual range.

Although Kirker overlooked the fact, in 1804 Bulfinch was negotiating about a new house in New York for Rufus King, who over a long and distinguished career was a lawyer, delegate to the Continental Congress, U.S. senator, minister to Great Britain, and presidential nominee.[9] Nothing came of that negotiation as far as I know. But there was again contact between the two in August 1818 when Bulfinch, then superintendent of the National Capitol, wrote to Senator King recommending architectural publications for acquisition by the Library of Congress.[10] The library, he said, "will probably be for many years the most important collection of books for general reference in the Southern division of the country," so it was "of consequence to make it as complete as the appropriations will allow." He went on to say that he was taking the liberty "to mention some books in the Science which I profess & a few others of more general nature." He listed fifteen titles. Bulfinch may not have owned them, but he certainly knew them.

At the top of the list was the bible of the Greek Revival: James Stuart and Nicolas Revett's *Antiquities of Athens,* which, he observed, "has had a material influence in directing the public taste of late years."[11]

He also recommended Edmund Aikin's 1810 *Essay on the Doric Order of Architecture* and William Wilkins's *Atheniensia, or, Remarks on the Topography and Buildings of Ath-*

ens (published in London in 1816). To these we can add another title from another source: Stephen Riou's much earlier *Grecian Order of Architecture* (1768), for Riou's name and a copy of one of his plates appear on folio 7 of the "Bulfinch Sketchbook" now in the Library of Congress. In a large gathering of copper-engraved plates which he dedicated to James Stuart, Riou reduced to system the three orders of Greek Classicism, then applied them to Palladian schemes. None of the works Bulfinch recommended to King represented the older Roman Classicism; by the mid-1810s, it seems, the designer had—at least in his literary leaning—left that episode behind.

Did Bulfinch apply his interest in the Grecian style to any of his own designs? The answer is yes: minimally, tentatively, and late in his career.[12] One piece of evidence is a stiff drawing in the Library of Congress that is unpublished so far as I know (figure 6.1). It shows a 215-foot-high monument in the form of an obelisk with Greek Doric columns *in antis* set into its blocky base.[13] In a letter to his son Thomas on 22 June 1825, just five days after Daniel Webster's celebrated speech at the laying of the cornerstone of the Bunker Hill Monument, Bulfinch mentioned that project; he had thought of submitting a design himself, he wrote, but rejected the idea. Could the Library of Congress sketch be Bulfinch's abandoned proposal for the Bunker Hill Monument? Bulfinch told his son that in order "to meet the high raised expectations of the publick it [that is, an obelisk] must be very large and lofty; and is singly, of itself, a very uninteresting figure; built only of plain courses of stone it will require to be accompanied by Collonades [*sic*] or groups of sculpture to make it an honourable specimen of the arts," and he thought the budget would not allow for such expenditure.[14] That seems to me the description of a project like that shown in his sketch. Here is suggestive material for future research.[15]

Finally, Kirker had already noticed the Grecian drift of Bulfinch's last building, the Maine State House of 1829. A comparison of its principal colonnade to that of its antecedent in Boston clearly reveals the Greek robustness of the late Bulfinch's work, a drift that may have been given impetus by his encounters with such Grecophiles as William Strickland, with whom he consulted about the ceiling of the Capitol's Hall of Representatives in Washington in 1826.[16]

The *Essays on Gothic Architecture* of Thomas Warton and others, which appears on Kirker's list, was published by I. and J. Taylor in London in 1800, suggesting Bulfinch's study of that style at least that early. John Frew first emphasized his serious interest in medieval building in 1986. Bulfinch's copy of the *Essays*, as I have shown in a 1991 coda to Frew's note, is now at the Massachusetts Historical Society and contains, among

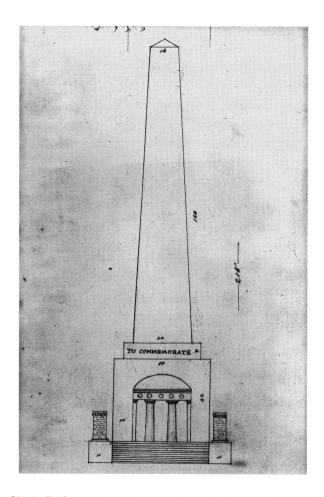

FIG 6.1 Sketch by Charles Bulfinch, ca. 1825, probably for the Bunker Hill Monument. Library of Congress.

other tipped-in sheets of Gothic material, the architect's sketch of St. John of Acre, a sketch published by Charles Place in the 1920s and thought by Frew to have been lost.[17] The view of St. John's is in fact a copy of a plate in Edward Daniel Clarke's *Travels in Various Countries of Europe Asia and Africa*, part 2, *Greece, Egypt, and the Holy Land*, published in 1814. This is the title that had been so anticipated by Bulfinch's mother and one that also appears in the catalogue of the Boston Library Society in 1815. Clarke cites St. John as "evidence that the pointed stile originated in the east," as Bulfinch noted beneath his copy of Clarke's illustration. Bulfinch's use of Clarke cautions us to look beyond mere architectural publications, to draw as wide a circumference as possible in search of the designer's sources—sources for intellectual inquiry as well as for architectural design.

By the time he copied Clarke's view of St. John, Bulfinch had already designed William Ellery Channing's Federal Street Church with Gothic accents. In 1818 he included among his recommendations for the Library of Congress George Downing Whittington's *Historical Survey of the Ecclesiastical Antiquities of France, with a View to Illustrate the Rise and Progress of Gothic Architecture* (published by I. and J. Taylor in 1809) and—going well beyond professional reading—Joseph Berington's *Literary History of the Middle Ages* (1814).[18]

The names I. and J. Taylor, publishers of Whittington's *Survey,* demand more than passing mention, for their "Architectural Library" in Holborn, London, was a constant source of Bulfinch's book purchases, as Frew pointed out. (Taylor was swallowed by Batsford in the nineteenth century. My request to the existing publishers for information related to Bulfinch, alas, turned up nothing but the lament that there has always been a shortage of storage space and "therefore priority has never been put on keeping archives or records.")[19] It can nonetheless be shown through the Taylor connection that Bulfinch's interest in Gothic stems from early in his career. In 1795 Taylor published James Murphy's *Plans, Elevations, Sections, and Views of the Church of Batalha . . . in Portugal* (figure 6.2), a work Georg Germann characterized as the "first reproduction of a Gothic building comparable with the splendid and precise reproductions of antique temples made some forty years before"—that is, by Stuart and Revett.[20] The Irish architect's plates are dated 1795, but the preface is signed 1792. As early as that year, then, Bulfinch supported the production of this handsome folio, for his name appears on its list of distinguished subscribers—showing once again how far we must go beyond the architect's surviving library to measure the range of his interests.[21]

But enough of style. How did an amateur like Bulfinch—for whom architecture was a moonlight job until, at the age of fifty-four, he moved to Washington to take over the completion of the National Capitol from Benjamin Henry Latrobe—learn enough structural engineering to be able to supervise the erection of, say, the Capitol's original dome? Again, the books in his library and those we know he at least knew of become important in assessing his career. He could have garnered information about building from such architectural works as Stephen Riou's *Grecian Order,* for Riou discusses construction, but Bulfinch consulted engineering works as well. He had, for example (and MIT retains), George Atwood's *Dissertation on the Construction and Properties of Arches,* a work published in 1801 to which Bulfinch appended pages filled with notes on the

FIG 6.2 Decorated title page from James Murphy, *Plans, Elevations, Sections, and Views of the Church of Batalha* (1795).

subject transcribed from volume 10 of the *Philosophical Magazine*. (These manuscript pages have been characterized as original observations, by the way, but like so much of the surviving Bulfinch manuscript material they are in fact mostly quotations from published sources.)

There is good reason to believe that Bulfinch's professional library was larger than what has been preserved at MIT. We know, for example, that several books were sold after his death. There exists a letter from his son S. G. Bulfinch to the book dealer

Charles S. Storrow of Boston—a letter written in September 1846, or roughly two and a half years after the architect's death—in which the younger Bulfinch requests an appraisal of some volumes that once belonged to his father because he wants to dispose of them. Unfortunately, the list of works seems to be missing, but not all is lost, for the writer says he understands that Storrow would like the work on the Edystone Lighthouse and might also want to take the *"Belidor,"* which is "said to be a scarce and valuable work."[22]

No more bibliographic detail is provided about these two books, but I would not hesitate to guess that the first was John Smeaton's *Narrative of the Building and a Description of the Construction of the Edystone Lighthouse,* probably in the second edition of 1793. Smeaton's volume reported on his single success at erecting a lighthouse in treacherous waters off the coast of England, and his experiments with hydraulic mortar. The second book mentioned by the younger Bulfinch is more difficult to pinpoint, for Bernard Forest de Belidor, that eighteenth-century *savant ingénieur français,* produced several important publications on civil, military, and hydraulic architecture. I would like to think that Bulfinch owned *La Science des ingenieurs dans la conduite des travaux de fortification et d'architecture civile.* Published in Paris in 1729, followed by many later editions and translations, it discusses masonry, vaults, materials, construction, the orders, and so on. Since Belidor also published *Architecture hydraulique* in 1737–39, I am shooting in the dark, but in any event, Smeaton and Belidor join Atwood—and others—as Bulfinch's mentors in structural matters.

Those others include the physicists Peter Barlow and Antoine Parent, and the civil engineers Thomas Telford and John Rennie, all reporting on the strength of materials. On a drawing now in the Library of Congress, Bulfinch jotted down notes from "Barlow on strength of timber" and commented that the author agreed with Parent and Belidor.[23] Among the many possible publications connected with the name of Barlow, Bulfinch could have used *An Essay on the Strength and Stress of Timber . . . [with] an Appendix on the Strength of Iron, and Other Materials* (1817 and later editions). Whether he knew Parent's *Eléments de mechanique et de physique* of 1700 or some other publication, or learned of Parent's work secondhand, I cannot say. On another sheet in the same collection are notes on Telford's and Rennie's experiments with the strength of iron bars.[24] I will not hazard to guess in which of (I assume the elder) John Rennie's and Thomas Telford's many reports on bridges, canals, railroads, and breakwaters Bulfinch found useful information.

One more reference merits attention under the rubric of structure, although its

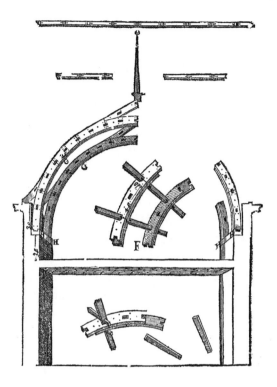

FIG 6.3 "Comme les courbes & Hemicycles pour fair les Combles, se commencent a assembler sur les murs," from Philibert Delorme, *Nouvelles inventions pour bien bastir* (1561).

worth is at the moment merely intriguing and difficult to assess. In 1791, Bulfinch ordered a number of books through James Cutler in Paris, a request that points up the fact that he did not rely entirely on the Taylors in London to supply his literary needs. Among other volumes, he wanted one that he described as "Des Instructions sur le procede de Philibert Du Lorme apres lequel la cupole de la nouvelle Halle au bled a Paris fut construite."[25] Although he added that he was not certain any such work had ever been published, this sounds to me like Philibert Delorme's *Nouvelles inventions pour bien bastir* of 1561 (figure 6.3). The construction of the dome of the Halle au Blé was of great interest to many of Bulfinch's contemporaries (especially Thomas Jefferson, who owned a copy of the *Inventions* and may have directed Bulfinch's attention to this engineering marvel when they were both in Paris in the mid-1780s). Whether or not Bulfinch ever received a copy of Delorme's work, we know that his interest in the subject did not wane: both Delorme and the Halle au Blé are mentioned in a letter from Latrobe to Bulfinch—the only known correspondence between the two—written in March 1807.[26]

Through Jefferson's influence a number of Delorme-inspired domes were erected along the eastern seaboard in the early nineteenth century. Douglas Harnsberger has shown that two were built in Boston, both by Alexander Parris: one on the Massachusetts General Hospital and the other on the center building at Quincy Market.[27] The hospital dome was probably conceived by Bulfinch before he left for Washington in 1817, for although Harnsberger has demonstrated that the dome Parris erected in 1821–23 was not identical to that shown in the earliest drawings, Bulfinch's role in this work cannot be fully discounted. Moreover, Harnsberger was not aware of Bulfinch's 1791 request for a copy of Delorme's *Inventions,* so his elaborate search for Parris's possible sources of information about Delorme's method overlooked the one closest to home. In any event, whatever Bulfinch's knowledge of this construction technique, we profit in our understanding of his aspirations by knowing that he sought to learn about it through Delorme's publication.

Bulfinch's manuscript "Principles of Perspective," now in the Library of Congress, introduces his perusal of works on that subject.[28] His study began at Harvard with Joshua Kirby's *Dr. Brook Taylor's Method of Perspective Made Easy* (a work also known, in Harvard's copy, by John Trumbull, Jonathan Fisher, and others): the first illustration in his manuscript is taken line for line from Kirby. But by the time he compiled his "Principles," sometime after 1813, he had studied a long list of works both specialized and— in the limited sense in which one can apply the word to his period—popular. He listed Joshua Kirby's more beautiful and more important *Perspective of Architecture* (1761), Thomas Malton's *Compleat Treatise on Perspective* (1776), and Joseph Priestley's *Familiar Introduction to the Theory and Practice of Perspective* (1770) among the dozen specialized works he had consulted; he also used George Gregory's *Dictionary of Arts and Sciences,* which first appeared in 1806–7.

Bulfinch laboriously copied the rules of linear perspective from the masters, for unlike Latrobe, he was not a gifted artist. His approach to the subject of three-dimensional representation was pedantic, dry, stiff; witness his perspective of the Hollis Street Church of 1788.[29] But one must not minimize the importance of Bulfinch's perspectival perusal, for I think it was an essential ingredient in his leap from the design of individual buildings such as the first Harrison Gray Otis house to his desire, as both politician and architect, to shape the town of Boston as a coherent ensemble of visually related parts.

Bulfinch's concern for the urban dimension of architectural design may have sprung from his travels in Europe, and it is reflected in books such as two from his library preserved at MIT: a grangerized edition of James Ralph's *Critical View of the Public Buildings . . . in London* (1783), and William Watts's *Select Views of the Principal Buildings . . . of Bath and Bristol* (1794). But there is more than just these works to be considered here.

As chief administrative officer of the town of Boston in the early years of the nineteenth century, Bulfinch willy-nilly developed a comprehensive view of his own urban environment. During and for a long period after his residency there, Bulfinch and Boston became synonymous. As Walter Whitehill wrote, Boston owed Bulfinch "a unique debt for his skill in transforming an eighteenth-century town into a nineteenth-century city."[30] He developed not just single units but whole stretches of the town. He projected a large rectangular square for John Singleton Copley's land on Beacon Hill. For the Mill Pond development he created a Neoclassical pattern of streets and market within a triangular periphery. The Tontine Crescent and Franklin Place, Park Row, and the Tremont Street Colonnade brought British Neoclassical sophistication to Boston's domestic life.

This mode of thinking in terms of urban dimension was an important element in Bulfinch's contribution to North American design, and I think it was one that required an ability to envision spatial continuities and architectural relationships—an ability enhanced by, among other things, a knowledge of linear perspective. Although he was not the first American architect to use linear perspective, he was the subject's first serious student in this country. Among Bulfinch's drawings are a number of small sketches of urban vistas, or thumbnail visions of urban continuity (figure 6.4). Such perspectival exercises could have been derived from any of the dozen or more books on the subject which Bulfinch perused, but they also trained his eye to the harmonies of city planning.

Those harmonies depended on building continuity. We know that Bulfinch knew Stephen Riou's 1768 *Grecian Order* because he copied, in undated sketches now in the "Bulfinch Sketchbook" in the Library of Congress, Riou's plate 7 of part 2, "Design for a new street in the City." Riou based his work on Inigo Jones's connected houses at Covent Garden, so the Grecian aura is minimized. He suggested that a domestic street

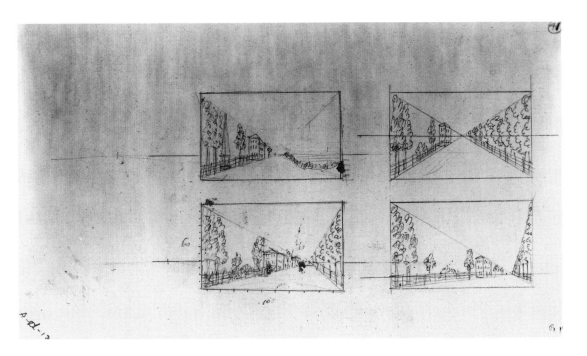

FIG 6.4 Urban vistas (perspectival studies) by Charles Bulfinch, 1813 or later. Library of Congress.

front should show a continuous cornice, and his design presented a house row with central salient and lateral terminals. Bulfinch learned of continuous urban domestic development firsthand, of course, in London and perhaps Bath, but his sketch after Riou demonstrates that designs such as those of the Tontine Crescent or the Park Row development had literary inspiration as well. Riou recommended straight, broad streets lined with rowhouses proportional to them, and Bulfinch must often have ground his teeth about Boston's twisted lanes and mismatched houses. Still, he achieved what he could within the given conditions. The vista up Bulfinch's Park Row toward Bulfinch's State House once applied at urban scale Bulfinch's study of linear perspective (figure 6.5).

The State House terminated this vista as a focal monument in the urban pattern. As a city planner Bulfinch recognized the function of major architectural monuments to punctuate the otherwise continuous matrix. His Boston Theatre of 1793–94 was prominently sited at the end of the Tontine Crescent. He kept its important location in mind as he designed the building, for he reported that "as it stands in a conspicuous situation, it has been thought necessary to observe a strict symmetry on the outside."[31] Kirker pointed out that the designer derived the main facade from plate 35 of John Crunden's *Convenient and Ornamental Architecture,* and he published Bulfinch's redraft

FIG 6.5 Park Row (erected 1803–5) and the Massachusetts State House (erected 1795–97), Boston. Both by Charles Bulfinch. Courtesy of the Bostonian Society / Old State House.

(now in the Library of Congress) of that plate. The design and its source reflect the Roman Classicism of Bulfinch's early works.

Kirker also names three theaters—two American and one English—that Bulfinch could have studied as he began to design the Boston building. To reflect a moment on that suggestion, it seems to me that the designer of a theater needs special knowledge of the way such a room has to function. He must not merely copy forms he sees in other theaters but understand how to achieve certain desirable properties in the hall. What Kirker overlooked is the fact that in his 1791 letter to James Cutler in Paris, Bulfinch requested a copy of Pierre Patte's *Essai sur l'architecture theatrale ou de l'ordenance le plus avantageuse a une salle de spectacles, relativement aux principles de l'optique e de l'acoustique*, published in 1782 (figure 6.6). Patte discussed theater design from such use-

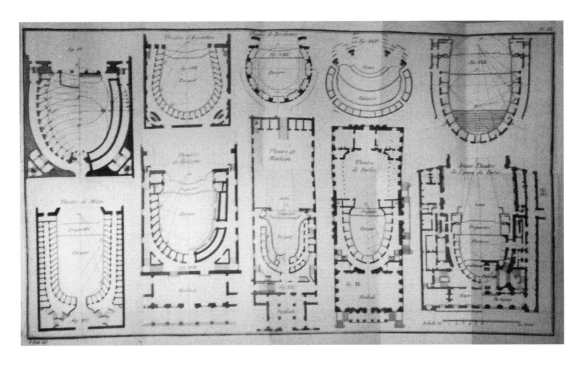

FIG 6.6 European theater plans, from Pierre Patte, *Essai sur l'architecture theatrale* (1782).

ful points as sight and hearing, and he also published the plans and characterized the various qualities of the most important theaters in Europe—those in Milan, Bologna, Parma, Naples, Turin, Venice, Bordeaux, Mannheim, Berlin, and Paris—and an example of the ancient theater as well. Again I cannot prove that Bulfinch actually received this work, but he was certainly hoping to receive it at a time when he was contemplating the design of the Boston Theatre. Although Patte concluded, it might be noted, that the ellipse is the best plan for a theatrical hall, he illustrated some that were based on other shapes, including the circle. Bulfinch based his hall on the circle.

I have barely scratched the surface of a potentially richly rewarding inquiry into Bulfinch's literary sources. What is really wanted, however, is a completely new study of the man and his work in general, one that proceeds from a biographical point of view—however old-fashioned that may sound—and above all places the moonlighting architectural work of his earlier years in just proportion to his daytime political profession. Further, it would examine the richness of his intellectual life through a better understanding of the broad range of his literary perusal.

Such a study would round out a historical figure who seems at present, I think, rather flat. Let me give one example of what I mean. We don't think of Bulfinch as a designer of landscapes, or as an advocate of the picturesque aesthetic, yet he thought enough about such subjects to include three works in these categories among the fifteen he recommended to Rufus King in 1818 as desirable acquisitions for the Library of Congress. They were works by the three giants of the English landscape theory: Humphry Repton's *Observations on the Theory and Practice of Landscape Gardening* (1803), Richard Payne Knight's *Analytical Inquiry into the Principles of Taste* (1805), and Uvedale Price's *Essay on the Picturesque* (1794). Knowing that he admired these books enough to recommend them to the nation's premier library puts Bulfinch in a different light for me. And I hope my observations have done the same for future students of the man.

NOTES

1. Ellen Susan Bulfinch, *The Life and Letters of Charles Bulfinch, Architect* (Boston: Houghton Mifflin, 1896), 169, 171–72.

2. Ibid., 83.

3. Harold Kirker, *The Architecture of Charles Bulfinch* (Cambridge, Mass.: Harvard University Press, 1969), 387–88. Kirker's monograph is basic to the further study of Bulfinch, and this essay is dedicated to him.

4. See Michael Wentworth with Elizabeth Lamb Clark, *The Boston Library Society, 1794–1994* (Boston: Athenaeum, 1994), 7–15.

5. Harold and James Kirker, *Bulfinch's Boston, 1787–1817* (New York: Oxford University Press, 1964), 214.

6. See James F. O'Gorman, "Bulfinch's Perspectival Perusal," in *Das Bauwerk und die Stadt; The Building and the City*, ed. Wolfgang Boehm (Vienna: Boehlau Verlag, 1994), 252–64.

7. Jack Quinan, "Some Aspects of the Development of the Architectural Profession in Boston between 1800 and 1830," *Old-Time New England* 68 (July–December 1977): 32–37; *The Constitution of the Proprietors of the Architectural Library of Boston* (Boston: T. Kennard, 1809). See also Christopher P. Monkhouse, "Parris' Perusal," *Old-Time New England* 58 (fall 1967): 51–59.

8. Eileen Harris, *British Architectural Books and Writers, 1556–1785* (Cambridge: Cambridge University Press, 1990), 455–56.

9. Charles R. King, *The Life and Correspondence of Rufus King* (New York: Putnam, 1894–1900), 6:159–60.

10. Kirker, *Bulfinch*, 12 n. 23, mentions this letter but names only three of the books.

11. When Charles King published Bulfinch's letter to his father (*Rufus King*, 159–60), he omitted the list of books, but it can be found in the Rufus King Papers at the New-York Historical Society.

12. The description of Bulfinch's New South Church of 1814 contained in Samuel Thacher's dedicatory sermon calls the portico "Grecian Doric," which only suggests that he no more remarked the differences between Greek and Roman orders than do my undergraduate students. See Samuel C. Thacher, *An Apology for Rational and Evangelical Christianity* . . . (Boston: T. B. Waite, 1815), 42–43 (a reference I owe to Kenneth Hafertepe).

13. See my section on Bulfinch in *Capital Drawings* (Washington, D.C.: Library of Congress, forthcoming), a catalogue of architectural drawings in the library.

14. Bulfinch, *Life and Letters,* 248.

15. The entire Bulfinch drawing collection in the Library of Congress requires intensive study.

16. Kirker, *Bulfinch,* 354–63, 325.

17. John Frew, "Bulfinch on Gothic," *Journal of the Society of Architectural Historians* 45 (June 1986): 161–63; James F. O'Gorman, "Bulfinch on Gothic Again," *Journal of the Society of Architectural Historians* 50 (June 1991): 192–94; Charles A. Place, *Charles Bulfinch, Architect and Citizen* (Boston: Houghton Mifflin, 1925), 287–88.

18. In 1821 Bulfinch donated a copy of a book by Thompson on Boston in Lincolnshire to the Boston Athenaeum (Bulfinch Papers, Boston Athenaeum). I assume this to be Pishey Thompson, *Collections for a Topographical and Historical Account of Boston and the Hundred of Skirbeck in the County of Lincolnshire,* which adds one more title to his (now) known perusal. It appeared in 1820 while Thompson was living in Washington, D.C., so Bulfinch might have known the author.

19. Mrs. Clare Sunderland of Batsford to author, 27 August 1991.

20. Georg Germann, *Gothic Revival in Europe and Britain: Sources, Influences, and Ideas* (Cambridge, Mass.: MIT Press, 1972), 32.

21. It is probably worth mentioning that the Architectural Library of Boston in 1809 had a couple of volumes by Batty Langley but little else on Gothic.

22. S. G. Bulfinch to Charles S. Storrow, Essex Company Collection, Merrimack Valley Textile Museum, North Andover, Mass. (copy held by Massachusetts Historical Society).

23. Bulfinch drawing collection, ADE 11-A-Bulfinch 77, Library of Congress.

24. Ibid., ADE 11-A-Bulfinch 78.

25. Bulfinch to James Cutler, 2 May 1791, Massachusetts Historical Society.

26. *The Correspondence and Miscellaneous Papers of Benjamin Henry Latrobe,* ed. John C. Van Horne et al. (New Haven, Conn.: Yale University Press, 1984–88), 2:399–400.

27. Douglas James Harnsberger, " 'In Delorme's Manner—.': A Study of the Applications of Philibert Delorme's Dome Construction Method in Early 19th Century American Architecture" (master's Thesis, University of Virginia, 1981).

28. I have written at length else where about Bulfinch's study of linear perspective: see O'Gorman, "Bulfinch's Perspectival Perusal," and James F. O'Gorman, *The Perspective of Anglo-American Architecture* (Philadelphia: Athenaeum, 1995), 6–40.

29. Kirker, *Bulfinch,* 20.

30. Walter Muir Whitehill, *Boston: A Topographical History,* 2d ed. (Cambridge, Mass.: Harvard University Press, 1968), 47–72.

31. Quoted in Kirker, *Bulfinch,* 67.

VII

THE ARCHITECTURAL LIBRARIES OF
BENJAMIN HENRY LATROBE

Jeffrey A. Cohen

In the latter part of the eighteenth century and the early part of the nineteenth, architectural books were a critical resource for those who designed buildings of any cosmopolitan pretension, whether they were genteel amateurs, building tradesmen, or among the relatively few early professional architects in this country. These publications were a potent means of transmission, coursing with favored new forms and justifying ideas, and providing precisely recorded particulars of noted landmarks, current possibilities for specific building types, and a storehouse of appropriate detail. Forms and ideas on paper offered themselves up for ready application in stone, brick, wood, and plaster and were soon transported into the varied landscapes of the colonies and the early nation.

The tripartite cast among those providing building designs at the start of the nineteenth century was concisely described by Benjamin Latrobe (figure 7.1), one of the earliest professional architects to practice in the United States and in several ways the most influential. Writing to his student Robert Mills in July 1806, he explained: "The profession of Architecture has been hitherto in the hands of two sets of Men. The first, of those, who from travelling or from books have acquired some knowledge of the Theory of the art, but know nothing of its practice, the second of those who know nothing but the practice, and whose early life being spent in labor, and in the habits of a laborious life, have had no opportunity of acquiring the theory. The complaisance of

FIG 7.1 Portrait of Benjamin Henry Latrobe by Charles Willson Peale, ca. 1804. Courtesy of The White House.

these two sets of Men to each other, renders it difficult for the Architect to get in between them."[1]

The first sort of designer, whom Latrobe labeled the "Gentleman architect," had reference to books presenting views of faraway places, the forms of approved new modernities, and the theories that supported them. These were often expensive folio or quarto volumes with many plates, which such men held individually or borrowed from elite subscription libraries. Most of the library titles that can be traced have been ably compiled into lists by Helen Park (through 1775) and Janice Schimmelman (through 1800).[2] The collections of architectural books held by individuals have proved less susceptible to modern compilation except where they were recorded in detailed inventories or can be glimpsed at the time of their purchase, often recently imported, through the newspaper advertisements of booksellers—also rich sources for Park and Schimmelman.

The second kind of designer, the kind Latrobe called the "Building mechanic," was also served by architectural books, if frequently of a different sort. Often octavo or smaller, these volumes were usually more formulaic, with greater focus on correct forms for specific details that could be readily adapted to a wide range of buildings, including frontispieces, mantels, and moldings on relatively modest houses. But toward the end of the eighteenth century there was a good deal of convergence in the use made of architectural books by these two types of designer—especially where a master builder had risen to the gentlemanly standing of a Robert Smith, Thomas Dawes, or William Buckland, or where builders pooled their resources, as in the case of the Carpenters' Company of the City and County of Philadelphia.

Designers of the third sort mentioned in Latrobe's account, professional architects like himself, emerged in a significant and lasting way in this country only during the last decade of the eighteenth century. This small but growing and influential group turned even more avidly to books, although theirs was a different kind of dependency. Whereas the key books of the midcentury used by amateurs and builders alike had been mostly contemporary English or earlier Italian publications that guided their users in the harmonies and proprieties of neo-Palladian design, the early professionals looked to a broader set of more current books whose formal range and aesthetic theory had diversified greatly. These books offered the necessary grist for the mills of both the Neoclassicism and the stylistic eclecticism just then emerging and soon to become dominant in the early nineteenth century. As architectural fashion turned toward models and styles rarely broached in the New World, this more wide-ranging class of books served a population of architects and then builders as well—most of whom had not seen such examples in modern European cities, nor their referents farther afield. They served even the few who had done so, though, by providing the useful currency of scaled drawings that could be readily adapted in new building designs marked by forms from distant times and places.

Advances in building technology and systems were also transmitted through publication in these decades. But the greater hunger was for books more directly addressing architectural form and style, for the tides of architectural form had begun to evolve and even reverse at an astonishingly accelerated rate from the 1790s on, if usually paralleling similar shifts in European architectural centers. Such changefulness, of which patrons were widely aware, required that building designers tap much more frequently into what was still an almost entirely westward flow of publications—at least until American architectural books achieved wider circulation in their own country during the middle decades of the nineteenth century. Architectural books and journals were the lifeblood of antebellum designers, and the wills of even modest housebuilders often mentioned sundry illustrated volumes to which they had made productive recourse.

This chapter explores the professional library of Benjamin Henry Latrobe, expanding the term to comprise the set of architectural and engineering books that, evidence indicates, Latrobe knew, and usually seemed to know well, whether or not he actually owned them. The word might also be pluralized, for he gathered and lost his own collection of books more than once.

Latrobe probably began to collect architectural books in the mid-1780s in England, as he adopted his vocation in his early twenties, but they were mostly lost when he emigrated to the United States in the mid-1790s. As he recalled in 1804, "When I came to America 10 Years ago I brought part of my library with me, the remainder being sent in another vessel about 1,500 valuable books, and several instruments was captured by the French and sold, so that I could never recover any part of it. By this means I have lost many professional books."[3] Latrobe subsequently began a new collection of books, creating what may have been one of the largest professional architectural libraries in this country until that brought together by Ithiel Town a few decades later. But like those of his leading pupils, Robert Mills and William Strickland, his second library too was dispersed, and no inventory or substantial survival of its contents seems to be known.[4]

In the surviving writings of these early professionals, however, one finds a good deal of evidence of the presence of architectural books. References to them in Latrobe's writings between the 1780s and his death in 1820 were collected by the staff of the Papers of Benjamin Henry Latrobe, an editorial project initiated by the Maryland Historical Society which gathered, researched, and through Yale University Press published many of Latrobe's writings and drawings.[5] From such citations, mostly in letters, one can construct an "inferred" library of books and journals that the architect knew. Latrobe's many mentions of particular authors and books, with his keen and sometimes mordant comments, offer the perspective of a remarkably well-read architect; he set a formative example for his students, and the profession at large, in thinking of books as essential tools of the architect, and of architecture as a high-minded liberal art and science.

Continuing on the subject of the 1,500 books lost at sea, he recalled: "This loss would have rendered me almost incapable of doing business here, had not my memory been tolerably good, and I even designed and executed the bank of Pennsylvania without any assistance from books; the part of my library which I had saved been then in the custody of a friend." Despite that feat of memory, he clearly saw books as critical to his practice as architect and engineer, as he explained further on in the same letter: "I find a recurrence to books daily more convenient, and there are two or three works which are become almost indispensibly necessary to me. I have made several attempts to procure them, but have failed, the promises of my friends who have gone to France having been lost at Sea, I suppose."[6] As this last line indicates, he was particularly eager to put his hands on books from the Continent, in addition to the many English titles he would mention.

He expanded a bit on the importance of books to the professional in an 1806 letter to his pupil Robert Mills: "Every architect who has been regularly educated knows what has been done before in the Same line. This knowledge he necessarily acquires in the office in which he studies not only from the books, and designs which he finds there, but in the instructions, and *actual practice* of the principal, provided [he] be a man of intelligence, candor, and of business." He illustrated his point with an example, recalling that when he had been "applied to for a design" for the Virginia State Penitentiary in 1796 or 1797, he enjoyed the advantage that "no one there could have the same means of information on this subject as myself, for independently of my general professional character I had been surveyor of the police [in] the districts of London, and had not only erected the buildings belonging to that branch of the government of the metropolis but necessarily acquired a knowledge of all that others had done in the erection and improvement of prisons."[7]

But not all architectural books were of equal interest to him. He was supremely aware of what he perceived as a revolution in taste, to which he enthusiastically adhered. Writing to the members of Congress in 1806, he explained his reaction upon first encountering the design of William Thornton (and others) for the U.S. Capitol: "I frankly confess that, excepting in a few of the details, all my ideas of good taste, and even of good sense in architecture were shocked by the style of the building. I am well aware that in what I shall say on this subject I am probably in a minority. All the books for the last three or four hundred years up to 1760, are against me, and many that have been published since stand on the same ground. But as the arts continue to be improved,—simplicity gains daily more admirers."[8] This taste brooked no heterodoxy: hence Latrobe's confident view expressed in 1805 to John Lenthall, his clerk of the works at the U.S. Capitol, about the taste of his client, President Thomas Jefferson. Latrobe saw himself as "cramped in this design by his [Jefferson's] prejudices in favor of the architecture of the old french books, out of which he fishes every thing."[9]

His students got the message. William Strickland recalled this generational shift in taste in an autobiographical sketch that he composed about 1825, looking back two decades to the time he had entered Latrobe's office: "I remained in this Office 4 years . . . At night I copied the Engraved plates and read the letter press of Stuarts Athens, Ionian Antiquities &c; and was soon enabled, by contrasting these works with *Batty Langley, Swan* & my father's *bench mate,* to discover the graceful forms of Grecian Architecture."[10] Robert Mills echoed this sense of a sea change in one of his later autobiographical accounts:

> Mr. Jefferson was a Roman in his views of architecture, as evidenced in Monticello House, his late residence, which was designed by him . . . The example and influence of Mr. Jefferson at first operated in favour of the introduction of the Roman style into the country, and it required all the talents and good taste of such a man as Mr. Latrobe to correct it by introducing a better. The natural good taste and the unprejudiced eye of our citizens required only a few examples of the Greek style to convince them of its superiority over the Roman for public structures, and its simplicity recommended its introduction into their private dwellings.[11]

One must qualify this oversimplified opposition of Greek versus Roman, for in some respects Latrobe's work was more Roman then Greek. He and his pupils often combined Greek detail and simplicity with a Roman monumentality and spatial complexity; their building techniques and planning for large projects often drew on those of the great Roman bath complexes. In their work in the first decades of the nineteenth century these architects also ventured a bold element of invention, celebrating a potent contemporaneity and a breadth of possibility through the vehicle and individuality of the architect. Latrobe would probably have been more circumspect than Mills, who was typically blunt about this license to invent:

> Many useful hints now are to be gathered from French works on Architecture; but the author has made it a rule never to consult books when he had to design a building . . . Books are useful to the student, but when he enters upon the practice of his profession, he should lay them aside and only consult them upon doubtful points, or in matters of detail or as mere studies, not to copy buildings from.[12]

One could certainly take Latrobe's students' references to books further, especially by turning to the manifold mentions in Strickland's Franklin Institute lectures of the mid-1820s or, a generation later, those of Thomas Ustick Walter in the early 1840s.[13] Mills's papers, recently published on microfilm, would similarly reveal a long list of references to architectural books.[14] This chapter, however, focuses on those mentioned by Latrobe.

Over the course of several years the staff of the Latrobe Papers maintained a file of the architect's references to books on all subjects—culled from the thousands of letters and other documents that survive from the architect's hand—and gathered them into a seventeen-page typescript list.[15] Titles and partial references were matched with likely identifications as an internal tool for the project. Additional indications of his reading appear in other documents and even in some drawings or designs. Taken together, they help sketch out the range of the architect's reading and often give some indication of what he thought of these books. What follows is a selective list by likely author and title (editions are often uncertain), first of architectural books and then of engineering works, accompanied by the evidence from Latrobe's writings or elsewhere.

Taking the architectural books in roughly chronological order, one can start with Vitruvius.

• Vitruvius, *The Ten Books of Architecture*

> The book of Vitruvius, a Roman, is indeed the only one on architecture, which has survived the rage of barbarians and the decay of time. But this work is of very inferior rank both in its literature, its taste, and its science, and is not now entirely intelligible. The only edifice which has been sometimes suspected to be of his design, the amphitheatre of Verona, has no extraordinary merit. (Latrobe, "Anniversary Oration to the Society of Artists," 8 May 1811, *BHL Corr.*, 3.73)

Latrobe's critical stance was not unparalleled among cosmopolitan architectural writers of the time, but it still seems quite a departure from the unqualified respect that Vitruvius had been widely accorded since the Renaissance. Some inkling of that respect, nevertheless, is implied by Latrobe's citing chapter and verse, along with his indication that he had consulted multiple editions of the text:

> This question [of acoustics] has not occupied the attention of architects as much as its importance deserves. Even Vitruvius dismisses the subject in two paragraphs at the end of his

chapter on Theatres, recommending only that a *place* shall be chosen in which the voice is neither rendered confused by a distinct echo, nor by its continuance beyond the utterance of the speaker: for this is in my opinion the full meaning of the somewhat obscure passages . . . nor do I find it satisfactorily explained either by his English or his German Translators. (See Vitruvii Lib. V Cap. VIII). (Latrobe, "Remarks on the Best Form of a Room for Hearing and Speaking," c. 1803, *BHL Corr.,* 1:400)

• Andrea Palladio, *I Quattro Libri dell'architettura* (Venice, 1570)

Palladio and his successors and contemporaries endeavored to establish fixed rules for the most minute parts of the orders. The Greeks knew of no such rules, but having established *general* proportions and laws of form and arrangement, all matters of detail were left to the talent and taste of individual architects . . . Of this license in detail, I think it right to avail myself on all occasions. There are however practices in respect to some of their arrangements which Palladio and his school, have totally rejected, although among the Greeks they were so general, as scarcely to have been arbitrary. (Latrobe to John Lenthall, 5 August 1804, *BHL Corr.,* 1:528)

Latrobe's modern stance also questioned Renaissance theorists, testing their prescriptive Classicism against the emerging evidence of a far more wide-ranging ancient Classicism now brought to Neoclassical eyes precisely drawn and measured through books, even if many of the examples, in Greece, southern Italy, Dalmatia, and the Near East, had not been seen in person by most architects of Western Europe and the New World. Latrobe would be similarly critical of subsequent Renaissance authors, though still willing to rely on the details and proportional schemes they offered in publications.

Palladio was more of an authority in the eyes of Thomas Jefferson, Latrobe's frequent correspondent and initial client for work on the U.S. Capitol, who directed Latrobe to writings of Lord Burlington on Palladio, most likely his *Fabbriche antiche disegnate da A. Palladio date in luce da Riccardo, Conte di Burlington* (London, 1730):

Ld. Burlington in his notes on Palladio tells us that he found most of the buildings erected under Palladio's direction and described in his architecture to have their columns made of brick in this way and covered over with stucco. (Jefferson to Latrobe, 28 February 1804, *BHL Corr.,* 1:440)

- Vincenzo Scamozzi, possibly *L'Idea dell'architettura universale* (1615)
- Giacomo Barrozi da Vignola, *Regole delli cinque ordini d'architettura* (Venice, 1596)

> The books *lie,* as regards ancient architecture. They tell you what Palladio and Scamozzi and Vignola *opined,* not what the greeks or Romans actually *did.* Your columns are Doric ... Behold how much I have yielded to oeconomy in making the diam. only 17, or 1/8, being exactly Palladio's proportion, or that of Theatre of Marcellus." (Latrobe to Joel Barlow, June 1810, *BHL Corr.,* 2:873)

> The specimen of the Doric Order which you showed to me was in a work which I do not possess, but it was so similar to Vignola's representation of the Doric of the Theatre of Marcellus, that I shall use his proportions in speaking of it." (Latrobe to Thomas Jefferson, 29 March 1804, *BHL Corr.,* 1:470)

- Antoine Barbuty Desgodetz, *Les édifices antiques de Rome dessinés et mesurés très exactement* (Paris, 1682)

> If you will be pleased to refer to Degodetz you would see that there is a rim projecting above the arch of the Pantheon at the opening. (Latrobe to Thomas Jefferson, 21 May 1807, *BHL Corr.,* 2:429)

In this case Latrobe was making reference to one of those "old french books" that he knew Jefferson placed more confidence in than did Latrobe himself.

Illustrated travel books bringing back images of exotic sites beyond western Europe were another staple of this more worldly century which made Classicism a conscious choice.

- *Persepolis Illustrata* (1739), possibly

> In the Palace of forty Columns at Persepolis are represented battles and civil transactions in Sculpture. (Latrobe to Thomas Law, 10 November 1816, *BHL Corr.,* 3:828)

Latrobe was aware of similar books, such as one by James Bruce on the source of the Nile (1790); one by Patrick Brydone on Sicily and Malta (1773) and another on Sicily by Lazzaro Spallanzani (1792–97); by Jean Baptiste Tavernier on Turkey and Persia (1676); by David Cranz on Greenland (1765); and by William MacIntosh on travels that reached into Africa and Asia (1782).

Others, though, were less works of exoticism than of wider possibilities in modern Classical design spurred by new discoveries in buildings of antiquity.

• Robert Wood, *The Ruins of Baalbeck* (London, 1757)
• Robert Wood, *The Ruins of Palmyra* (London, 1753)

> In Grecian architecture, I am a bigotted Greek, to the condemnation of the roman architecture of Balba, Palmyra, Spalatro, and of all the buildings erected subsequent to Hadrian's reign. (Latrobe to Jefferson, 21 May 1807, *BHL Corr.*, 2:428)

• Robert Adam, *Ruins of the Palace of the Emperor Diocletian at Spalatro in Dalmatia* (London, 1764)

> My allusion was . . . to the palace of Dioclesian at Salonica (Spalatro) which is yet very entire, and which abounds more in bad taste and absurd decoration, than almost any other building of that age, though it must also be confessed that some parts, especially the front towards the port has very great merit. (Latrobe to Jefferson, 7 December 1806, *BHL Corr.*, 2:322)

Some of these sites brought into contemporary Classical work new elements that Latrobe clearly rejected. But others, specifically from ancient Greece, were fundamental to his generation's reconceptualization of Classicism. The most important source, alluded to by his student Strickland (above), were the works of Stuart and Revett, along with a glimpse of their discoveries perhaps first offered to him by a French source.

• Julien-David Le Roy, *Les ruines des plus beaux monuments de la Grèce* (Paris, 1758)

In Latrobe's so-called English notebook (ca. 1791–93), at the Library of Congress, there are sketches identified in his table of contents as "Capital & Base of the Columns of the Temple of Erectheus at Athens from le Roi." Much later in his career, Latrobe would repeat a story told by Le Roy:

Both Iron and Timber when completely buried in Lime or Mortar, and entirely secluded from the Action of the Air are as indestructible as Marble, a proof of which has been discovered in a Temple at Athens built 2000 Years ago, in which the Cedar pieces inserted between the Marble Blocks of which the Columns were composed, to the perfect exclusion of Air, were found in perfect preservation. (Latrobe, "Memorial to Congress in Vindication of His Professional Skill," 8 December 1818, *BHL Corr.*, 3:1015)

For the principal voice of authority in such matters, however, Latrobe would repeatedly turn to Stuart and Revett.

• James Stuart and Nicholas Revett, *The Antiquities of Athens Measured and Delineated*, 3 vols. (London, 1762–94)

The Athenian capital I allude to, is of the best Age of Athenian architecture, as is to be found in the 1st. or 2d Volume of Stuart's *Athens*. (Latrobe to Jefferson, 29 April 1804, *BHL Corr.*, 1:486)

I have packed and sent to Baltimore the Volume of Stuart's *Athens* containing the choragic Monument of Lysicrates . . . (Latrobe to Jefferson, 17 November 1804, *BHL Corr.*, 1:572)

This kind of [Greek] painting Stuart tells me still exists upon the internal frieze of the temple of Theseus at Athens, on white marble. If on trial you do not like it, then the ground should be a little *bluer*, and the fret broke with yellow. (Latrobe to S. M. Fox, 8 July 1805, *BHL Corr.*, 2:98)

The Columns are of the Attic order, a very beautiful specimen of which is to be found in the Clepsydra in Athens, commonly called the Temple of the Winds, (see Stuart's *Athens*). (Latrobe to Jefferson, 29 March 1804, *BHL Corr.*, 1:469–70)

• Nicholas Revett, *Ionian Antiquities*, 2d ed. (London, 1769, 1797).

This work, mentioned by Strickland during his pupilage in Latrobe's office, may also have been the one Latrobe himself referred to a few years later:

As the Work [a portico thought to be of the period of Diocletian] is not mentioned in the very minute and accurate work of Rivett, I doubt its existence in a very intelligible state. (Latrobe to Jefferson, 7 December 1806, *BHL Corr.*, 2:321)

At the same time that he was looking off to such distant horizons of both the past and the future course of architecture, Latrobe was supremely aware of what was being built and had been built by his and previous generations of British architects, from the standpoint both of building technologies and of taste.

• Christopher Wren, *Parentalia; or Memoirs of the Family of the Wrens* (London, 1750)

> The enormous dome and cone of St. Pauls (see Wrens *Parentalia*) the Double Dome of the Invalids and the Triple dome of St. Genieve and I may say all the great Domes that spring above their lower piers and abuttments, are thus confined and in fact could not have been constructed by any other method [than by using iron chains or bands]. (Latrobe, "Memorial to Congress in Vindication of His Professional Skill," 8 December 1818, *BHL Corr.*, 3:1015)

St. Paul's was deeply imprinted in his consciousness. In fact, he penciled its plan and elevation in an undated sketchbook, perhaps calling on these from memory when he was starting out his design of the Baltimore Cathedral.[16]

The establishment voice for the British Classicism of the time was that of William Chambers, who engaged in a diachronic dialogue with Italian and French treatises from previous centuries to arrive at models for a monumental British classicism. Latrobe would sometimes turn to Chambers as an authority, but at other times treated him as a foil against which newer ideas would play.

• William Chambers, *A Treatise on Civil Architecture, in which Principles of the Art are laid down* (London, 1759)

> The Cornice will of course make out the *2 diameters* of the Column, and have the projection of Sir William's Corinthian cornice. (Latrobe to John Lenthall, 13 May 1805, *BHL Corr.*, 2:72)

> In the lower block enough additional allowance must be made for the projection of the Cincture. What it must be, you will find in Chambers. (Latrobe to John Lenthall, 13 July 1804, *BHL Corr.*, 1:521)

> I have followed the Greek rather than the Roman style, in spite of Sir William Chambers. (BHL to John Lenthall, 29 October 1804, *BHL Corr.*, 1:553)

Chambers would strike notes quite different from the Classical in his 1772 *Dissertation on Oriental Gardening,* of which a parody was published the following year.

• Mason, William, *An Heroic Epistle to Sir William Chambers* (London, 1773).

In a journal entry of 17 June 1796, Latrobe paraphrased Mason's parody, writing of landscape, "Search, as you will the whole creation round, 'Tis after all but water, trees, and ground."[17]

Latrobe was also quite aware of eighteenth-century architecture in Dublin, including great models of neo-Palladian practice and works by followers of Chambers. Buildings such as the Irish House of Commons, the Royal Exchange, and Leinster House were of particular pertinence, as they had offered models for America's new federal buildings of the 1790s: William Thornton's proposed congressional chambers at the U.S. Capitol, Samuel Blodget's First Bank of the United States in Philadelphia, and James Hoban's design for the president's house. Latrobe cited a publication illustrating all three models, commenting on the third.

• Robert Pool and John Cash, *Views of the Most Remarkable Public Buildings, Monuments, and other Edifices in the City of Dublin* (Dublin, 1780)

> If the plan of the house were his [Hoban's] design, I should be guilty of great professional impropriety in interfering with his operations. But as it is acknowledged to be that of the palace of the duke of Leinster, which I have now before me, in a book containing the principal edifices of Dublin, he cannot be offended even if he should see these remarks. (Latrobe to William Lee, 22 March 1817, *BHL Corr.,* 3:872)

Latrobe was also demonstrably aware, though generally disdainful, of another class of contemporary British architectural books that tended to followed neo-Palladian models, either adapting them for a more middling clientele and local builders or introducing their authors' own design innovations.

• James Paine, possibly *Plans, Elevations and Sections of Noblemen and Gentlemen's Houses* (London, 1767)
• Abraham Swan, various titles of the 1740s–60s, possibly including *A Collection of Design in Architecture* (London, 1757)
• William Thomas, *Original Designs in Architecture* (London, 1783)

If the Capitol were a mass of straight walls and timber floors, and a roof copied from Paine or Swan . . . then I should be as well satisfied with Leroy or Meade as with Davis. (Latrobe to Elias B. Caldwell, 26 June 1816)[18]

Excepting when books describe and delineate works of merit, actually executed, they generally have been published by men, whose want of business, and of course, of experience, has given them leisure to speculate, and to build *castles in the Air.* Of this kind are almost *all* the books of Architecture with which I am acquainted, as Thomas's, Paine, Swan's, &c. &c. &c. out of all which a judge of architectural merit, can gather valuable materials; but in which those, who usually have recourse to them, are incapable of distinguishing beauties from defects. (Latrobe to John Ewing Colhoun, 17 April 1802, *BHL Corr.,* 1:203)

Latrobe did draw instruction from the practice of other architects, particularly the most prominent London offices. In a letter of 19 July 1806 to his father-in-law, Isaac Hazlehurst, about his itinerant practice, he cited as examples the buildings of "Adams, Chambers, Wyatt, Soane, &c., whose works are scattered over two Islands" (*BHL Corr.,* 2:248). Of these, he apparently took the greatest inspiration from the work of John Soane. Although there does not appear to be definitive evidence that Latrobe saw such books as Soane's *Sketches in Architecture* (London, 1793), a number of strong resemblances to Soane's published designs suggest his familiarity with them.

Like Soane, he would be particularly attentive to modern French Neoclassicism, especially the work of Claude-Nicolas Ledoux. One potent model, Ledoux's Guimard house, was at hand in multiple views in a publication borrowed from Jefferson.

• Johann Karl Krafft and Pierre Nicolas Ransonette, *Plans, coupes, élévations des plus belles maisons et des hôtels construits à Paris* (Paris, 1801–2)

Since my return a bilious fever and inflammation of the head has confined me entirely. My amusement has been the tinting of the Drawings in your Maisons de Paris. The paper is very bad, and they cannot be as well done as I wish. My pupil has worked with fear, and has done little on this account. (Latrobe to Jefferson, 13 September 1805, *BHL Corr.,* 2:146)

Latrobe later advised the president that he would "find the designs however considerably improved by shadows and tinting" (28 May 1807, *BHL Corr.,* 2:146 n.)

Latrobe was also aware of other modern European publications—some of them, like Krafft and Ransonette, volumes published subsequent to his emigration—which he must have seen or heard about while in this country.

• Armand Guy Simon de Coetnempren, Comte de Kersaint, *Discours sur les monuments publics, prononcé au conseil du departmente de Paris, 15 Décembre 1791* (Paris, 1792)

> The Board of Architects, with Kersaint at their head, in their report to the National Convention of France, upon the public Buildings, (and which I possess but cannot just now find) proposed to convert the unfinished Church of St. Madelaine into a Building for the meeting of the National Legislature. (Latrobe, "Remarks on the Best Form of a Room for Hearing and Speaking," c. 1803, *BHL Corr.,* 1:405–6)

• Jean Nicolas Louis Durand, *Recueil et parallèle des édifices de tout genre, anciennes et modernes, remarquables par leur beauté,* 2 vols. (Paris, 1799–1800)

> Import for me, if possible early next spring . . . *Recueil et Parallèle des edifices de tout genre, anciens et modernes,* par Durand, two Volumes, one of plates the other of description. (Latrobe to Charles Ghequiere, 12 November 1804, *BHL Corr.,* 1:570)

• David Gilly, *Handbuch der Landbaukunst* (Berlin, 1800)

> In looking over my books, I find Professor Gilly's great work on practical Architecture (Berlin 1800) a very compleat treatise on the *Delorme* roof. Every thing that has been done or written on the subject has been collected by him with German industry and correctness. (Latrobe to Jefferson, 19 July 1805, *BHL Corr.,* 2:108)

> I have not yet been able to prepare my extract from Gilli, on the Del'orme roof for you. But it shall not be long withheld. (Latrobe to Jefferson, 13 September 1805, *BHL Corr.,* 2:146)

• Baron Dominique Vivant Denon, *Voyage dans la basse et la haute Egypte, pendant les campagnes du Général Bonaparte,* 2 vols. (Paris, 1802)

Latrobe's letters reveal that he borrowed this French publication, a rich font of Egyptian forms that would find their way into his works, from the American Philosophical Society in 1808.[19]

He was quite attuned, even before his departure from England, to the emerging literature of the Picturesque and the Gothic Revival, which also found a place in his work. Such books, too, he would sometimes borrow.

• [?] William Gilpin, *Remarks on Forest Scenery, and other Woodland Views (relative chiefly to picturesque beauty)*, 2 vols. (London, 1791)

> . . . the sooner I get *my Gothic hints,* & Gilpins picturesque scenery the more I shall thank you. Perhaps you will trust me with two or three of the Volumes. (Latrobe to Joshua Gilpin, 14 May 1804, *BHL Corr.,* 1:499)

> I cannot quarrell with you if you have forgotten my Gothic Cathedral, and my Gilpinian landscapes. (Latrobe to Joshua Gilpin, 19 May 1804, *BHL Corr.,* 1:502)

• Richard Payne Knight, *The Landscape, a Didactic Poem, in three books* (London, 1794)

> Knight in his *Landscape* quotes some Poetaster . . . ridiculing the employment of Park making. (Latrobe, journal entry, 17 June 1796)

> Mr. Knight in his elegant, but illnatured poem on Landscape gardening . . . (Latrobe, "Essay on Landscape," 1798–99)[20]

• John Britton, *The Architectural Antiquities of Great Britain, represented and illustrated in a series of views, elevations, plans, sections, and details of various English edifices, with historical and descriptive accounts of each,* 5 vols. (London, 1807–26)

When working on his Gothic design for the Bank of Philadelphia in 1808, Latrobe sent his assistant, Robert Mills, "the first part of Britton's Gothic Antiquities."[21]

As much as Latrobe is remembered as an architect, engineering was also a major part of his practice, and he was equally, if not more, aware of the critical need for reference to certain books on civil and military engineering, some more than a century old.

• John Smeaton, *A Narrative of the Building, and a Description of the Construction of the Edystone Lighthouse* (London, 1791)

Latrobe, who had trained with Smeaton in the 1780s, copied excerpts from this in his "English notebook" (ca. 1791–93, now in the Library of Congress).

• Johann Albert Eytelwein, *Praktische Anweisung zur Konstrukzion der Faschinenwerke und den dazu gedringen Anlagen an Flüssen und Strömen nebst einer Anleitung zur Beranschlagung dieser Baue* (Berlin, 1800)

Latrobe drew from this publication, even translating excerpts, when recommending flood-controlling fascine works to New Orleans authorities in 1816.[22]

• Bernard Forest de Belidor, *Architecture hydraulique, ou L'Art de conduire, d'élever et de ménager les eaux pour les différens besoins de la vie,* 4 vols. (Paris, 1737–53)
• Jean-Rudolphe Perronet, possibly *Description des projets et de la construction des ponts de Neully, de Montes, d'Orleans et autres,* 2 vols. (Paris, 1782–83)

> Whether I am growing more lazy, or more aged, or whether the increase of my business is the cause, I find a recurrence to books daily more convenient, and there are two or three works which are become almost indispensibly necessary to me . . . I therefore take the liberty to request of you *as a matter of business* to import for me, if possible early next spring the following Works, which are expensive ones and not to be had but at Paris, I believe.
>
> 1.) *L'Architecture Hydraulique, par* M. Belidor. This is an old work and perhaps scarce, of course, dear.
>
> 2.) All the works of M. Peronet. Peronet was without exception the greatest Bridge-builder in the world. His works are voluminous, and the numerous plates render them expensive. I could wish to have *them all.* (Latrobe to Charles Ghequiere, 12 November 1804, *BHL Corr.,* 1:569–70)

Writing in 1820 to his son John H. B. Latrobe, then studying at West Point, Latrobe offered him some of his volumes on military engineering, and mentioned others.

• Possibly Simon-Francis Gay de Vernon, *Traité élémentaire d'art militaire et de fortification, à l'usage des élèves des Écoles militaires,* 2 vols. (Paris, 1805)
• Carnot, Lazare Nicolas Marguerite, possibly *De la défense des places fortes* (Paris, 1810)
• Sebastien Le Prestre, Marquis de Vauban, *Traité de l'attaque et de la défense des places* (La Haye, 1737)

In rummaging over my books I found a parcel of odd Volumes on military subjects which I send to New York . . . I have also the polytechnic Elementary work on Engineering and military Tactics: I have thought it too valuable to send to You now; but it awaits Your service when you shall be farther advanced; and altho I understand that much in this work is not any longer useful, further improvement and perfection having been attained since it was written, Still, it must always remain one of the best elementary works in existence. Even Carnot's new suggestions add only to the practice not to the *principles* of destruction or defence. Vauban will always be the Newton of Engineers, tho' now dead more than 100 Years ago. (Latrobe to John H. B. Latrobe, 12 January 1820, *BHL Corr.*, 3:1038)

Latrobe also mentioned Vauban in a letter of 10 October 1814 to Maximilian Godefroy (*BHL Corr.*, 3:580).

• Marc-René, Marquis de Montalembert, *La fortification perpendiculaire*, 6 vols. (1776–86)

On 9 February 1807, Latrobe discussed another publication on fortified works with West Point superintendent Jonathan Williams: "I want to talk to you at large on Montalembert's system . . . I do not wish to throw cold water on a system of fortification of which the theory appears so perfect, and so seducing." (*BHL Corr.*, 2:371).

Latrobe flirted repeatedly with the idea of writing a book on architecture himself. He was approached in early 1812 by Philadelphia publisher Joseph Delaplaine but declined, inasmuch as he felt he was "not the Man to write one which could be either popular, or useful to the mechanic"—presumably what Delaplaine told him (or Latrobe had inferred) was wanted. Instead, Latrobe envisioned writing different sorts of books:

I have long ago contemplated the publication of two professional works, one, in folio, a technical description of all my great works, expressly calculated for the use of professional Men, as well as adapted to the taste of those who collect books as they do furniture, or who have a taste for the Arts without practising them; the other, a collection of Essays in a convenient form on the principles on which public as well as private buildings ought to be constructed. (Latrobe to Delaplaine, 1 Jan. 1812, *BHL Corr.*, 3:222)

Latrobe prepared versions of several of his drawings that seemed destined less for his clients than posterity, and his letters show a continual inclination to discuss his thoughts about architecture with clients, students, and friends. But his was a rather nomadic life filled with professional activity in which, as he foresaw, such literary enterprises would require a critical ingredient he had not had:

> When I therefore take up the pen, it must be with a certainty that I shall have leisure to write a book that will be worth reprinting and rereading. My talents I cannot encrease but to make the most of what little I possess I must [take] care of *leisure* . . . I want several months before I would put a line to press. (Latrobe to Delaplaine, 23 January 1812, *BHL Corr.*, 3:237)

He was not able to fulfill either of these writing ambitions in what was to be a foreshortened lifetime.

NOTES

1. Latrobe to Mills, 12 July 1806, in *The Correspondence and Miscellaneous Papers of Benjamin Henry Latrobe*, 3 vols., ed. John C. Van Horne et al. (New Haven: Yale University Press, 1984–88), 2:239. This title is hereafter cited in notes and text as *BHL Corr.*

2. Helen Park, *A List of Architectural Books Available in America before the Revolution* (Los Angeles: Hennessy & Ingalls, 1973); Janice G. Schimmelman, *Architectural Treatises and Building Handbooks Available in American Libraries and Bookstores through 1800* (Worcester, Mass.: American Antiquarian Society, 1986).

Further evidence of various kinds of architectural book collections is scattered, but in many cases ownership information can be drawn from inscriptions in surviving books. (One might propose to find a way to collect and disseminate such information through the World Wide Web.)

3. Latrobe to C. Ghequiere, 12 November 1804, in *BHL Corr.*, 1:569.

4. One of the few known surviving books owned by Latrobe is not an architectural title but Sir Humphrey Polesworth's *Fragments of the History of John Bull* (London, 1791). The copy at the Library of Congress bears the inscription "Lydia Latrobe from her very affectionate husband B. H. Latrobe." The text was heavily annotated by Benjamin Latrobe, according to a note by his son John H. B. Latrobe. Larry E. Sullivan to Edward C. Carter II, 1 December 1993, photocopy in project archive, Papers of Benjamin Henry Latrobe, American Philosophical Society Library, Philadelphia.

5. Accounts of the editorial project itself are given in Edward C. Carter II, "The Papers of Benjamin Henry Latrobe and the Maryland Historical Society, 1885–1971: Nature, Structure, and Means of Acquisition," *Maryland Historical Magazine* 66 (1971): 436–55; John C. Van Horne, "The Latrobe Papers: A Retrospective," and Jeffrey A. Cohen, "Life and Afterlife of an Editorial Project: The Papers of Benjamin Henry Latrobe, 1970–1995," *Annotation: The Newsletter of the National Historical Publications and Records Commission* 27, no. 2 (1999): 13–15, 16–18.

The publications of the Latrobe Papers from the 1970s through the 1990s have included a microfiche edition of the manuscripts known at the commencement of the project (1976), three letterpress volumes of Latrobe's journals (1977–80), three more of his correspondence (1984–88), one of his watercolors (1985), one of his engineering drawings (1980), and one (in two parts) of his architectural drawings (1994).

6. Latrobe to C. Ghequiere, 12 November 1804, in *BHL Corr.*, 1:569.

7. Latrobe to Mills, 12 July 1806, in *BHL Corr.*, 2:242–43.

8. Latrobe, "A Private Letter to the Individual Members of Congress, on the Subject of the Public Buildings of the United States at Washington," 28 November 1806, in *BHL Corr.*, 2:306.

9. Latrobe to Lenthall, 3 May 1805, quoted in BHL, *Corr.* 2:197 n. 1.

10. William Strickland, autobiographical fragment, c. 1825, J. K. Kane Papers, American Philosophical Society Library, Philadelphia. The books he refers to are English, unspecified titles by Batty Langley (1696–1751) and Abraham Swan (fl. 1740s–60s); the last was most likely Batty Langley, *The Builders' Director, or Bench-mate* (London, 1747).

11. Robert Mills, "The Architectural Works of Robert Mills," in H. M. P. Gallagher, *Robert Mills, Architect of the Washington Monument, 1781–1855* (New York: Columbia University Press, 1935), 169.

12. Ibid., 170.

13. Jeffrey A. Cohen, "Building a Discipline: Early Institutional Settings for Architectural Education in Philadelphia, 1804–1890," *Journal of the Society of Architectural Historians* 53 (June 1994): 139–83.

14. *The Papers of Robert Mills, 1781–1855,* Pamela J. Scott, ed. microfilm ed. (Wilmington, Del.: Scholarly Resources, 1990).

15. Geraldine S. Vickers, Thomas E. Jeffrey, and John C. Van Horne, comps., "Notes on the Latrobe Library," typescript [ca. 1980?], project archive, Papers of Benjamin Henry Latrobe. This effort probably also reflected the efforts of staff members Charles E. Brownell, Angeline Polites, Lee W. Formwalt, Tina H. Sheller, Darwin H. Stapleton, and others.

16. Jeffrey A. Cohen and Charles E. Brownell, *The Architectural Drawings of Benjamin Henry Latrobe* (New Haven: Yale University Press, 1994), fig. 153.

17. *The Journals of Benjamin Henry Latrobe,* 3 vols., ed. Edward C. Carter et al. (New Haven: Yale University Press, 1977–80), 1:153.

18. *The Microfiche Edition of the Papers of Benjamin Henry Latrobe,* ed. Thomas E. Jeffrey (Clifton, N.J.: James T. White, 1976), 131/F13; *BHL Corr.,* 3:964 n.

19. Latrobe to John Vaughan, 9 and 10 January 1808, Latrobe, *Microfiche Edition,* 62/C5.

20. Latrobe, *Journals,* 1:153, 2:469.

21. Latrobe to Mills, 13 February 1808, Latrobe, *Microfiche Edition,* 62/F1.

22. Darwin H. Stapleton, ed., *The Engineering Drawings of Benjamin Henry Latrobe* (New Haven: Yale University Press, 1980), 208–13.

VIII

THE COUNTRY BUILDER'S ASSISTANT:

TEXT AND CONTEXT

Kenneth Hafertepe

The portrait of Asher Benjamin which hangs in the hall of the Federal-era Asa Stebbins House in Deerfield, Massachusetts, presents a man who is successful, prosperous, and serene (figure 8.1). He is perhaps sixty years old and enjoying a renaissance in his dual career as an architect and an author of architectural books. This image of the mature Benjamin—his only known portrait—does not give us a sense of the young housewright, starting out in the Connecticut River Valley, when he produced his first book, *The Country Builder's Assistant.*

The Asher Benjamin who worked in Northampton, Deerfield, and Greenfield was not successful and settled but young, restless, and ambitious. In these characteristics he was completely in accord with the tenor of his times. In the 1790s the new nation was coming out of the postrevolutionary economic doldrums of the previous decade, and the possibilities for success seemed endless. In Rhode Island the Englishman Samuel Slater erected the first textile mill in the United States, the earliest sign of the coming Industrial Revolution. A new national capital city was being built in the District of Columbia, where real estate speculation was perhaps the original form of Potomac fever. Land deals were being offered in western New York, in Ohio, and in the area that now constitutes Alabama and Mississippi. Banks and insurance companies were being founded in major American cities, and lotteries and tontine associations (like the one that funded the Tontine Crescent in Boston) were attracting investors—

FIG 8.1 Portrait of Asher Benjamin, artist unknown, ca. 1830. Oil on canvas, 40.75 × 35.38 in. Historic Deerfield, Inc., Deerfield, Mass.

though frequently not enough investors to keep these schemes afloat. This was the atmosphere in which Asher Benjamin launched his career.

I try in this essay to place *The Country Builder's Assistant* in several contexts: the context of Connecticut River Valley architecture, the context of Asher Benjamin's career as architect and author, and the context of American architectural publication. The fact that it was the first original book on architecture produced by an American— or at least the first American architectural book with aspirations to originality—is made all the more extraordinary by Benjamin's relative youth, his relative inexperience as an architect, and his roots in rural New England rather than in a publishing hub such as Boston.

Little is known of Asher Benjamin's upbringing in rural Hartford County, Connecticut, or about his training.[1] In a letter of 1802—five years after the publication of his first book—Gideon Granger described him as "a poor boy unaided by friends" who had "raised himself to the first rank of his profession."[2] As Abbott Lowell Cummings has pointed out, Benjamin makes his first appearance on the stage of architectural history at the Oliver Phelps House in Suffield, Connecticut: in late 1794 and early 1795 he carved the Ionic capitals of the door for the new wing that Phelps was adding.[3] The twenty-one-year-old Benjamin was assisting the construction of one of the earliest Neoclassical buildings in New England; in so doing, he worked with Thomas Hayden, the master builder from Windsor with whom Benjamin may have apprenticed and through whom he was introduced to the books of the British architect William Pain.

Pain's early works promoted the British version of Andrea Palladio's Renaissance style, but his later work publicized the new European Neoclassicism, particularly that of the Scottish architect Robert Adam. Pain's *Practical House Carpenter* was published in London in 1788, and American editions were produced by John Norman in Boston in 1796, and by Thomas Dobson in Philadelphia in 1797. Since both American editions postdated the Phelps House, it is clear that Thomas Hayden owned the London edition. And since Asher Benjamin had the responsibility of carving the capitals of a frontispiece out of Pain, he certainly had the opportunity to look through its pages.

Later in 1795, Benjamin built the circular staircase in the new Connecticut State House in Hartford. Begun in 1793 and completed in 1796, it was based on a design by the young gentleman architect Charles Bulfinch of Boston. There is no evidence that Bulfinch actually visited Hartford in connection with this project; nevertheless, in this earliest phase of his career Benjamin worked on an early building by New England's leading Neoclassical architect.[4]

As with the Phelps House, Benjamin's work was only one aspect of the project, but it was a job that he long remembered. Years later he recalled that "in the year 1795, I made the drawings and superintended the erection of a circular stair case in the State House at Hartford, Connecticut, which, I believe, was the first circular rail that was ever made in New England."[5] Since the method for building such stairs had only recently been published by the British architect Peter Nicholson, it is clear that Benjamin was familiar with Nicholson's work. And his statement that he made the *drawings* tells us not only that he was responsible for the design of the staircase but also that by 1795 he was skilled in architectural drawing.

How did Benjamin win this choice job on a major public building? It may have helped that he knew Gideon Granger, who represented Suffield in the General Assembly of Connecticut and went on to become postmaster general of the United States under Thomas Jefferson. When Benjamin decided to enter the competition for the U.S. Naval Hospital in Charlestown, Massachusetts, he wrote to Granger in Washington invoking his help and reporting on the projects that he had done since he left Suffield.

One of the projects Benjamin listed was a house for Samuel and Dorothy Hinckley in Northampton, Massachusetts, Hinckley was a Yale graduate who had come to Northampton to study law with Caleb Strong, a leading Federalist lawyer and politician; he not only studied with Strong but also married his younger sister, Dorothy, in 1786. Hinckley served as Hampshire County's register of probate for thirty years and judge of probate for another seventeen.[6] Like Oliver Phelps, he invested heavily in western lands; it has been said that at one time he owned all of what is now Rochester, New York, although he sold out too soon to make a profit. Meanwhile, he took on law students of his own, and one of these students was Gideon Granger, who had lived with the Hinckleys in the late 1780s. Ten years later Granger may have introduced the Hinckleys to his friend Asher Benjamin, who designed and built their new house on Pleasant Street in 1796.

On the Hinckley House, Benjamin emphasized the three central bays by projecting them forward slightly and accentuated them further with a pediment. A balustrade mounted with neoclassical urns screened the low, hipped roof (figure 8.2). Although the Hinckley House was demolished in 1902, its interior arrangements can be determined from a drawing (figure 8.3) in the collections of the Society for the Preservation of New England Antiquities (SPNEA). Although unsigned, it was acquired with a group of signed Benjamin drawings, and—by comparison with Samuel Hinckley's 1840 probate inventory (figure 8.4), photographs of the exterior, and insurance maps showing the footprint of the house in the late nineteenth century—can be identified as the plan of the Hinckley House. As such, it is the earliest known Benjamin drawing.[7]

The house had a central passage, with two rooms on each side. The two front rooms were parlors; behind the south parlor was a bedroom, and behind the north parlor was the dining room. The kitchen and other work-related spaces were relegated to a rear ell on the north side. The drawing shows that the ell had a gambrel roof, making the Hinckley House one of the earliest in western Massachusetts to use the gambrel for an ell.

The house is compelling evidence that by 1796 Benjamin had not only *worked* on a building by Charles Bulfinch but had also been to Boston himself and had seen the early works of Bulfinch firsthand. In particular, Benjamin seems to have studied the house of Joseph Coolidge Sr., a three-story house with a hipped roof and a pediment three bays wide, built 1791–92 (figure 8.5). The Coolidge House did not have Doric overlintels, but Benjamin could have seen those on the quite similar house of Thomas Dawes Jr., built about 1795. And the Hinckley House is equally compelling evidence that Benjamin owned his own copy of Pain's *Practical House Carpenter,* in which plate 107 shows both in plan and elevation the subtle projection of the three central bays (figure 8.6).[8]

By January 1797, Benjamin was in Greenfield, Massachusetts. A drawing at SPNEA is marked "Greenfield 29 of January 1797 Asher Benjamin." A second drawing for a frontispiece in the Ionic order is signed and dated "Greenfield 4th of March 1797." Meanwhile, in the 16 February issue of the *Greenfield Gazette,* Benjamin advertised for "7 or 8 journeymen joiners for the next Summer." The number of joiners suggests that he anticipated building two houses in the 1797 season, and that is what happened. His clients were the two attorneys in town, Jonathan Leavitt Jr. and William Coleman.

Leavitt was a minister's son and a 1785 Yale graduate who had taught school in New Haven and studied law before moving to Greenfield in 1789. In April 1796 he married Emilia Stiles, third daughter of Yale's President Ezra Stiles. The Leavitts soon had four daughters and one son. In addition, the Leavitt household included African American servants: Eliza the cook, Jim the manservant, and Vincy the nursemaid. When President Stiles died in 1795, Amelia inherited her father's two elderly slaves, Newport and his wife Nabby. They came to live in Greenfield for a while, but Newport missed the college, and they moved back to New Haven.[9]

In late 1796 and early 1797, Jonathan and Emilia were thinking about building a new house. Possibly Benjamin made contact with them through Gideon Granger—who was in the Yale class of 1787, just two years behind Leavitt—or through Samuel Hinckley, who, like Leavitt, specialized in probate law. Jonathan Leavitt's name is not on the list

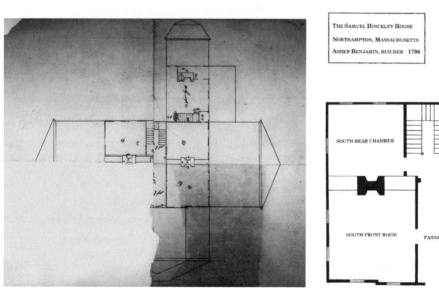

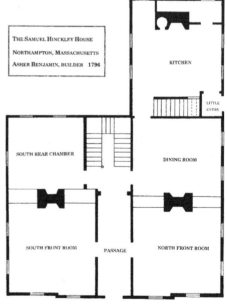

THE SAMUEL HINCKLEY HOUSE

NORTHAMPTON, MASSACHUSETTS

ASHER BENJAMIN, BUILDER   1796

KITCHEN

LITTLE ENTRY

SOUTH REAR CHAMBER

DINING ROOM

SOUTH FRONT ROOM

PASSAGE

NORTH FRONT ROOM

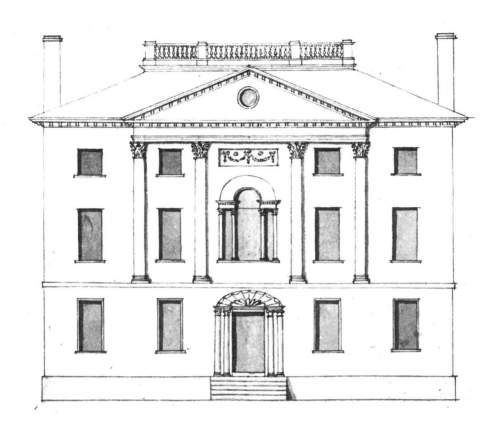

FIG 8.2 (*opposite, top*) Samuel and Dorothy Hinckley House, Northampton, Mass., by Asher Benjamin, 1796. Photo published in *Northampton: The Meadow City* (1894).

FIG 8.3 (*opposite, bottom left*) Asher Benjamin's preliminary floor plan for the Hinckley House, Northampton, Mass., 1796. Courtesy of the Society for the Preservation of New England Antiquities, Boston.

FIG 8.4 (*opposite, bottom right*) Preliminary floor plan for the Hinckley House with room designations from Samuel Hinckley's 1840 probate inventory. Drawing by the author.

FIG 8.5 (*above*) Charles Bulfinch, front of the Joseph Coolidge House, Boston, 1791–92. Pen and ink drawing. Courtesy of the Print Collection, Miriam and Ira D. Wallach Division of Art, Prints and Photographs, New York Public Library, Astor, Lenox and Tilden Foundation.

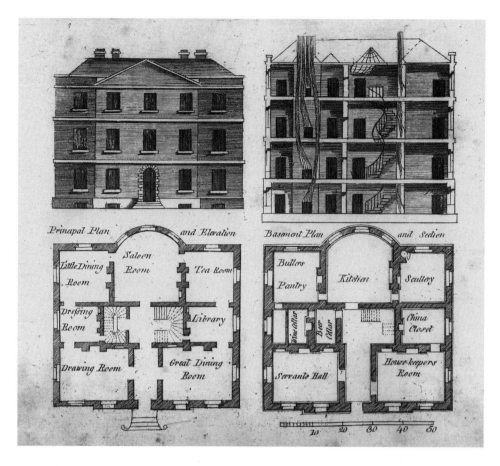

FIG 8.6 William Pain, *The Practical House Carpenter* (1788), plate 107. Courtesy of the Society for the Preservation of New England Antiquities, Boston.

of clients which Benjamin sent to Granger, but there is considerable formal evidence to link him with the Leavitt House. A Benjamin drawing at SPNEA of a wing and connector adjoining a "Great House" may well have been done for the Leavitts.

The house that Benjamin built for Jonathan and Emilia Leavitt still stands and is used as the Greenfield Public Library (figure 8.7). Alas, however, it has been almost entirely rebuilt and the interior completely remodeled. The original house was very simple, both because it had limited ornamentation and because its ornamental features—such as the cornice and the one-story porch—were of the Doric order (the mutules of the cornice would soon be illustrated in plate 8 of *The Country Builder's Assistant*). The house relates closely to plate 25 in *The Country Builder's Assistant*, which shows a rather horizontal format and a low, hipped roof (figure 8.8). The horizontality is emphasized by the stringcourse, a motif that Benjamin found in William Pain's *Practical House Carpenter;* Pain himself found it on the streets of London, in designs such as that of Home House in Portman Square, by Robert Adam. The notion of a five-part plan with Great House, connectors, and wings can also be found in Pain. The five-part plan is usually associated with the Palladianism of the mid-eighteenth century, as in the Hammond-Harwood House in Annapolis by William Buckland, but the Leavitt House also looks forward to the Neoclassical villas of the next decade— particularly Gore Place in Waltham, Massachusetts.

Benjamin's other client in Greenfield was William Coleman. Although born in the Boston poorhouse, Coleman enrolled in the first class at the Phillips Academy in Andover and later studied law with Robert Treat Paine, first attorney general of Massachusetts. Living in Greenfield by 1790, he practiced law and founded the local newspaper. Coleman represented Greenfield in the state legislature in 1795 and 1796, serving alongside such New England luminaries as Harrison Gray Otis, Jonathan Mason, and Elias Hasket Derby Jr., all once or future clients of Charles Bulfinch. On Christmas Day of 1796, Coleman married Mehitable Haviland in Trinity Church in New York City.[10]

Like Jonathan Leavitt, then, William Coleman was newly married and looking to build a new house in 1797. The William and Mehitable Coleman House still stands southwest of the town common in Greenfield (figures 8.9, 8.10); now known as the Coleman-Hollister House, it serves as the McCarthy Funeral Home. Although aluminum siding somewhat obscures Benjamin's original intentions, the house is reasonably intact. The present porch is a later addition, but even without it the Coleman House is an advanced statement of Neoclassical ideals. Four two-story Ionic pilasters accentuate the center of the facade. The cornice projects forward for the three central bays, as on the Hinckley House. Between the first- and second-floor windows are panels with a swag motif. The frontispiece has a circular window and sidelights—repeated on the rear door—and above it on the second floor is a handsome Palladian window. Like the Hinckley House, the Coleman House suggests that Benjamin had closely studied Bulfinch's Boston works. Indeed, Abbott Cummings has pointed out that the pilasters on the Coleman House closely relate to those on the Tontine Crescent.[11]

A description from December 1797 reveals that the house was "fifty feet in front by thirty-nine or forty feet deep, with twenty-four foot eight inches posts, has a piazza of ten feet or eight feet by the whole depth of the south side of the house and octagonal room extending out on the north side about ten feet; a cellar supporting on brick pillars

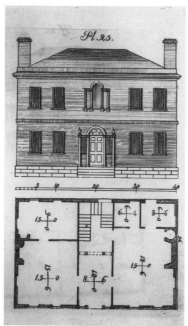

FIG 8.7 Jonathan and Emilia Leavitt House (Leavitt-Hovey House), Greenfield, Mass., by Asher Benjamin, 1797. Photo taken between 1866 and 1907. Courtesy of the Historical Society of Greenfield, Mass. FIG 8.8 (*bottom*) Asher Benjamin, *The Country Builder's Assistant* (1797), plate 25. Courtesy of the Society for the Preservation of New England Antiquities, Boston.

FIG 8.9 William and Mehitable Coleman House (Coleman-Hollister House), Greenfield, Mass., by Asher Benjamin, 1797. Photo by the Historic American Buildings Survey, 1934. Library of Congress.

the frame and extending over the whole of the said house; with a large and convenient back kitchen, wood house and necessary."[12] This document makes clear that the octagonal projection is original—similar oval or octagonal rooms could be found in other Federal-era houses in Boston and elsewhere—and that the kitchen was not in the main block of the house but in the back, probably in the ell, though the present ell has been completely rebuilt. The piazza or porch on the south side, with its Ionic columns, is visible in several views of the house from the 1820s (when it became a young ladies' high school). Later in the nineteenth century the Hollister family replaced it with an Italianate piazza, which in turn was removed in the 1950s.

The interior of the house is no less impressive. The central passage runs straight through to the rear door, and a grand circular stairway rises beyond the hall. The hall is plastered in imitation of vaulting, and Ionic pilasters continue the rhythm established by the pair of columns in front of the stairway. This stairway, probably similar to the one Benjamin erected in the Hartford State House, may be the earliest circular stair still extant in New England. The front parlors, although quite restrained in their ornamentation, echo the patterns of Pain's *Practical House Carpenter*. Most elaborate is

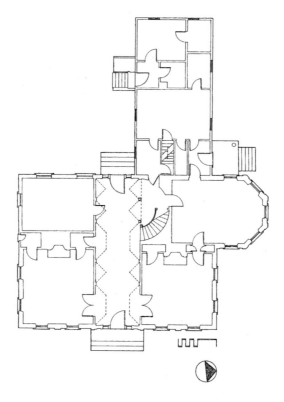

FIG 8.10 Floor plan of the Coleman-Hollister House, Greenfield, Mass. Historic American Buildings Survey drawing by Fred E. S. Sawyer, 1934, redrawn by J. Ritchie Garrison. Original drawing, Library of Congress.

the northwest room, which, adjoining the kitchen ell, presumably served as a dining room. The semi-octagonal bow on its north side gave it a distinctive shape, and it was graced with a plaster Doric entablature.

The Colemans lived only briefly in the house, if ever. In October 1796 Coleman had purchased large tracts in the southern part of what is now Mississippi (then still part of Georgia's western holdings), known as the Yazoo Lands. This speculative enterprise seduced many other members of the New England elite, including Elias Hasket Derby Jr., Joseph Barrell, Thomas H. Perkins, Charles Bulfinch, and Oliver Phelps of Suffield. Unfortunately for the investors, the Georgia legislature annulled the Yazoo purchases late in 1796, claiming that that the entire project was a corrupt scheme of the previous legislature. Coleman sold his house in Greenfield in July 1797 and was soon living in New York, where he became the founding editor of the *New York Evening Post*.[13]

William Coleman had given Asher Benjamin his biggest opportunity to build a dazzling house, and he may well have encouraged Benjamin to think of producing an architectural book. Coleman had financed the local newspaper and recruited the editor, Thomas Dickman, who had apprenticed in Boston and then worked for Isaiah Thomas in Worcester. In the 1790s, Dickman was editor of the newspaper and the local postmaster; he also kept a bookstore in his office and published three or four books a year. The books tended to be local sermons and public orations but also included Alexander Pope's *Essay on Man,* Chesterfield's *Principles of Politeness, A Collection of the Newest Cotillions and Country Dances,* and a new edition of that Deerfield classic, the Reverend John Williams's *Redeemed Captive.*[14]

The *Greenfield Gazette* of 31 August 1797 announced that *The Country Builder's Assistant* was available at Thomas Dickman's bookstore and also at Russell and Ripley, watch- and clockmakers and jewelers, both in Greenfield (figures 8.11, 8.12). The book comprised prints from thirty engraved copper plates with brief explanations—though for the plates illustrating two houses and a meetinghouse, Benjamin wrote not a word but passed over them in silence. This may suggest a brisk, let's-get-down-to-business attitude, but it may also reflect Benjamin's awareness of his lack of formal education and consequent unwillingness to write anything more than he absolutely had to.

The only previous American books on architecture were American editions of or compilations from older British architectural books. In Philadelphia in 1775 the English émigré John Norman, who styled himself an architect and engraver, brought out an edition of Abraham Swan's *British Architect,* a work originally published in 1745. Norman was in Boston by 1781, and there in 1786 he published *The Town and Country Builder's Assistant,* which was a compilation of plates from Swan and Isaac Ware, among others. And, as noted earlier, Norman published the first American edition of Pain's *Practical House Carpenter,* in 1796.

It is well known that Benjamin considered the houses illustrated in British pattern books to be too large and too ornamented for American use and particularly for country use, and in *The Country Builder's Assistant* he seems to have consciously chosen to illustrate houses that were more simple than the Hinckley, Leavitt, and Coleman houses. All three of those houses had their kitchens and other service rooms in an ell or wing, reserving all the rooms in the main block for more genteel purposes, but both houses in his first book had the cooking hearth within the main block. At the same time, Benjamin drew the bake oven flush with the facade of the hearth. This meant that the cook would not have to step into the fireplace to remove the contents of the oven, but it also meant the additional cost of building a separate flue—not at all typical

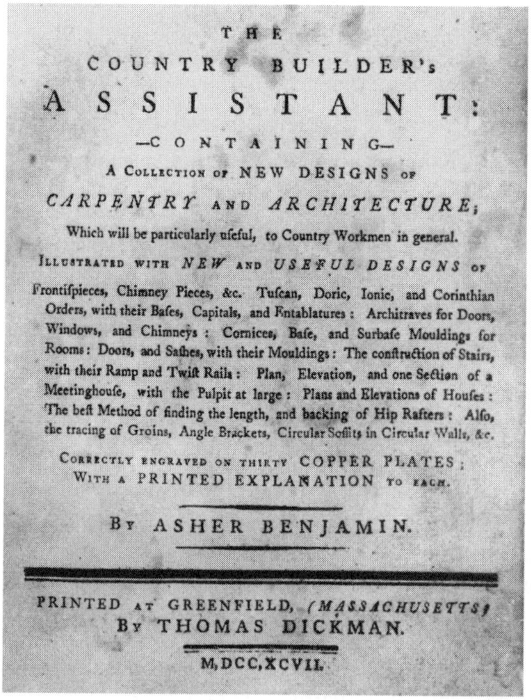

THE
COUNTRY BUILDER's
ASSISTANT:
—CONTAINING—
A COLLECTION OF NEW DESIGNS OF
CARPENTRY AND ARCHITECTURE;
Which will be particularly useful, to Country Workmen in general.
ILLUSTRATED WITH NEW AND USEFUL DESIGNS OF
Frontispieces, Chimney Pieces, &c. Tuscan, Doric, Ionic, and Corinthian
Orders, with their Bases, Capitals, and Entablatures: Architraves for Doors,
Windows, and Chimneys: Cornices, Base, and Surbase Mouldings for
Rooms: Doors, and Sashes, with their Mouldings: The construction of Stairs,
with their Ramp and Twist Rails: Plan, Elevation, and one Section of a
Meetinghouse, with the Pulpit at large: Plans and Elevations of Houses:
The best Method of finding the length, and backing of Hip Rafters: Also,
the tracing of Groins, Angle Brackets, Circular Soffits in Circular Walls, &c.

CORRECTLY ENGRAVED ON THIRTY COPPER PLATES;
WITH A PRINTED EXPLANATION TO EACH.

BY ASHER BENJAMIN.

PRINTED AT GREENFIELD, (MASSACHUSETTS)
BY THOMAS DICKMAN.
M,DCC,XCVII.

FIG 8.11 Title page of Asher Benjamin, *The Country Builder's Assistant* (1797). Photo by Penny Leveritt. Courtesy of Historic Deerfield, Inc., Deerfield, Mass.
FIG 8.12 (*bottom*) Frontispiece in Asher Benjamin, *The Country Builder's Assistant* (3d ed., 1800). Photo by the author. Courtesy of Historic Deerfield, Inc., Deerfield, Mass.

for the Connecticut River Valley in 1797 but quite the norm thereafter, as in the new kitchen ell of the Sheldon-Hawks House in Deerfield.

The most famous and widely imitated plate in *The Country Builder's Assistant* is that of the meetinghouse (figure 8.13). It was derived not from Pain but from Charles Bulfinch, specifically his Taunton meetinghouse and Pittsfield meetinghouse, both built in 1790–92. The leading characteristics are a projecting entry lobby, which creates a pseudoportico on the exterior, and a steeple with several stages, including one with an open colonnade.[15] Benjamin built his own version of this meetinghouse in Windsor, Vermont, for a new and obviously not well-off congregation. Since both of the Bulfinch meetinghouses have been demolished, and Benjamin's remodeled mercilessly, the plate in *The Country Builder's Assistant* is the best image of the interior. Traditional box pews fill the floor; there are galleries above on three sides; the pulpit is approached by circular stairs from both sides; and a Venetian window behind the pulpit provides the light. This Bulfinch-Benjamin design was adopted across New England, from Middletown, Connecticut, to Bennington, Vermont (both erected by the master builder Lavius Fillmore) and from Manchester-by-the-Sea to Otis in the Berkshires.

In 1798, Samuel Etheridge and William Spotswood of Charlestown brought out a Boston edition of *The Country Builder's Assistant*. Etheridge continued to work with Benjamin in Boston, serving, with his new partner Elam Bliss, as publisher of *The American Builder's Companion* in 1806. Significantly, the title page of the second edition of *The Country Builder's Assistant* states that Etheridge and Spotswood printed the book *for the author* and for Alexander Thomas of Worcester, who was a distant relative and sometime partner of Isaiah Thomas Sr. and Jr. Presumably, Benjamin would handle distribution in the Connecticut River Valley, Thomas in Worcester, and Etheridge and Spotswood in the eastern counties.[16]

The 1798 edition had seven new plates, two depicting a house for which two octagonal buildings create a forecourt. It is notable that in this design Benjamin included a circular staircase, which had not been present in either of the houses shown in the first edition. Unlike the circular staircase in the Coleman House, which is tucked off to the north side of the hall, this stair is directly opposite the front door and would make an immediate impression upon entry. Such an arrangement was soon used for the Asa Stebbins House in Deerfield.

The third edition of Benjamin's book, published by Thomas Dickman at Greenfield in 1800, and the final edition, published by Dickman's successor John Denio in 1805, were identical to the second edition except for the addition of a frontispiece. The building it depicts is not identified, but the plate is based quite closely on a view of the

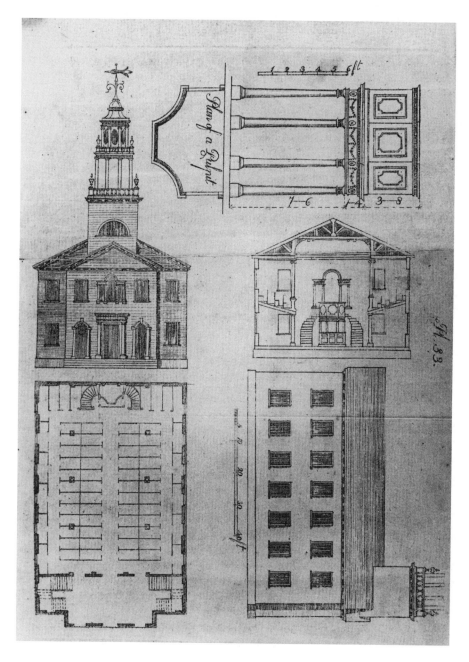

FIG 8.13 "Plan, Elevation, and one Section of a Meetinghouse, with the Pulpit at Large," plate 33 from *The Country Builder's Assistant* (1797). Photo by the author. Courtesy of Historic Deerfield, Inc., Deerfield, Mass.

Hancock House on Beacon Hill which had appeared in the *Massachusetts Magazine* in July 1789. That engraving had been done by Samuel Hill of Boston, but it seems likely that the plate in *The Country Builder's Assistant* was done by another hand and by someone *not* in Boston: in rearranging the trees the engraver was forced to show the side elevation and gave it a simple pitched roof rather than the Hancock House's actual gambrel. The adjacent carriage house was garbled in the translation as well. It seems clear that this plate was done elsewhere, probably back in Greenfield.[17]

It is striking that Benjamin chose to illustrate the Hancock House at all. Built in 1737, it was one of the most important Georgian houses in New England, but one would have expected Benjamin to present something a little more current than a sixty-year-old house. Perhaps Benjamin chose it out of admiration for John Hancock's role in the American Revolution or out of respect for an earlier manifestation of the classical tradition. Perhaps it was easier to copy an existing engraving than to design one from scratch. Or perhaps Benjamin had nothing to do with the choice at all: by 1800, when the frontispiece first appeared, Benjamin was working in Windsor, Vermont, so the decision to add a frontispiece may have been made by Thomas Dickman.

All this raises the question, who *did* engrave this plate, and all the other plates in *The Country Builder's Assistant?* One leading suspect in Greenfield is John Russell, jeweler, silversmith, and goldsmith. Russell and Ripley sold the book at their shop, so they were connected at least with its distribution. More to the point, John Russell had experience in engraving, owing to his training as a jeweler. When the cornerstone was laid for a new Congregational church in Greenfield in 1818, "a plate, engraved and presented by Maj. John Russell, was deposited in the cornerstone." And John Russell was the cousin of William Russell, the Wethersfield-born carpenter who worked with Asher Benjamin on the building for the Deerfield Academy in 1798. None of this is conclusive, to be sure, but certainly worth further investigation.[18]

The final edition of *The Country Builder's Assistant,* appearing in 1805, was final because the work was supplanted by Benjamin's next book, *The American Builder's Companion,* coauthored with Daniel Raynerd and published by Etheridge and Bliss in 1806. This work contained forty-four plates, seven more than the second *Country Builder's Assistant,* and the quality of the engravings, done in Boston by Gilbert Fox and Thomas Wightman, was immeasurably better. The work also demonstrated Benjamin's growth as an architect and his continued admiration of the work of Charles Bulfinch.

The Country Builder's Assistant provided carpenters and housewrights in New England and beyond with the forms of Neoclassical architecture—classical columns and pilasters, cornices and mantelpieces—and with technical information about hipped roofs, circular stairs, and bake ovens with separate flues. On the title page, Benjamin characterized his designs not as Neoclassical but as "new and useful." It is perhaps significant that he appreciated the novelty of Neoclassical forms rather than the antiquity of their associations. In later decades he would read the Scottish philosopher Archibald Alison's *Essays on the Nature and Principles of Taste* and incorporate many of Alison's principles in his last book, *Elements of Architecture.* But in neither his first book nor his second did Benjamin express the least bit of interest in the symbolism of the Neoclassical style. He valued the style for its formal qualities, for its good proportions, and for its elegant ornament. When illustrating Bulfinch's United States Bank in Boston, Benjamin praised it not as uniquely American or even as Neoclassical but as "the neatest public building in the state." He valued Bulfinch's architecture as much for its austerity and restraint as for its Neoclassical ornament. It can truly be said that Asher Benjamin would rather have his buildings be neat than Neoclassical.

The Country Builder's Assistant outlived its usefulness in less than ten years, but it had served its purpose. It had successfully launched the publishing career of a young man who was to become the best-known figure in American architectural publishing through the 1830s. It helped Benjamin along in his ultimate career goal of evolving from country builder to urban architect. And by introducing a generation of carpenters and housewrights to some of the key characteristics of Neoclassical design, it left the New England landscape a more graceful place.

NOTES

1. The starting points for research on Benjamin are two Ph.D. dissertations: Abbott Lowell Cummings, "An Investigation of the Sources, Stylistic Evolution, and Influence of Asher Benjamin's Builders' Guides" (Ohio State University, 1950), and Jack Quinan, "The Architectural Style of Asher Benjamin" (Brown University, 1973). Quinan subsequently edited and contributed to "Asher Benjamin and American Architecture," *Journal of the Society of Architectural Historians* 38, no. 3 (1979), a special number that includes a chronologically arranged list of projects and buildings by Benjamin and a bibliography of writings by and about Benjamin. Cummings's entry on Benjamin in *The Macmillan Encyclopedia of Architects,* ed. Adolf K. Placzek (New York: Free Press, 1982) 1:176–79, also includes a list of works and a bibliography.

2. Gideon Granger to Albert Gallatin, 13 August 1802, in the Albert Gallatin Papers at the New-York Historical Society, reprinted in Florence Thompson Howe, "More about Asher Benjamin," in *Journal of the Society of Architectural Historians* 13, no. 3 (1954): 16–17.

3. Abbott Lowell Cummings, "Asher Benjamin's Apprenticeship and Training: The State of Current Knowledge" (paper given at a colloquium, "Asher Benjamin: The State of Scholarship," at Historic Deerfield, Inc., 12 November 1993). On the Burbank-Phelps House, see William N. Hosley Jr., "Architecture,"

in *The Great River: Art and Society of the Connecticut Valley, 1635–1820*, ed. Gerald W. R. Ward and William N. Hosley Jr. (Hartford: Wadsworth Atheneum, 1985), 115–18.

4. On the State House, see Harold Kirker, *The Architecture of Charles Bulfinch* (Cambridge, Mass.: Harvard University Press, 1969), 54–65; Newton C. Brainerd, *The Hartford State House of 1796* (Hartford: Connecticut Historical Society, 1964); and Hosley, "Architecture," 121–24.

5. Asher Benjamin, *The Builder's Guide* (Boston: Perkins & Maruin, 1839), 40.

6. On Hinckley, see the *Hampshire Gazette*, 17 and 24 June 1840, 16 November 1886, and 2 December 1892; and Franklin Bowditch Dexter, *Biographical Sketches of the Graduates of Yale College* (New York: Henry Holt, 1907) 4:188.

7. On the Hinckley House, see Kenneth Hafertepe, "Asher Benjamin and the Hinckley House, Northampton," in *Old-Time New England* 77 (spring-summer 1999): 5–22. The house was illustrated in *Northampton: The Meadow City* (Northampton, 1894) as "The Kirkland Homestead, Pleasant Street." Other photographs are in the collections of the Society for the Preservation of New England Antiquities (SPNEA), Boston, and of Hinckley descendants. The footprint of the house can be seen on Sanborn Fire Insurance Maps for Northampton of June 1884, p. 7; May 1889, p. 7; March 1895, p. 10, and July 1902, p. 5. Samuel Hinckley's probate inventory of 3 October 1840 is at the Hampshire County Courthouse, Northampton. All this evidence correlates with the unlabeled drawing by Benjamin in the SPNEA collections which I have identified as for the Hinckley House.

8. For the Coolidge House, see Kirker, *Bulfinch*, 41–42 and plate 14; for the Dawes House, see Frederic C. Detwiller, "Thomas Dawes: Boston's Patriot Architect," in *Old-Time New England* 68 (summer-fall 1977): 14–15.

9. On the Leavitts, see Jonathan Leavitt's obituary in *Greenfield Gazette* and *Franklin Herald*, 4 May 1830, and biographies of Jonathan Leavitt Sr. and Jr. in Dexter, *Biographical Sketches*, 2:543–45, 4:423–24. For the Leavitt servants, see Amelia L. Hill, "Childhood in 1800," in *New England Magazine*, n. s., 15 (December 1896): 407.

10. The earliest biographical notice of Coleman is in David Willard, *Willard's History of Greenfield* (Greenfield, Mass.: Kneeland & Eastman, 1838), 162–64; see also Francis M. Thompson, *History of Greenfield*, (Greenfield, Mass.: [T. Morey], 1904–31), 2:944–45. His attendance at Phillips Academy can be found in *Biographical Catalogue of the Trustees, Teachers, and Students of Phillips Academy, Andover, 1778–1830* (Andover, Mass.: Andover Press, 1903), p. 25; on his legislative career, see *Greenfield Gazette and Courier*, 11 June 1795 and 16 June 1796; on his marriage, see *Greenfield Gazette and Courier*, 5 January 1797.

11. Considerable scholarly attention has been focused on the house, most recently by Hosley in "Architecture," 118–21. The house itself is one of the best pieces of evidence of Bulfinch's influence, supported by an excellent set of Historic American Buildings Survey drawings from 1934 (in the Library of Congress). It was illustrated in several engravings from the 1820s onward, including the frontispiece of the *Outline Plan of Education Pursued at the Greenfield High School for Young Ladies* (Greenfield, Mass.: 1829). The Hollister family has an extensive collection of photographs of the interior from the latter half of the nineteenth century and the first decade of the twentieth.

12. This description is from an indenture between William Coleman of New York City and Apollos Kingsley of Hartford, dated 18 December 1797, filed 14 March 1798, in the Franklin County Deed Records, bk. 11, p. 392.

13. *American State Papers, Class VIII: Public Lands. Documents, Legislative and Executive, of the Congress of the United States*, ed. Walter Laurie and Matthew St. Clair Clark, (Washington, D.C.: Gales & Seaton, 1832), 1:231. See also C. Peter Magrath, *Yazoo: Law and Politics in the New Republic; The Case of Fletcher v. Peck* (Providence, R.I.: Brown University Press, 1966). Coleman's later career is detailed by Allan Nevins in *The Evening Post: A Century of Journalism* (New York: Boni & Liveright, 1922), 14–33.

14. On Dickman, see Joseph T. Buckingham, *Specimens of Newspaper Literature* (Boston: Charles C. Little & James Brown, 1850) 2:318–25.

15. For the Taunton and Pittsfield meetinghouses, see Kirker, *Bulfinch*, 25–32.

16. On Alexander Thomas, see Clifford K. Shipton, *Isaiah Thomas: Printer, Patriot, and Philanthropist, 1749–1831* (Rochester, N.Y.: Leo Hart, 1948), 50. An advertisement in the *Weekly Museum*—reproduced in Rita Susswein Gottesman, *The Arts and Crafts in New York, 1777–1799* (New York: New-York Historical Society, 1954), 191—reprinted the contents of the entire title page; among other things, its reference to thirty-seven plates demonstrates that it was the second edition that was for sale.

17. On the Hancock House, see Walter Kendall Watkins, "The Hancock House and Its Builder," in *Old-Time New England* 17, no. 1 (1926): 2–19; and Hugh Morrison, *Early American Architecture: From the First Colonial Settlements to the National Period* (New York: Oxford University Press, 1952), 480–84.

18. On John Russell, see George Sheldon, *A History of Deerfield, Massachusetts* (Deerfield, Mass.: E. A. Hall, 1895–96), 2:276; the advertisement in *Greenfield Impartial Intelligencer,* 23 May 1792; and the notice of the laying of the cornerstone of the Congregational Church in *Franklin Herald,* 11 May 1819. On William Russell, see Susan McGowan and Amelia F. Miller, *Family and Landscape: Deerfield Homelots from 1671* (Deerfield, Mass.: Pocumtuck Valley Memorial Association, 1996), 51–52, 67–69, 132–34.

IX

OWEN BIDDLE AND

THE YOUNG CARPENTER'S ASSISTANT

Michael J. Lewis

In 1805 the Philadelphia architect Owen Biddle published The Young Carpenter's Assistant; or, A System of Architecture, Adapted to the Style of Building in the United States. Preceded only by Asher Benjamin's *Country Builder's Assistant* (1797), it was the second work of architectural instruction written and published in the United States.[1] A manual of architectural education in the eighteenth-century sense—in which builders and carpenters became architects by mastering drawing and, in particular, the drafting of the classical orders—Biddle's book also anticipated the restless architectural culture of the nineteenth century, with its profusion of pattern books and increasing preoccupation with matters of fashion and style.

Only the barest sketch of Biddle's life is known.[2] The son of a Quaker clockmaker, Owen Biddle Sr., he was born in 1774. Trained as a carpenter, he became a member of the Carpenters' Company in 1800. Although he practiced from 1799 to 1801 with fellow carpenter Joseph Cowgill, for most of his life he worked independently, drawing from Quaker society his principal patronage. Biddle was counted among the city's most prominent master builders and often served as builder for structures designed by others. Such was the case with the Pennsylvania Academy of the Fine Arts (1805–6), which he built according to the designs of gentleman architect John Dorsey (c. 1759–1821).

Biddle's own conception of architecture was of a piece with that of his generation; he stood neither in the vanguard nor the rear guard. In 1790, as an apprentice of sixteen, he would have imbibed the fashionable taste of the age, with its mixture of Adam detail draped over Palladian planning. His early work would have been in the spirit of the late Georgian style; his mature work showed the increasing grace of Federal architecture. Late work was not to be: Biddle died in 1806 at the age of thirty-two.

The chief events of Biddle's formative years were the arrival of the new sense of form and proportion brought about by European Neoclassicism. When the decade of the 1790s began, the city's most sophisticated architect was perhaps Pierre Charles L'Enfant; at its close, it was Benjamin Henry Latrobe. And Biddle, like every builder in the city, took note of Latrobe's work. Nonetheless, Latrobe's arrival was not a formative experience; in 1800 Biddle was already twenty-six years old and settled in taste, method, and outlook. He would fit Latrobe into his system; he would not make a new system to fit Latrobe.

In addition to *The Young Carpenter's Assistant,* Biddle is known by two projects. In 1805–6 he built the superstructure for the Schuylkill Permanent Bridge (figure 9.1); he also published a description of the project in the *Literary Magazine and American Registry* in October 1805.[3] Until its destruction by fire in 1875, the bridge was a conspicuous landmark in Philadelphia. But Biddle's principal work was the Arch Street Meeting House, still standing at Third and Arch Streets, which he both designed and built. Begun in 1803, it was the greatest of Philadelphia's meetinghouses—although in respectable Quaker fashion it was stylistically unfashionable, its Plain Style architecture as taut and laconic as that of any meetinghouse of the eighteenth century. But Biddle was able to present his proposal for the building in ink-wash drawings of considerable sophistication, depicting it in accurate perspective, with constructed cast shadows (figure 9.2).[4]

Biddle was no professional architect in the modern sense, however; to him the process of design was but a necessary adjunct to the act of construction, which was his principal livelihood. Even his most prominent projects seem to have involved the work of other designers: Latrobe was a consultant on the Arch Street Meeting; the Schuylkill bridge involved assistance from Dorsey and Judge Richard Peters (1744–1828). Biddle apparently never regarded himself as anything more than a "House Carpenter and Teacher of Architectural Drawing," which is how he identified himself on the title page of his book.

Biddle began to teach architecture some time around 1800. He was not the first to do so. Philadelphia's first formal school of architecture had been established as early as the mid-1760s when the prominent carpenter John Nevell took pupils, offering to teach any person "of common capacity" the rudiments of architecture "in two months

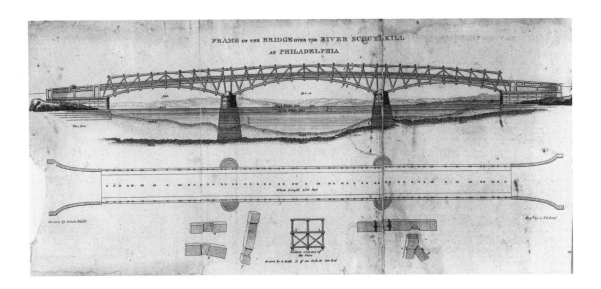

FIG 9.1 Owen Biddle, elevation of the Schuykill Permanent Bridge, Philadelphia, 1798–1805. From *The Young Carpenter's Assistant* (1805), plate 41. Courtesy of the Athenaeum of Philadelphia.

FIG 9.2 (*bottom*) Owen Biddle, perspective, detail of presentation drawing for the Arch Street Meeting House, Philadelphia, 1803. Courtesy of the Athenaeum of Philadelphia.

at most."⁵ Although his program lasted but a few years, architecture was again taught in 1794 at an academy founded by Peter Lacour and Claudius Falize.⁶ And in late 1796, Stephen Hallet (ca. 1760–1825) announced the opening of a "School of Architecture, In the Academy, north Fourth, near Mulberry street, from six to nine in the evening." Hallet's school is the most intriguing of all. A French émigré, he had been superintending the erection of the United States Capitol in Washington until his feuding with William Thornton, the architect, prompted his resignation. Hallet's academy must have had some success, since he was again advertising for pupils in 1797.⁷ We do not know the name of a single one of them, but presumably they were trained carpenters who sought education in architectural drawing, composition, and formal design—in other words, men precisely like Owen Biddle, then in his early twenties. And given the scarcity of opportunities to learn architectural rendering in Philadelphia, it seems quite likely that Biddle was among Hallet's young men.

All that we know of Biddle's own drawing school comes from a stray remark in the preface of his book: "Having been for some time past in the practice of teaching the rudiments of Architecture, I have experienced much inconvenience for want of suitable books on the subject. All that have yet appeared have been written by foreign authors, who have adapted their examples and observations almost entirely to the style of building in their respective countries, which in many instances differs very materially from ours."⁸ Biddle's book was the outgrowth a project that preoccupied him for much of 1804, a plan to establish a formal school of architecture in Philadelphia that would be affiliated with the Carpenters' Company. In January 1804 he proposed that "a Committee of five Members be appointed to take into consideration the expediency of forming an establishment under the patronage of this Company, for the purpose of Teaching the different branches of Architecture &cc. and if in the opinion of this Committee such an establishment should be proper, they are directed to draw out a plan for carrying the same into efect [sic], and lay it before the Company at the next stated meeting."⁹ Biddle's proposal was studied, and defeated in a vote the following November. Perhaps the Carpenters' Company was more concerned with regulating competition than with the grooming of competitors. In any event, Biddle's rebuff seems to have prompted him to begin compiling his book.

By the end of 1804 the project would have been under way. Biddle's printer was Benjamin Johnson, who had a shop on 31 Market Street and who copyrighted the manuscript on 5 July 1805. Biddle must have spent a good deal of time in lining up purchasers, for in good eighteenth-century fashion his book was paid for by subscription in advance. He had at least 198 subscribers, who bought 221 copies. The vast majority of these men were themselves builder and carpenters, among them his partner Joseph Cowgill, John C. Evans, John Ogden, and the amateur architect John Dorsey, with whom he had worked—names familiar to the Philadelphia profession. But the most prominent name on the list was Richard Peters, the Philadelphia judge, close confidant of George Washington, and chief patron behind Biddle's Schuylkill bridge. Conspicuously absent was Latrobe, who might well have had nothing but scorn for the book had it not marked his own first appearance in an American architectural book.

Biddle's subscribers were concentrated chiefly in and around Philadelphia, although there were far-flung patrons in Lancaster, Pittsburgh, and even Bristol, Rhode Island, where a certain David Leonard bought one. Perhaps not surprisingly, seven different builders in Baltimore subscribed. The single biggest subscriber was an enterprising patron named Lewis Sanders in Lexington, Kentucky, who ordered ten copies, apparently to sell them to the carpenters of the backwoods region. Thus the architectural culture of Philadelphia was carried to the very edge of the frontier.

Biddle explicitly aimed his book at the young carpenter rather than the young architect. Clearly this distinction is crucial: Biddle was teaching men like himself, men who had already swung tools and formed calluses, who knew how to build but not how to draw or design. And to judge from the text of his book, his curriculum was crafted to produce men like himself: that is, to produce Biddles rather than Latrobes—carpenters who could devise serviceable designs, and could communicate them effectively by graphic means.

This accounts for some of the oddities in *The Young Carpenter's Assistant*, which does not pretend to present an education in architectural design. Instead, it is intended as a supplement to classroom study, a reference book devoted chiefly to drawing and the classical orders. Following the model of architectural treatises since the Renaissance, it begins with a design for a drawing board and T-square and progresses to the laying out of ellipses and arches; plates 4 through 6 depict moldings and cornices; at plate 7 the orders commence, beginning with the Tuscan and proceeding apace through the Doric, Ionic, and Corinthian. Following the orders comes a succession of porticos, pedimented frontispieces, dormer windows, Venetian windows, mantles, roof trusses (figure 9.3) and stairs. In all these examples, Biddle's proportions are the same as Palladio's, or "pretty nearly" so: "Paladio has been allowed to have been the best judge among the Moderns, who have given the proportions of the remains of Antiquity; the proportions in this book are pretty nearly the same as his."[10]

Biddle was no slavish copyist, and through his book runs the pragmatism of the experienced carpenter. Where circumstances forced him to alter his proportions, as

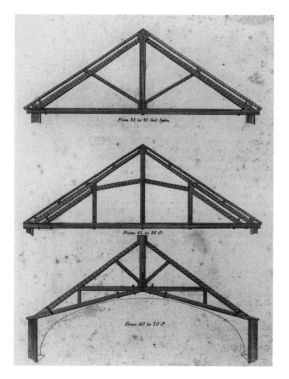
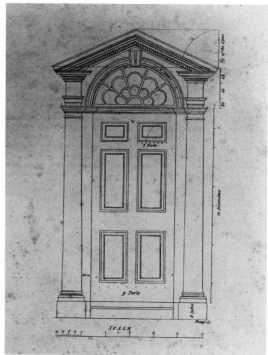

FIG 9.3 Owen Biddle, design for three roof trusses. From *The Young Carpenter's Assistant,* plate 24. Courtesy of the Athenaeum of Philadelphia.

FIG 9.4 (*bottom*) Owen Biddle, design for a classical frontispiece to a town house. From *The Young Carpenter's Assistant,* plate 15. Courtesy of the Athenaeum of Philadelphia.

with a townhouse of constricted frontage (figure 9.4) he was willing to do so, although he still upheld the notion of ideal proportions: "[If] the door is for a town house with a narrow front . . . the true proportions of the Orders may be dispensed with, and regard had to the general proportion of the building; but in country houses where the front may be well proportioned, the nearer we adhere to the Orders, the better will be the appearance in general." But Biddle also conceded that some modifications in proportion were made necessary by the vagaries of changing taste, and here too he recommended a posture of discriminating flexibility. When showing his cornice design on plate 28, for example, he recommended that it be gauged at one-nineteenth the height of the building. But, he remarked, "every thing is in some degree regulated by fashion," and "the present fashion would be something smaller than the above proportion."[11] Whether by the "present fashion" he meant the bold Neoclassicism of Latrobe or the general shift in taste to the attenuated forms of Federal architecture is not entirely clear; in fact, he did not necessarily distinguish between these categories.

From time to time a glimmer of the man's own taste appeared. In a discussion of mantlepieces he recommended that the design should "always have a due proportion of plain surfaces, as a contrast to the ornamented parts"; the workman should by no means "cover his work with unmeaning holes and cuttings of a gouge."[12] In this is something of the voice of a conservative Philadelphia craftsman, for whom a mantle must always remain an architectonic composition in good Palladian fashion—as in Nevell's Mount Pleasant—and not an overwrought piece of Federal woodwork (of the sort that still survives in a number of houses in New Castle, Delaware).

Biddle himself made no claim whatsoever to originality, freely acknowledging his debt to English sources. He derived the proportions of the orders from William Pain (ca. 1730–1790), whose *Builder's Companion* (London, 1762) was among the most accessible of eighteenth-century architectural manuals and the closest model for Biddle's book. But the geometric exercises at the start of the book he credited not to Pain but to the Scottish architect Peter Nicholson (1765–1844), "whose works are held in deserved estimation." Biddle likely meant *The Principles of Architecture*, Nicholson's chief work. He did not accept products of a different building culture uncritically, however; his plate 25 depicts a wooden dome, which was copied as he tells us from Nicholson but which, he complained, "to me appears abundantly too strong."

These English books were assuredly in Biddle's own possession. According to his estate inventory, he owned fifteen "books of Archititure [*sic*]" which would have included the works by Pain and Nicholson and presumably an edition or two of Palladio.[13] What were the others? If we consider the principal works of James Gibbs, Colen Campbell, William Chambers, and William Halfpenny, it is possible to envision a useful architectural reference library of fifteen books, particularly if the owner himself already knew how to build.

But Biddle was not merely pirating from contemporary English sources. Many of his designs, including his classical frontispieces and roof trusses, follow quite closely the illustrations made by John Nevell for the *Articles of the Carpenters Company of Philadelphia: and Their Rules for Measuring and Valuing House-Carpenters Work* (1786).[14] Previously, these designs had been precious commodities, but their appearance in Biddle's book shows how the company's role and influence were changing. When Biddle joined it, the company had been dominating the building trades since 1724, acting much like a medieval guild, enforcing standards of workmanship, consistent fee scales, and corporate solidarity among its members. And it was guildlike not only in its organization but also in its secrecy, guarding its trade secrets as the arcane knowledge of a privileged conventicle. In fact, it could be argued that the 1786 *Articles* was America's first architectural book, even though it was a publication without a public.[15] Copies were numbered and signed, and on the death of a member his widow would find herself visited by a somber delegation from the company to reclaim his volume. By publishing variants of the plates from the Carpenters' Company rule book, however, Biddle was hardly risking expulsion, for most of those plates were themselves stolen goods, cribbed from English originals.[16] Furthermore, a pirated edition of the rule book had already appeared in 1801.[17]

The vast bulk of Biddle's book, then, is derivative. Until the final half-dozen or so plates, which illustrated Philadelphia architecture, he was original only in the selection and arrangement of his borrowed pieces. But even selection is a category of originality. Biddle took great pains, he emphasized, to eliminate the unessential information that clogged European books.

Up to plate 36, Biddle presented little that would have been out of place in a book half a century older. Only his final section—a portfolio of illustrations of recent buildings and two townhouse designs—shows any awareness that he was writing in a time of extraordinary architectural change. Three of his examples were rather recent: his own bridge over the Schuylkill River, Samuel Blodgett's Bank of the United States, and Benjamin Latrobe's Bank of Pennsylvania. (The two banks were shown in elevation, and the illustrations, rather than being measured drawings, were apparently based on the original drawings of their respective architects.) These designs for new and prominent public buildings would have been of intense interest to Biddle's pupils. But the final illustration in his book, plate 56, is something of an anomaly: the steeple of Christ Church, designed and built by Robert Smith in 1753. This tribute to Smith, a fellow Carpenters' Company member and designer of its building, showed that he was still held in high esteem, even though he had died in 1777. An exhibition of architectural drawings in 1795 at the Columbianum (or American Academy of Painting, Sculpture, and Architecture) had shown several of his drawings; perhaps they were lying around in the collections of the company.

Clearly, it was no contradiction to Biddle to bring together America's most modern building, Latrobe's bank, with a steeple a half-century old. In fact, his description of the steeple scarcely noticed its venerability:

> For the justness of its proportions, simplicity and symmetry of its parts [it] is allowed by
> good judges to be equal if not superior in beauty to any Steeple of the spire kind, either in

Europe or America . . . The superstructure of this steeple is composed of three distinct well-proportioned parts of Architecture, the first story, with its small Pediments and Attics, forming one; the octagonal part, with its ogee formed dome, being the second; and the spire and its pedestal, the third. These three parts are very dissimilar, no one having any thing in it that is common to the others and yet they agree very well with each other, forming one complete and consistent whole.[18]

For him the steeple was no superannuated curiosity; it was to be judged as a piece of design, on its own merits. Perhaps there was also some sentimental attachment to the most venerable symbol on the Philadelphia skyline. To be sure, William Strickland himself made a drawing of the same mid-Georgian relic a few years later. Moreover, in an architecturally conservative city, the study of the Georgian past was not useless knowledge. It was this very immersion in local tradition which made Strickland's own neo-Georgian steeples so satisfying—those he later added to Independence Hall and St. Peter's Episcopal Church.

Biddle judged the more recent architecture, the two banks by Latrobe and Blodgett, on the same neutral scale. Latrobe's was a "beautiful building" and a "neat specimen of the Ionic order, taken from an ancient Greek Temple"; Blodgett's was a "superb building" and an "elegant specimen of the Corinthian Order; the proportions taken from a Roman Temple called the *Maison Quarree,* at Nismes, in the south of France."[19] To our eyes these buildings leap apart as if electrically charged, but Biddle did not think in categories of the sort we do: those rigid stylistic divisions of Neoclassical, Federal, and Georgian architecture. His understanding of architecture permitted him to judge all these things, even Smith's steeple, as part of the same flexible, elastic system, so that even Latrobe's building was a neat Ionic "specimen" rather than a revolutionary essay in correct Classicism and America's first great masonry-vaulted dome.

The Anglo-American Palladianism that dominated Philadelphia architecture permitted an extraordinary latitude in the design of details, but within certain conventional channels. Such a system could absorb the stylistic innovations of George Dance or the Adam brothers and yet remain in the end fundamentally unchanged. In this mixture of permissive eclecticism and underlying conservatism lies the peculiar character of Philadelphia's architectural culture. It was the very conservatism of Philadelphia which allowed it to absorb fads and innovations with abandon yet never lose its strongly local character. Such a result was possible in a city for whom style was simply a dressing of carpentry applied to a brick shell; the style of the portico or cornice might change according to the vagaries of taste, but the underlying brick building did not.

This approach is apparent with Biddle's own designs for a freestanding urban townhouse (figure 9.5): a bewildering variety of lunettes, bull's eyes, and fanlights cluttered a facade that was otherwise a taut planar form, in substance not that different from Biddle's own laconic meetinghouse.[20] Here is the taste, above all, of a carpenter. Although he understood the orders, he understood them as two dimensional affairs rather than plastically, as sculpture. But this is no surprise; after all, the sculptural handling of the orders cannot be separated from masonry construction. To be sure, Philadelphia's brick Palladianism had always tended toward planarity, its ornamental motifs always resting lightly on the surface of the building. But even in his interior planning Biddle languished behind the vanguard of taste (figure 9.6). The geometric sequence of spaces throughout the house is varied, but more in the interlocking Palladian sense than the dynamic sense of Woodlands, Alexander Hamilton's celebrated estate, a local building that was already sixteen years old when Biddle wrote his book. With these competent but rather ungainly and additive designs, which recall much of the anonymous architecture of turn-of-the-century Philadelphia, Biddle's book closes.

Biddle practiced in a swiftly changing world in which competent professionals such as Latrobe would increasingly shape and dominate architectural culture. But his response to change was not so much to embrace the new as to solidify the old. He strove to elevate carpenter-builders to the level of their professional competitors, regularizing a previously informal system of education even as the substance of such education remained that of the eighteenth century. Nonetheless, in conservative Philadelphia, where the vast bulk of building activity was still the domain of bricklayers and carpenters, such a response was entirely appropriate. In fact, Biddle's book remained a useful compendium for at least another generation.[21] As late as 1833, at the apogee of the Greek Revival, John Haviland produced a second edition of it (adding at the end a few plates of his own "particularly adapted for country use").

Haviland's relationship to Biddle indicates how complex the relationship was between the supposedly distinct categories of architects and builders. An English émigré who arrived in Philadelphia in 1816, Haviland had benefited from an apprenticeship to the English architect James Elmes. But although he was a professional like Latrobe, Haviland also learned from the example of Biddle. He too (together with Hugh Bridport) conducted a drawing school where architecture was taught from 1818 to 1822. And like Biddle, he published a book aimed at the upwardly ambitious carpenter: *The Builder's Assistant, containing the five orders of architecture . . . for the use of builders, carpenters, masons, plasterers, cabinet makers, and carvers,* which appeared in three successive volumes between 1818 and 1821.[22]

PLATE XXXVII.

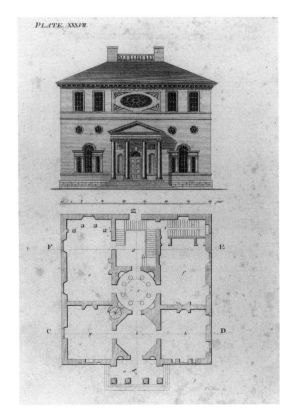

PLATE XXXVIII

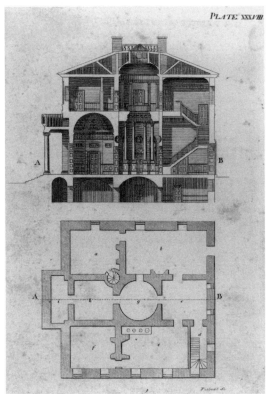

FIG 9.5 Owen Biddle, plan and elevation of a town house. From *The Young Carpenter's Assistant*, plate 37. Courtesy of the Athenaeum of Philadelphia.

FIG 9.6 (*right*) Owen Biddle, plan and section of a town house. From *The Young Carpenter's Assistant*, plate 38. Courtesy of the Athenaeum of Philadelphia.

The Builder's Assistant was a more substantial book than Biddle's, with a more sophisticated text, but it was still basically a book of the orders, augmented with the customary leaven of original designs. And Haviland seems indeed to have followed Biddle in becoming Philadelphia's principal architectural educator, for upon closing his own school of drawing he became chief instructor at the Franklin Institute's school of architecture.[23] And throughout this time Biddle's book seems to have remained in constant use; why else would Haviland have worked so diligently to republish it in 1833?

In that same year the Carpenters' Company at last established the architectural drawing school that Biddle had proposed in 1805. Thus the eighteenth-century system of architectural education—aimed at builders and based on the drawing of simplified versions of the classical orders—passed into the mainstream of Philadelphia architecture in the nineteenth century. The story of American architecture is told primarily as a triumph of professionalism, but it is equally remarkable how enduring and adaptable the country's builder-architects remained. Many of Philadelphia's key figures of mid-century design, including Samuel Sloan, John McArthur Jr., and even T. U. Walter, enjoyed much the same sort of education that Biddle and Haviland had provided.[24]

Against this backdrop, Biddle's book plays a more prominent role than its humble wood engravings might suggest. Even up to the end of the eighteenth century, American architecture was a regional affair, based on local building practices and materials. Training was controlled by the building trades, making building a local matter in much the same way that medieval architecture was local. This is not to say that ideas did not move from place to place; they did, but they moved on foot and through individuals. If there was an overall national character to American architecture—a collective set of typical ideas and forms—it was one borrowed from England. The means whereby Americans learned about English architecture were modern—that is, publications and mass-produced, accurate illustrations—whereas the means whereby Americans learned about their own architecture were medieval: personal travel, second hand accounts, drawings and sketchbooks. American carpenters were more reliably informed about the buildings of London than about those in Boston, Baltimore, or Charleston.

Not all aspects of American culture were still so regional in character. For example, the United States had already achieved a national political culture by the 1790s. The various local models of self-government had been interacting for a generation, throughout the Revolution and the Constitutional Convention, during which period there came into being a national political literature of vigor and vitality. But American builder-architects still worked within a limited radius, and even a city such as Philadelphia remained profoundly provincial—so far as its building went—into the nineteenth century.

From the standpoint of the history of ideas, then, Biddle's book is not remarkable. It is a provincial variant of a European publishing genre of considerable antiquity and is highly formulaic in character. But with its publication—and that of Benjamin's book—the character of American architecture changed decisively and permanently, for these books were nothing less than the beginning of a national architectural culture.

NOTES

1. Biddle does not mention Asher Benjamin in his book, and seems to have been completely unaware of him: "Nothing on Architecture has heretofore appeared in this country, where the field for improvement in every useful art and science is, perhaps, more extensive, than in any other. Why there has not, appears

to me matter of surprise, whilst we have among us men of talents, fully acquainted with the subject, some of whom are also men of leisure: perhaps they have not viewed the subject in the same light, or given to it the same degree of importance that I have." Owen Biddle, *The Young Carpenter's Assistant; or, A System of Architecture, Adapted to the Style of Building in the United States* (Philadelphia: Printed by Benj[amin] Johnson, 1805), 3.

2. See Jeffrey A. Cohen, "Owen Biddle," in *Drawing toward Building: Philadelphia Architectural Graphics, 1723–1986,* ed. James F. O'Gorman (Philadelphia: University of Pennsylvania Press, 1986), 48–49; Sandra Tatman and Roger Moss, *Biographical Dictionary of Philadelphia Architects* (Boston: G. K. Hall, 1986), 68; Henry D. Biddle, *A Sketch of Owen Biddle* (Philadelphia: privately printed, 1922).

3. George B. Tatum, *Penn's Great Town* (Philadelphia: University of Pennsylvania Press, 1961), 164–65.

4. A drawing by Biddle for the Arch Street Meeting survives in the Quaker Collection, Haverford College, Haverford, Pa.

5. For this training, Nevell charged ten shillings to start, and an additional twenty each month. See Tatman and Moss, *Biographical Dictionary,* 568–69.

6. Lacour's school treated architecture as a branch of drawing, to judge by the advertisement in the *General Advertiser* of 19 April 1794, which refers to an "academy of drawing, architecture, figures, landscape, animals, flowers, ornaments, plans and charts." Tatman and Moss, *Biographical Dictionary,* 261, 462.

7. *Pennsylvania Packet,* 21 December 1796, and *Federal Gazette,* 25 November 1797, both cited in Tatman and Moss, *Biographical Dictionary,* 332.

8. Biddle, *Young Carpenter's Assistant,* 3.

9. Carpenters' Company minutes, quoted in Jeffrey A. Cohen, "Building a Discipline: Early Institutional Settings for Architectural Education in Philadelphia, 1804–1890," *Journal of the Society of Architectural Historians* 53, no. 2 (1994): 140.

10. Biddle, *Young Carpenter's Assistant,* 27.

11. Ibid., 34.

12. Ibid., 28.

13. Will 1806:50, Philadelphia City Hall.

14. For example, the roof trusses shown on Biddle's plate 24 match quite closely those of plates 6 and 7 of the Carpenters' Company book.

15. One must say first *original* architectural book, since a version of Abraham Swan's *British Architect* had already been published in Philadelphia in 1775. When the rule book was revised in 1805, Biddle himself drew some of the new plates.

16. Plate 22, for example—a design for "a fine open newel stairway"—apparently came from William Halfpenny's *Art of Sound Building* (London, 1725).

17. Cohen, "Building a Discipline," 141.

18. Quoted in ibid., 56.

19. Quoted in ibid., 54–55.

20. Biddle argued, however, that his overcrowded facade was intended to provide a complicated drawing assignment for his students: "In these plans it has been more my object to throw as great a variety into a small compass as was readily practicable than to give eligible plans for the builder, thereby aiming at instruction for the student, which indeed has been my object throughout this work" (*Young Carpenter's Assistant,* 44).

21. One of the first to acknowledge Biddle's importance was Asher Benjamin himself, who, in the preface to his own second book, remarked that "the American Mechanic is, therefore, in purchasing European publications, under the necessity of paying two thirds the value of his purchase for what is of no real use to him." This is a clear paraphrase of Biddle, who wrote that "the American student of Architecture has been taxed with the purchase of books, two thirds of the contents of which were, to him, unnecessary."

Likewise, Biddle's 1805 title, *The Young Carpenter's Assistant; or, A System of Architecture, Adapted to the Style of Building in the United States,* was paraphrased in that of Benjamin's 1806 book: *The American Builder's Companion; or, a New System of Architecture particularly adapted to the present style of Building in the United States of America.* How Benjamin so quickly became aware of Biddle's work remains unclear.

22. John Haviland, *The Builder's Assistant,* was published in Philadelphia by John Bioren in 1818, 1819, and 1821.

23. Cohen, "Building a Discipline," 145.

24. This was especially conspicuous in the 1832 competition for Girard College in Philadelphia, in which the entries of the builder-architects were in many instances indistinguishable from those of the professionals, and in several cases distinctly better. See Bruce Laverty, Michael J. Lewis, and Michelle Taillon Taylor, *Monument to Philanthropy: The Design and Building of Girard College, 1832–1848* (Philadelphia: Girard College, 1998), 48.

X

ARCHITECTURAL BOOKS IN NEW YORK:

FROM McCOMB TO LAFEVER

Damie Stillman

On 15 March 1828, Alexander Jackson Davis wrote in his daybook of his "first study of Stuarts Athens, from which I date Professional Practice."[1] In this way this major American architect of the second quarter of the nineteenth century stated definitively the role of architectural books in the American republic a half-century after the Declaration of Independence. Nine years later Davis would publish his own *Rural Residences,* thus demonstrating the other side of the coin: the contribution that Americans made to the genre.

But Davis was not alone in exemplifying the twofold role of architectural books on these shores at this time. In the six decades between 1790 and the middle of the nineteenth century, New York—which grew dramatically from the second city in the new United States to by far its largest metropolis—illustrates this tendency both forcefully and beautifully. On the one hand, it provides in the case of John McComb Jr., its leading architect during the 1790s and the first quarter of the new century, a classic demonstration of the use of architectural pattern books as source material. And, on the other, it witnessed not only Davis's *Rural Residences* but the outpouring of a series of books from the pen of Minard Lafever, whose volumes spread the taste for the Greek Revival throughout the country during the second quarter of the century. During that same period New York also saw the publication of a group of books that both espoused the glories of the Picturesque and provided patterns for its efflorescence, from Davis's book of 1837 through the works of Andrew Jackson Downing in the 1840s and early 1950s. We can add to these the designs of Calvin Pollard, an architect who bridges the gap between the two tendencies and provides an illustration of Lafever's influence in New York itself.

For all of this there is a wealth of evidence. There are, of course, the books of Davis, Downing, and Lafever, as well as statements in Lafever's about his use of European models, and catalogues of Davis's library and that of his mentor and partner, Ithiel Town, from whom he tells us he borrowed James Stuart and Nicholas Revett's *Antiquities of Athens.* There are Pollard's drawings. And there are McComb's catalogues of his library, comments in his papers, and a list he made of specific sources for New York City Hall.[2]

McComb's library can be discerned from three different lists preserved among his papers at the New-York Historical Society. Two shorter ones are undated, but a "Catalogue of Books on Architecture etc. Belonging to John McComb Jun.ʳ," dated 1808, contains fifty-two titles, with the number of volumes and the cost of each (figure 10.1): all together there are sixty-two volumes, their prices totaling $557.31.[3] Most, as might be expected of a builder-architect turned architect, are in the English traditions of the second half of the eighteenth century: the continued and modified Palladian, the Adamesque, and the new Greco-Roman revival. His collection included such grand folio volumes of the earlier eighteenth century as Colen Campbell's *Vitruvius Britannicus* and James Gibbs's *Book of Architecture,* as well as their later counterparts, among them *The Works in Architecture of Robert and James Adam* (1773–79) and Sir William Chambers's *Treatise on the Decorative Part of Civil Architecture* (3d ed., 1791).

There were also the standard handbooks, the octavo and pocket-sized productions of Batty Langley, William Salmon, William Pain, and Peter Nicholson. Exoticism was represented by Chambers's book on Kew, and the Langley's *Gothic Architecture* was also present. He owned two furniture design books—Thomas Chippendale's *Gentleman and Cabinet-Maker's Director* and Thomas Sheraton's *Cabinet-Maker and Upholsterer's Drawing Book*—and a number of engineering guides and treatises on canals. There were books on decoration, on iconology, on fortifications, on lighthouses, and on various other aspects of architecture. Most were in English, but there were a few in French and at least one each in Italian and German. The most expensive was the Adam, which cost $78.50; next came the two-volume *Vitruvius Britannicus* at $55.9 the cheapest, at fifty cents, was a book in German on fortifications by Leonard Christoph Sturm, who died in 1719.

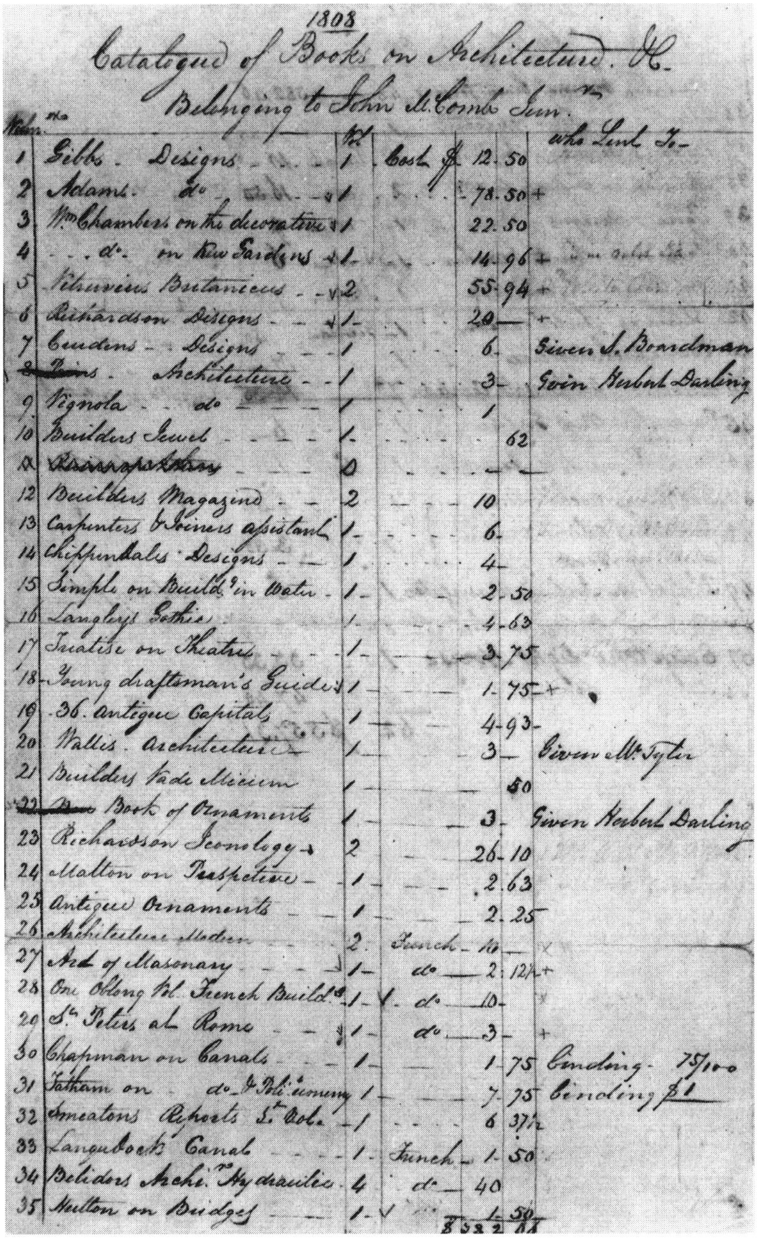

1808

Catalogue of Books on Architecture &c.
Belonging to John McComb Jun.

No		Vol.		Cost $	who Lent To
1	Gibbs . Designs	1	Cost $	12. 50	
2	Adams . do	1		78. 50 +	
3	Wm Chambers on the decoration	1		22. 50	
4	.. do . on Kew Gardens	1		14. 96 +	
5	Vitruvius Britanicus	2		55. 94 +	
6	Richardson Designs	1		20 +	
7	Gardens . Designs	1		6	Given S. Boardman
8	Pain . Architecture	1		3	Goin Herbert Darling
9	Vignola . do	1		1	
10	Builders Jewel	1		62	
11	Bisnopsldsus	0			
12	Builders Magazine	2		10	
13	Carpenters & Joiners assistant	1		6	
14	Chippindales Designs	1		4	
15	Simple on Build in Water	1		2. 50	
16	Langleys Gothic	1		4. 63	
17	Treatise on Theatres	1		3. 75	
18	Young draftsman's Guide	1		1. 75 +	
19	36. antique Capitals	1		4. 93	
20	Wallis . Architecture	1		3	Given Mr Tyler
21	Builders Vade Mecum	1		50	
22	Book of Ornaments	1		3	Given Herbert Darling
23	Richardson Iconology	2		26. 10	
24	Malton on Perspective	1		2. 63	
25	Antique Ornaments	1		2. 25	
26	Architecture Modern	2	French	10	
27	Art of Masonary	1	do	2. 12½ +	
28	One Oblong Vol. French Build.	1	do	10	
29	St Peters at Rome	1	do	3	
30	Chapman on Canals	1		1. 75	binding — 75/100
31	Tatham on do & Returning	1		7. 75	binding $1
32	Smeatons Reports 3 Vol.	1		6. 37½	
33	Langubocks Canal	1	French	1. 50	
34	Belidors Archi Hydraulics	4	do	40	
35	Mutton on Bridges	1		1. 50	
				352. 2. 85	

FIG 10.1 John McComb Jr., "Catalogue of Books on Architecture &c. Belonging to John McComb Jun.ʳ," 1808. No. 73154. © Collection of The New-York Historical Society.

Needless to say, McComb made extensive use of his library—from Smeaton's *Narrative of the . . . Edystone Lighthouse*, which served him well in his work in that area, to a host of pattern books that provided models or details for houses, churches, and public buildings galore. Of these, the volume that seems to have had the strongest appeal early on was John Crunden's *Convenient and Ornamental Architecture* of 1767, whose inspiration can be seen in McComb's earliest datable designs: those for Government House in New York (1790).[4] Although there is some question as to McComb's actual role in the building erected to house the governor of New York on the site now occupied by Cass Gilbert's Customs House—he was paid £3.4s for his designs but is not mentioned in the newspaper accounts[5]—he produced at least five different designs, three of which were derived from Crunden.

The most obviously indebted design (figure 10.2), as Fiske Kimball noted years ago, is derived from Crunden's plate 53 (figure 10.3). There are, of course, a number of differences, but the basic format, the colonnaded entrance hall, and the projecting circular saloon surely come from this volume, for which McComb paid $6.00.[6] Despite its dependence on an English architectural book, it provides the first appearance in America, even if only on paper, of that leitmotif of Neoclassicism, the projecting semicircular exedra. Various other plates from Crunden—also with exedrae but semi-octagonal ones—seem to have been the twenty-seven-year-old McComb's source for other designs for Government House. Some of these contain a single rear projection or twin rear projections; others feature a central or twin flanking projections on the entrance front. For the latter, Crunden's plate 12 is a likely source, though McComb's plan is a good deal grander. The same can be said of another with a rear exedra vis-à-vis Crunden's plate 41.[7] Still, although these may well have been his sources, in both these cases there are other Neoclassical books that could have provided the inspiration.

Another collection of Neoclassical designs that seems to have furnished McComb with at least one model is John Carter's *Builder's Magazine*, published in London from 1774 to 1786. McComb owned two volumes, for which he paid $10, and one of these probably contained the design for a town house, dated 1774, which McComb used in his own design for a town house of about 1799, albeit somewhat modified.[8]

McComb's employment of books such as these indicates his interest in the new Neoclassical manner that was just catching fire in America following the Revolution, but he also relied on such standards of the earlier part of the century as Gibbs's *Book of Architecture*, (1728), for which he had paid $12.50. This can be seen not only in his utilization of the familiar executed version of St. Martin-in-the-Fields—as for the facade of his St. John's Chapel of about 1803—but also in his playing with Gibb's

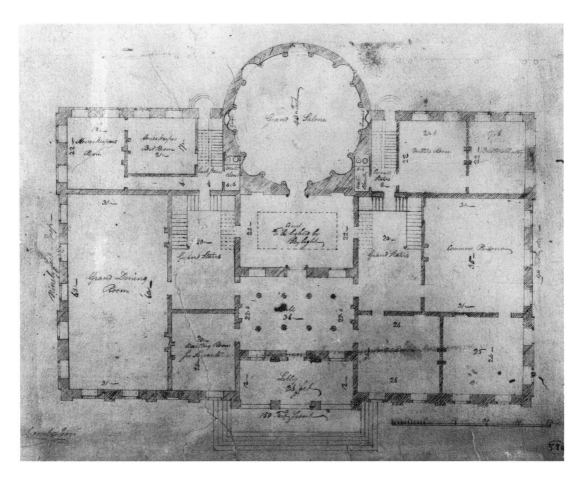

FIG 10.2 John McComb Jr., floor plan of a semi-public building resembling the Government House, New York, ca. 1790. No. 60538. © Collection of The New-York Historical Society.

circular alternative for St. Martin from the same volume. In an undated and unexecuted drawing McComb adapted this Gibbs alternative design for a church of his own, demonstrating a far more innovative approach than in his use of Gibbs's exterior.[9]

Despite the obvious borrowings cited here, a perfectly natural practice for someone of McComb's date and training, the one project of his that illustrates most closely his use of such books is New York City Hall of 1802–12. One's first reaction to that statement might be surprise, for although McComb not only was appointed Architect by the Common Council but certainly built the building, he did not in fact design the winning entry in the competition of 1802. Even though the premium was awarded to the entry submitted jointly by McComb and Joseph-François Mangin, that entry was

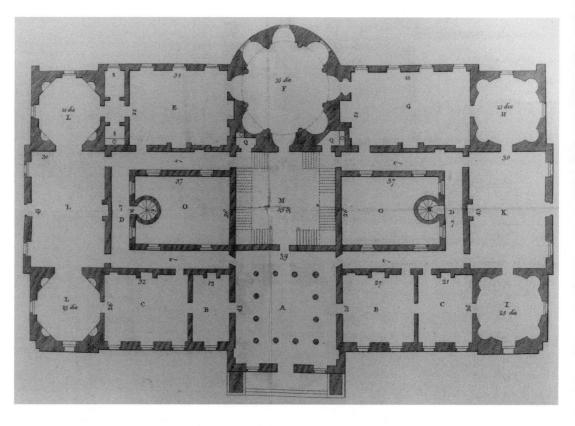

FIG 10.3 John Crunden, "Plan of a Mansion for a Person of Distinction," from *Convenient and Ornamental Architecture* (1767), plate 53. Courtesy of the University of Delaware Library, Newark.

the work of Mangin, a French émigré, who was undoubtedly not only the draftsman but the designer, for the elevation drawing is wholly in the manner of Louis XVI France.[10] In his execution of Mangin's design, however, McComb substituted a variety of English details for the French conceptions of his erstwhile collaborator, some of which are evident in the 1826 engraving of the building by John Hill after a drawing by W. G. Wall. The most obvious difference is in the cupola, for which McComb made a number of studies, three of which are shown on one of his drawings.[11] A comparison of these with the executed version demonstrates how important McComb's role was.

Nor was it limited to such major features; many of the details too were transformed with the aid of McComb's familiar English architectural books. In fact, he says so straight out in a note attached to his own copy of Chambers's 1791 edition of his *Trea-*

tise on the Decorative Part of Civil Architecture, preserved at the New-York Historical Society, a book for which he paid $22.50. On this list of plates that he found useful are sources for Corinthian capitals, moldings, and balusters.[12]

Given McComb's extensive use of Chambers's *Treatise,* it is no wonder that in an unfinished letter to a Mr. Colman, responding to an inquiry as to the best work of education for an aspiring architect, he recommended reading the Introduction to that book.[13]

If Chambers was the source for myriad details of New York City Hall, his rival Robert Adam seems to have inspired McComb even more profoundly. Although his copy of Adam's *Works in Architecture,* the most expensive item on his library list of 1808, has not survived, one can certainly see the result of its ownership in McComb's creation of interior spaces within the building. Thus, in the Board of Estimate Committee Room (figure 10.4), he transformed a square room into a circular one by inserting a round entablature topped by a dome, eliding the corners—a spatial sleight-of-hand akin to Adam's conversion of a rectangular room into a square one by introducing a screen of columns away from the wall, seen beautifully in the anteroom at Syon (ca. 1761–65; see plan at bottom right of figure 10.5). In addition to this and other similarities between McComb and Adam, McComb specifically advises himself in his manuscript "Notes on St. Paul's" to look at Adam's Duchess of Derby's antechamber for the second-floor gallery at City Hall and at the end of the Porter's Hall at Adam's Shelburne House for the shortening of the large courtrooms of the new governmental building.[14]

Besides his library and such notes as the ones just cited, there are other clues to McComb's use of European subjects. For example, among the prints he owned is that of the Middlesex Sessions House in London's Clerkenwell, designed by Thomas Rogers about 1778–82. It may possibly have inspired one of McComb's designs for Washington Hall in New York, the home of the Washington Benevolent Society, the Federalist counterpart to the Democratic Republicans' Tammany Hall. His drawing of about 1809 for that edifice has some differences, but the rusticated base, attenuated orders, arches, and ornamental panels all relate to the English model.[15]

In other cases, we have what must be McComb's copies of architectural plates, such as a drawing of the entrance screen in front of the Hôtel de Salm in Paris of 1782.[16] As this building was converted in 1804 into the Palace of the Legion of Honor, which is inscribed on the McComb drawing, this elevation must have been drawn from a book or a print, for McComb was certainly not in France after 1804. Still another example is furnished by a McComb drawing of the plans of three English asylums: the London

FIG 10.4 John McComb Jr., Board of Estimate Committee Room, New York City Hall, 1802–12. Photo by Underhill Studios, New York.

Asylum for the Care and Cure of the Insane of 1814; the Lunatic House at Guy's Hospital, also in London; and the Asylum of the West Riding of Yorkshire.[17] For someone involved in the designing of asylums and prisons, this sheet was undoubtedly extremely useful. So was Smeaton's book on the Edystone Lighthouse, for McComb was the designer of at least three lighthouses and possibly more.[18]

I have dwelt at substantial length on McComb because the catalogue of his library, his surviving copy of Chambers, his other manuscripts, and the obvious and extensive reflections of these in his drawings and executed buildings demonstrate so effectively the enormous importance of architectural books in New York in the 1790s and the first quarter of the nineteenth century. As indicated earlier, however, he was not alone among New York architects in his use of such sources.

Whereas McComb dominated the architecture of that city to about 1825, the next

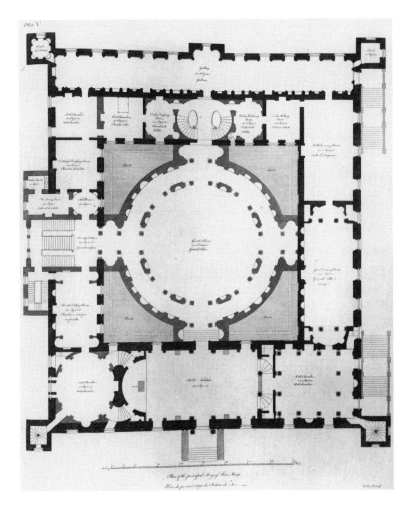

FIG 10.5 Robert Adam, plan (ca. 1761) for Syon House, Middlesex (now London), from Robert and James Adam, *The Works in Architecture*, vol. 1, no. 1 (1773), plate 5. Courtesy of the Winterthur Library: Printed Book and Periodical Collection, Winterthur, Del.

quarter-century found a substantial number of architects practicing there. Among them was Calvin Pollard, who began work about 1820 and died in 1850. Again, the New-York Historical Society preserves a number of his drawings, some of which clearly indicate their derivation from architectural books, even if we cannot always identify them. Typical are two designs for New York town houses, both dated 1847. One, for a house on Jane Street, features medievalizing label moldings above the windows and door and similarly inspired doorway, frieze, and cornice; the other employs a more classical vocabulary.[19] But for their quite similar format and plan and for such details as the doorway and iron railing of the Greek Revival house, Pollard undoubtedly relied on architectural books—as he did for the design of a set of parlor doors, dated 22 July 1844. This interior feature for Dr. Moffat's house on Broadway is related to three different plates in Minard Lafever's *Beauties of Modern Architecture* of 1835, Pollard combining aspects of all three interior sliding doorways for his own design for this popular motif of the day.[20]

And here we can link the use of architectural books as design sources in New York with the publication of such books in the same city, for Lafever (1798–1854) not only used models but provided them in his five works published between 1829 and 1856 (the last, of course, posthumously). The first of these, *The Young Builder's General Instructor,* is the most derivative, much of the text being based on Peter Nicholson's handbooks. Some of the plates, too, can be traced to specific models, as Lafever's biographer, Jacob Landy, has done.[21] Thus, plate 43, which Lafever called a "Gentleman's Summer Residence," has been related to the engraved view of John Raffield's St. John's Lodge of 1818–19 in London's Regent's Park, which was published in Thomas Shepherd and James Elmes's *Metropolitan Improvements* of 1827.[22] Similarly, Lafever's church in the Grecian Ionic order (plate 65) can be seen as a combination of two London churches, both also illustrated in Shepherd and Elmes and, as a matter of fact, on the same page: John Soane's Holy Trinity, Marylebone Road, of 1826–27, with its Ionic portico *in antis;* and the tower of Robert Smirke's St. Mary, Wyndham Place, of 1821–23.[23]

Although this first effort at publishing was apparently fairly successful, Lafever himself become disenchanted with it after a few years, choosing to publish a new work, *The Modern Builder's Guide* of 1833. As he explained in the preface to this second book:

> Those who are aware how flattering a reception and how ready a sale that work met with, will be somewhat surprised perhaps to learn, that, instead of issuing a second edition of it, I have, at considerable pecuniary sacrifice, entirely withdrawn the work from print. The truth is, though others seemed perfectly satisfied with the book, I myself was not. Subsequent investigation, and increased experience as an architect, enabled me to discover many defects and inaccuracies, which had at first escaped my notice; and, though I might have issued a corrected edition, yet, as I had much additional matter that I wished to present, and as this new matter, together with the numerous alterations to be made in the old, would have materially changed the character and well nigh destroyed the identity of the original, I, on the whole, preferred to suppress that work, and prepare a substitute.[24]

The frontispiece for the new book, showing a country villa, is signed "J. Gallier des. for Lafever" (figure 10.6). James Gallier (1798–1866), an Irish-born architect who had arrived in New York from London only the previous year, had, after a brief stint with James Dakin, entered into a partnership with Lafever in 1833. Their association was terminated the following year, and Gallier left for New Orleans, where he made his career. But in the first year of the partnership Gallier produced this design, which Landy relates to still another plate from Shepherd and Elmes's *Metropolitan Improvements:* Decimus Burton's Grove House, also in Regent's Park, of 1822–24 (figure 10.7). In this case, there appears to be an intermediate design by Lafever which is even closer to Grove House, with the Gallier villa being simplified and more abstract.[25] In this book, Lafever cites other sources as well, including both Nicholson and Stuart and Revett.

The Modern Builder's Guide, to which Dakin as well as Gallier contributed, was perhaps Lafever's most influential book. Subsequent editions appeared in 1841, 1846, 1849, 1850, 1853, and 1855, and its designs reappeared in buildings throughout the country—as far away, for example, as the Cooley House of 1853 in Racine, Wisconsin (figure 10.8).

In 1835 Lafever published his third book, *The Beauties of Modern Architecture,* which is probably his finest. It too ran through a number of later editions (1839, 1849, and 1855). Filled with Greek Revival details, its plates can be exemplified by the parlor doors that I compared with the Pollard drawing. Again, he acknowledges his debt to Stuart and Revett, as well as crediting both Dakin and C. L. Bell—the latter also briefly a partner of his—for drawings and inspiration. Two text sections appended to the plates indicate Lafever's borrowings from other books. First, there is an "Architectural History," clearly labeled as "Extracts from Elme's Dictionary," which turns out to be James Elmes's *Dictionary of the Fine Arts* of 1826. Here, in sixty-four pages, is a significant chunk of the history of the art from the Hebrews and Egyptians to the Greeks and Romans. This is followed by "Glossary of Names and Terms Used in Architecture," which Lafever again credits to a British source, the seventh edition of the *Encyclopaedia Britannica,* the first volume of which appeared in 1830.[26]

Lafever's fourth book, *The Modern Practice of Staircase and Handrail Construction,* appeared in 1838. Although primarily intended to provide instruction on this important but difficult aspect of the building trade, it also contained two villa designs. Again, Nicholson is an obvious source, perhaps along with Joshua Coulter of Philadelphia, whom Lafever had credited with suggestions on handrails in his earlier *Modern Builder's Guide.*[27] *Modern Practice* was followed by the nine subsequent editions of his two

FIG 10.6 "J. Gallier des. for Lafever," design for a country villa, from Minard Lafever, *Modern Builder's Guide* (1833), frontispiece. Courtesy of the University of Delaware Library, Newark.

FIG 10.7 (*opposite, top*) Decimus Burton, Grove House, Regent's Park, London, 1822–24, from Thomas Shepherd and James Elmes, *Metropolitan Improvements* (1827), opposite page 27. Courtesy of the University of Delaware Library, Newark.

FIG 10.8 (*opposite, bottom*) Cooley House, Racine, Wis., 1853. Photo by the author.

preceding works. His final book, *The Architectural Instructor,* was not published until 1856, two years after his death. In this, Lafever moved beyond the Greek Revival to include both Gothic Revival and Italianate designs.

All told, Lafever, who was also a practicing architect, was enormously influential as an author, primarily in spreading the Greek Revival taste throughout the country. So, from being a city that demonstrated the use of architectural books, New York in the second quarter of the nineteenth century became the place of publication of such works, which were, in turn, used very widely. (I am cheating slightly by claiming New York as the source for all these books, for Lafever's first one, of 1829, was published across the Hudson in Newark, New Jersey; all the others were, however, issued in New York.)

I began this discussion of the role of architectural books in New York with A. J. Davis, who cited his introduction to Stuart and Revett's *Antiquities of Athens,* borrowed from Ithiel Town in 1828, as the beginning of his architectural practice. Interestingly,

he was still reading that highly influential book as late as 1882, as he recorded in his journal.[28] In addition to his own library of architectural books, he also had access to that of Town (1784–1844), his sometime partner, who possessed the largest such library in the country; toward the end of his life it totaled approximately 11,000 books on architecture, art, and engineering, plus some 25,000 prints.[29]

But Davis not only relied on but also contributed to the literature of architecture with his own influential *Rural Residences,* whose title page bears the date 1837 (figure 10.9), though it was actually published the following year.[30] This book contained not the Greek Revival villas and details of Lafever's works but rather the Picturesque idiom as represented by the castellar house in the title-page vignette, a cottage orné, a farmer's house, a villa in the English Collegiate style, a gatehouse in the Rustic Cottage style, a villa in the Oriental style (which he defined as "East Indian"), and an American house that featured logs. Although Davis's imagination and his great facility as a draftsman contributed significantly to the character of the book, he was, like Lafever, indebted to English sources—especially John Claudius Loudon, whose *Encyclopedia of Cottage, Farm, and Villa Architecture and Furniture* he had acquired two years after its 1833 publication.[31]

Rural Residences did not sell particularly well, yet it was largely responsible for introducing the Picturesque to the United States. In particular, it was an inspiration to A. J. Downing, whose volumes of the 1840s and very early 1850s—some containing designs by Davis—spread the gospel of this taste throughout the country. Of these, especially characteristic was *Cottage Residences* of 1842, its title reminiscent of the Davis book of four or five years earlier. Here, Downing presented a whole panoply of Picturesque designs, including a "Cottage in the English, or Rural Gothic Style" and "A villa in the Italian Style."[32] Between them, they illustrate clearly the variety in domestic architecture which had become not only possible but actually desirable. And both this volume and Downing's others were published in New York, thus strengthening the contribution of that city to the field of architectural books.

Although other cities, especially Boston and Philadelphia, played significant roles in the story of architectural books in America before 1848, New York deserves a special place in that history. It was in New York that McComb demonstrated the full effect of the influence of these kinds of volumes, an effect that was strengthened by the publication there of the works of Lafever, Davis, and Downing. And those books in turn confirmed the role of architectural literature in spreading throughout the United States the Greek Revival and the taste for the Picturesque—the two dominant trends in American architecture in the second quarter of the nineteenth century.

RURAL RESIDENCES, ETC.

CONSISTING OF DESIGNS,

ORIGINAL AND SELECTED,

FOR

COTTAGES, FARM-HOUSES, VILLAS, AND VILLAGE CHURCHES:

WITH BRIEF

EXPLANATIONS, ESTIMATES, AND A SPECIFICATION

OF

MATERIALS, CONSTRUCTION, ETC.

BY ALEXANDER JACKSON DAVIS, ESQ,

AND OTHER ARCHITECTS.

PUBLISHED UNDER THE SUPERINTENDENCE OF SEVERAL GENTLEMEN, WITH A VIEW TO THE
IMPROVEMENT OF AMERICAN COUNTRY ARCHITECTURE.

NEW YORK.

TO BE HAD OF THE ARCHITECT, AT THE NEW YORK UNIVERSITY,
AND OF THE BOOKSELLERS GENERALLY, THROUGHOUT THE UNITED STATES.

MDCCCXXXVII.

FIG 10.9 Title page from A. J. Davis, *Rural Residences* (1838). Courtesy of the University of Delaware Library, Newark.

NOTES

1. A. J. Davis, Daybook, 13, New York Public Library, cited in Jane B. Davies, "Alexander J. Davis, Creative American Architect," in *Alexander Jackson Davis, American Architect, 1803–1892,* ed. Amelia Peck (New York: Metropolitan Museum of Art and Rizzoli, 1992), 18, 121 n. 16.

2. All these documents are at the New-York Historical Society (hereafter cited as N-YHS), both in Misc. MSS McComb and attached to the inside front cover of McComb's copy of William Chambers, *A Treatise on the Decorative Part of Civil Architecture,* 3d ed. (London: Printed by Joseph Smeeton, 1791).

3. Misc. MSS McComb, N-YHS.

4. McComb Drawings, nos. 54, 55, 56, 57, 58a, N-YHS.

5. "Account Book of Receipts & Payments Respecting the Government House" (1790), 1, Onondaga Historical Association, Syracuse, N.Y. I am grateful to Harley J. McKee for bringing this to my attention in 1956. McComb is not mentioned in the account in *New-York Magazine,* January, 1795, 1; there, the "direction of it" is assigned to "Messrs. Robinson, Moore, and Smith."

6. McComb's book payments are all from his "Catalogue of Books," in Misc. MSS McComb, N-YHS. The McComb design closest to Crunden's plate 53 is in McComb Drawings, no. 58a, N-YHS. Fiske Kimball discussed and illustrated the two in his *Domestic Architecture of the American Colonies and of the Early Republic* (New York: Scribner, 1922), 163–64 and figs. 117–18.

7. Cf. McComb Drawings, nos. 54–57, N-YHS, with the following plates in Crunden (in addition to 12 and 41): 8, with central front-facing exedra; 17, 18, 19, 22–23, 25–26, and 32–34, with central rear-facing exedra; 20, with one rear and two side-facing exedrae; 36, 64, 67, and 70, with two rear-facing exedrae. All of these are semi-octagonal. Plate 46 has one rear-facing oval exedra.

8. Cf. McComb Drawings, no. 104, N-YHS, and Andrew George Cook's reissue of Carter's plates in *The New Builder's Magazine* (London: H Hogg, 1820), plate 20.

9. For the now demolished St. John's Chapel on Varick Street, see, e.g., McComb Drawings, nos. 50 and 53, N-YHS; for his circular church design, see no. 44, which can be compared with Gibbs's plate 8.

10. See Damie Stillman, "New York City Hall: Competition and Execution," *Journal of the Society of Architectural Historians* 23, no. 3 (1964): 129–42, esp. 135–37.

11. McComb Drawings, City Hall, no. 55 1/2, N-YHS.

12. This note, listing twenty-six plates that he thought especially useful, is pasted inside the front cover of his copy of Chambers's *Treatise.* Cf. McComb Drawings, City Hall, nos. 22, 34, 35, 37, 38, 42, 53, and 93, N-YHS, with Chambers, *Treatise,* plates 2, 12, 22, 60, 102, and 110.

13. McComb to Mr. Colman, Misc. MSS McComb N-YHS.

14. "Notes on St. Paul's Church and Other Churches," n.d., Misc. MSS McComb, N-YHS.

15. Cf. McComb Drawings, no. 18 and no. 10a, the engraving sold by J. Walker, 1782, N-YHS.

16. McComb Drawings, no. 22a, N-YHS.

17. Ibid., no. 27.

18. For asylum and hospital designs, see, e.g., ibid., nos. 213, 266a, and 268. His bound volume "Memorandums & Estimates" (1798), in Misc. MSS McComb, N-YHS, lists estimates for six lighthouses: those at Sandy Hook, N.J.; Cape Henry, Va. (1791–92); Montauk Point, N.Y. (1795); Cape Henlopen, Del. (1797); Eaton's Neck, N.Y. (1798); and Faulkner's Island, Conn. (c. 1802). There are designs for Cape Henry, Montauk, and Eaton's Neck in McComb Drawings, nos. 75–78 and 82–84, N-YHS. Those three are definitely by him, the first with William Pers; Sandy Hook is definitely not.

19. Pollard Drawings, nos. 25 and 22b, N-YHS.

20. Cf. Minard Lafever, *Beauties of Modern Architecture* (New York: Appleton, 1835), plates 7, 13, 25, with Pollard Drawings, no. 24 N-YHS.

21. Jacob Landy, *The Architecture of Minard Lafever* (New York: Columbia University Press, 1970).

22. Cf. Thomas Shepherd and James Elmes, *Metropolitan Improvements* (London: Jones 1827), 24, 79, and illus. opp. 44. See also Landy, *Lafever*, 20–23.

23. The Lafever church, plate 65 in the *Young Builder's General Instructor*, can be compared with the two English churches shown in Shepherd and Elmes, *Metropolitan Improvements*, illus. opp. 81, noted by Landy, *Lafever*, 26–28.

24. Minard Lafever, *The Modern Builder's Guide* (New York: Paine & Burgess, 1833), 3.

25. See Shepherd and Elmes, *Metropolitan Improvements*, 24, illus. opp. 27. In Landy's discussion of these three designs (*Lafever*, 22, 24–26) he also acknowledges Denys Peter Myers's role in identifying Gallier's role.

26. See Lafever, *Beauties of Modern Architecture*, 5 and 69, respectively.

27. Lafever, *Modern Builder's Guide*, 4.

28. A. J. Davis, Journal, 322, Print Department, Metropolitan Museum of Art, New York, cited in Francis R. Kowsky, "Simplicity and Dignity: The Public and Institutional Buildings of Alexander Jackson Davis," in Peck, *Davis*, 123 n. 4.

29. Jane B. Davies, "Town, Ithiel," in *The Macmillan Encyclopedia of Architects*, ed. Adolf K. Placzek (New York: Free Press, 1982), 4:222.

30. Jane B. Davies, "Davies, Alexander Jackson," in Placzek, *Macmillan Encyclopedia of Architects*, 1:508.

31. Davis, Daybook, under September 1835, says that he purchased a copy of the book then, a fact noted in William H. Pierson Jr., *American Buildings and Their Architects: Technology and the Picturesque* (Garden City, N.Y.: Doubleday, 1978), 282.

32. A. J. Downing, *Cottage Residences* (New York: Wiley and Putnam, 1842), designs 2 and 8.

XI

ASHER BENJAMIN, ANDREW JACKSON DOWNING: TWO DIVERGENT FORMS OF BOOKMAKING

Charles B. Wood III

In the last quarter of the twentieth century a new academic discipline called "the history of the book" emerged in Europe and is today a rapidly growing field in the United States as well.[1] The American Antiquarian Society in Worcester, Massachusetts, has played a key role in studying the history of the book and is producing a five-volume work on the subject.[2] A new organization called SHARP (Society for the History of Authorship, Reading and Publishing) is publishing a journal. This new interdisciplinary field is rich in possibilities.

Historians of the book, at least in America, initially focused on literary works. More recently they have broadened their efforts to include popular literature, religious books, books for children and for women, and other specialized categories. But to the best of my knowledge there have been few, if any, studies of the American architectural book as object, as cultural icon; no scholar has applied any of the good work done in the study of bindings, illustrative processes, papermaking, publishing history, and related matters to architectural books. Amazingly enough, the most valuable and prescient study of nineteenth-century American architectural books was done fifty-three years ago by the late Henry-Russell Hitchcock. His *American Architectural Books: A List of Books, Portfolios, and Pamphlets on Architecture and Related Subjects Published in America before 1895* was issued initially in mimeograph in 1946 and published by the University of Minnesota Press in 1962. In 1976 Da Capo Press reprinted it, but now even that is out of print. Moreover, although it did include a useful and often quoted preface, Hitchcock's was not a "study" at all but a handlist of titles. More recently, a thoughtful piece by Dell Upton, "Pattern Books and Professionalism," was published in 1984, but it did not consider the books as objects for bibliographical study.[3]

Architectural historians have for many years investigated pattern books as carriers and disseminators of designs; anyone with the slightest interest in the subject knows of specific houses or churches inspired by Asher Benjamin's engraved plates. A few scholars have considered pattern books as statements on style, and a few have examined the extent to which they reflect the social and domestic culture of nineteenth-century America. But pattern books have so far escaped study by historians of the book. I am interested first in exploring them as objects and as products of the business of publishing, and then in looking at them in a broader cultural context.

To do this I have chosen to examine two books, the first by Asher Benjamin and the second by Andrew Jackson Downing, both published in the same year, 1841. Benjamin's is the 1841 printing of his fourth and most popular book, *The Practical House Carpenter,* which was originally published in Boston in 1830 (figure 11.1).[4] Downing's is the first edition of his first publication, *A Treatise on the Theory and Practice of Landscape Gardening Adapted to North America . . . with Remarks on Rural Architecture* (figure 11.2).[5] Benjamin's book was published by Benjamin B. Mussey, whom the *Dictionary of Literary Biography* identifies as "an obscure Boston publisher." Downing's was brought out by Wiley & Putnam, a famous publisher of textbooks whose successor firm is still in business today. Actually, the full imprint of the Downing book is "New York & London: Wiley & Putnam; Boston: C. C. Little & Co."; this has a bearing on the matter of the business of publishing which I touch on later.

Let us first look at the two authors whose books convey diverging architectural tastes. Asher Benjamin (1773–1845) was the author of the first American builder's guide and during his long life (he lived to age seventy-two) wrote seven guidebooks for builders. In a shift from his earlier three books, which focused on the Roman orders as adopted from William Pain and William Chambers, Benjamin's *Practical House Carpenter* was primarily concerned with the Greek Revival style; his two subsequent books, *The Practice of Architecture* (1833) and *The Builder's Guide* (1838), dealt entirely with Grecian material—both the orders and interior details. *The Practical House Carpenter,* which went through twenty-one recorded and several unrecorded reprintings between 1830 and about 1857, became the most popular American architectural handbook of the nineteenth century. As Abbott Cummings has identified Benjamin's significance, he was "essentially an instructor . . . he helped two, if not three generations

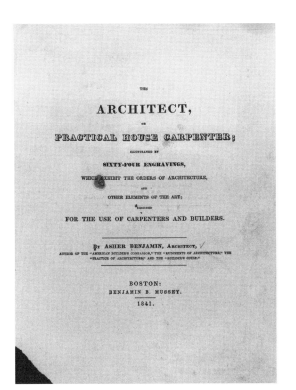

THE

ARCHITECT,
OR
PRACTICAL HOUSE CARPENTER;
ILLUSTRATED BY
SIXTY-FOUR ENGRAVINGS,
WHICH EXHIBIT THE ORDERS OF ARCHITECTURE,
AND
OTHER ELEMENTS OF THE ART;
DESIGNED
FOR THE USE OF CARPENTERS AND BUILDERS.

By ASHER BENJAMIN, ARCHITECT,
AUTHOR OF THE "AMERICAN BUILDER'S COMPANION," THE "RUDIMENTS OF ARCHITECTURE," THE
"PRACTICE OF ARCHITECTURE" AND THE "BUILDER'S GUIDE."

BOSTON:
BENJAMIN B. MUSSEY.
1841.

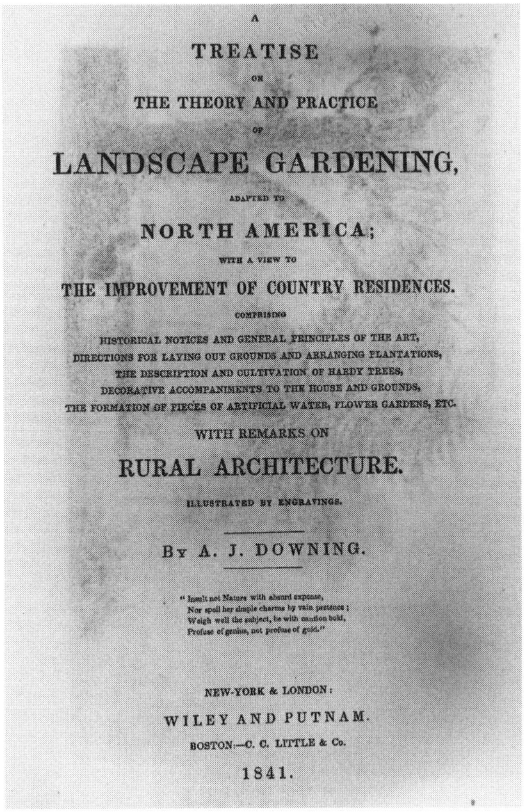

A
TREATISE
ON
THE THEORY AND PRACTICE
OF
LANDSCAPE GARDENING,
ADAPTED TO
NORTH AMERICA;
WITH A VIEW TO
THE IMPROVEMENT OF COUNTRY RESIDENCES.
COMPRISING
HISTORICAL NOTICES AND GENERAL PRINCIPLES OF THE ART,
DIRECTIONS FOR LAYING OUT GROUNDS AND ARRANGING PLANTATIONS,
THE DESCRIPTION AND CULTIVATION OF HARDY TREES,
DECORATIVE ACCOMPANIMENTS TO THE HOUSE AND GROUNDS,
THE FORMATION OF PIECES OF ARTIFICIAL WATER, FLOWER GARDENS, ETC.
WITH REMARKS ON
RURAL ARCHITECTURE.
ILLUSTRATED BY ENGRAVINGS.

By A. J. DOWNING.

" Insult not Nature with absurd expense,
Nor spoil her simple charms by vain pretence ;
Weigh well the subject, be with caution bold,
Profuse of genius, not profuse of gold."

NEW-YORK & LONDON:
WILEY AND PUTNAM.
BOSTON:—C. C. LITTLE & Co.
1841.

FIG 11.1 Title page of Asher Benjamin, *The Practical House Carpenter* (showing the expanded title of the 1841 edition). Courtesy of The George Peabody Library of The Johns Hopkins University, Baltimore.
FIG 11.2 (*right*) Title page of Andrew Jackson Downing, *A Treatise on the Theory and Practice of Landscape Gardening* (1841). Courtesy of the American Antiquarian Society, Worcester, Mass.

of American rural builders throughout the north, south and mid-west to achieve a measurable degree of sophistication."[6] One might add that all this influence was in the Classical style of architecture, and most of it in the Grecian mode.

Andrew Jackson Downing (1815–1852) was two generations younger than Benjamin; this simple fact of chronology explains some of the differences between them and their books. Unlike Benjamin, Downing was not a country builder who became an architect; he was a nurseryman and horticulturist. But the two men have one very important thing in common: they both wrote vastly influential books that had wide-ranging influences, especially on architecture in rural settings.

Benjamin has been the subject of many articles and two doctoral dissertations: the first, on his builders' guides, by Abbott Cummings in 1950; the second, on his architectural style, by Jack Quinan in 1973.[7] Downing's life and works, including his books, have been assiduously studied. He was the subject of a symposium in 1987 and a publication sponsored by the Athenaeum of Philadelphia and Dumbarton Oaks called *Prophet with Honor,* and a more recent biography by David Schuyler called *Apostle of Taste.*[8]

Downing was an advocate of the more modern styles coming into architectural fashion in England and America in the 1830s and 1840s. He was a great champion of the Picturesque Gothic, because it was considered more suited to the rural landscape, and also favored the Italianate, but he felt that Greek Revival dwellings were "unfit for American domestic life." Thus it is fair to say that by 1841, with respect to the architectural styles they promoted, Benjamin was advocating the Greek Revival style then in decline, whereas Downing was promoting the Gothic and other revival styles then on the rise. An examination both of 1841 publications shows that this backwardness/ forwardness was also true of their books. It is the thesis of this essay that the decade between 1830 and 1841 was a watershed because it saw the publication of two landmark books in the history of American architecture, representing two significant but quite different trends in the history of the book.

First, however, we should look at their respective audiences. Hitchcock was the first to note the essential differences between "builders' guides" and "house pattern books."[9] So-called builders' guides were intended primarily for the country carpenter rather than the homeowner or client; they consisted primarily of plates of the orders together with other plates of details, both structural and ornamental. A few such books included one or two plans and elevations of whole buildings, but these were clearly the exception rather than the rule. All seven of Asher Benjamin's books were builders' guides.

The first American house pattern book is generally considered to be Alexander Jackson Davis's *Rural Residences,* published by the author in 1837–38.[10] Because of hard economic times only two of its six proposed parts were issued, and relatively few copies were sold. In its physical makeup it was decidedly old-fashioned—illustrated with lithographic plates either uncolored or, for a higher purchase price, colored by hand— yet remarkably forward looking in its designs and concepts. The Davis scholar Jane Davies has called *Rural Residences* "the key to the beginnings of picturesque architecture in America."[11] But A. J. Downing's 1841 *Treatise* was the first fully developed American house pattern book, a work not intended for carpenters or craftsmen but for a lay audience of consumers or, to use a term of Downing's time "for those about to

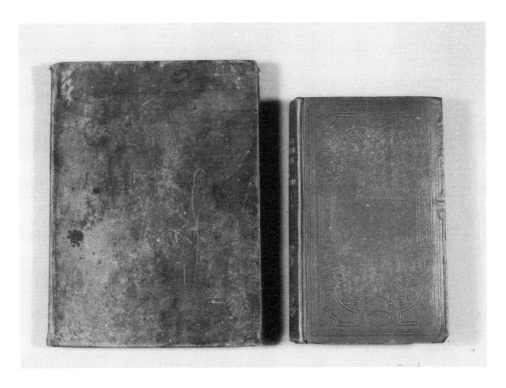

FIG 11.3 Benjamin's *Practical House Carpenter* (left) and Downing's *Treatise* (right), showing difference in size.

build." From this date on, house pattern books began to proliferate. For specific years in the third and fourth quarters of the nineteenth century, Hitchcock was able to correlate the numbers of house pattern books published with the curve of building production. This fact is an important insight into the function of such books in American society, and an early example of "book history."

As to the two books themselves, the first difference is in format, meaning their size and shape. In a bibliographical context the format indicates the size of a volume in terms of the number of times the original printed sheet was folded to form its constituent leaves.[12] One can see in figure 11.3 that the Benjamin book on the left is larger than the Downing on the right. That is as it should be, because each sheet of the Benjamin was folded once, making gatherings or *signatures* of two leaves (four pages); such a book is called a *folio*. (Most Benjamin books were small folios because of the relatively small size of the original sheets of paper.) For the Downing book the sheets were folded twice, making gatherings of four leaves (eight pages) and thus a smaller-sized book, called a *quarto*. The principal reason the Benjamin books were folios was that they had to be illustrated with large plates of the architectural orders and details; most of the similar Greek Revival builders' guides of the 1830s, including the books of Edward Shaw and Minard Lafever, were also in this format. Downing's book, on the other hand, could be produced in a smaller, more convenient, and more "modern" format because it did not have the same illustration requirements.

In the paper of the two books there is little difference. In both the paper is *mold-made wove:* that is, paper with an even, granulated texture, mostly made on a continuous, close-meshed wire screen or roll. This is in opposition to *laid paper,* which can be identified by the presence of chain lines in its texture, made by the wire mesh at the bottom of the tray in which it is formed. Most eighteenth-century American books were printed on handmade laid paper (including Benjamin's first book, *The Country Builder's Assistant* of 1797). But starting in the early nineteenth century, papermaking made great strides forward. During the 1820s and 1830s cylinder papermaking machines superseded hand manufacture, and in the 1840s and 1850s the so-called Fourdrinier machine, imported from England, became more and more widely used; by the middle of the nineteenth century, hand papermaking had virtually disappeared from the American scene. During this period Berkshire County, Massachusetts, because of its supply of pure water and available water power, assumed national leadership in the industry.[13] Early on, the Berkshire papermakers supplied large quantities to the New York City market; it is possible that the paper for Downing's *Treatise* was made there.

Almost all the paper manufactured during the second and third quarters of the nineteenth century was made from rags; the eminent authorities Lawrence Wroth and Rollo Silver have stated that "eighty-eight per cent of the paper produced during 1860 was still made from rags."[14] It was not until the 1880s and later that chemical wood pulp assumed widespread importance as a material for papermaking. Close observation suggests that the paper for the Downing book is very similar to that of the Benjamin book, with one difference: the plates in Benjamin's *Practical House Carpenter* were printed on a slightly heavier paper than the text; this so-called plate paper can be detected by touch and feel as well as by a paper gauge. The plates for the illustrations in Downing's treatise were in fact not plates at all but wood engravings printed integrally with the letterpress (this is an important feature that I will return to).

In considering the question of type, composition, the identity of the printer, and the actual printing of each book, one must first remember that throughout the nineteenth century there were more changes and advances in the technology of printing and book-making than there had been in the previous 350 years from the time of Gutenberg to the end of the eighteenth century. It should also, be said that determining the kind of press a nineteenth-century book was printed on is difficult at best, given no evidence other than the book itself. Certain generalizations can be made, however, especially for books from a specific decade such as 1830–41.[15]

First of all, both books most likely used American-made type, and both were set—that is, composed—by hand. Mechanical typesetting machines did not come along, at least in this country, until the 1870s and 80s. The Benjamin book, having first appeared in 1830, would have been printed from hand-cast type, each piece being an individual letter. We may assume that subsequent editions during the 1830s as well as the 1841 edition used the same hand-cast type. We know more about the printers. John Cotton was the printer of the first edition of 1830; his name appears on the verso of the title page. The printer of the third edition (1832) was S. Walker. For all the subsequent editions or issues (there were at least fourteen—Hitchcock numbers 120 to 134—and I have looked at about half of them), no printer was identified.

The identity of the printer of Downing's 1841 *Treatise* also appears on the verso of the title page: Hopkins & Jennings of 111 Fulton Street, New York. The question of type, however, is open. The first effective mechanical type-casting machine—invented and patented in the United States in 1838[16]—could have been in use in New York City by 1841; we know for certain that it was by 1855, because it was described and illustrated in that wonderful little book *The Harper Establishment; or, How the Story Books Are Made* (1855).[17]

It is reasonable to assume that both books were printed on iron presses. In contrast, one can say with virtual certainty that Asher Benjamin's first book, *The Country Build-er's Assistant* of 1797, was printed on a common wooden press with vertically applied power transmitted by a screw and powered by a human being. But by 1841 at least some of the printers in both Boston and New York had access to more modern printing technologies: iron flatbed presses, the power still vertically applied but transmitted by a fulcrum and lever rather than by a screw. Such presses were powered variously by men, horses, water, or steam.[18] Although I cannot prove this, my best guess is that both books were printed on flatbed presses but the Asher Benjamin on a hand press, the Downing on a steam-powered one.

Two aspects of the books are easier to compare, as they are more self-evident: the

FIG 11.4 Benjamin, *Practical House Carpenter,* plate 12, printed from copper or steel engraving. Collection of the author.

illustrations and the bindings. I noted earlier that the paper for the Asher Benjamin book was of two thicknesses, the heavier reserved for the illustrations (commonly referred to as *plates*). These were printed from full-page copper (or steel) engravings (also called *plates*) made by professional engravers after original drawings by the author (figure 11.4). It was quite common for engravers to sign their work; the plates in *The Practical House Carpenter* are signed by Annan and Smith. They were printed on other presses, than the text and probably in different shops, because engravings, as intaglio prints, needed much greater pressure than letterpress. The plates were printed on a hand-worked rolling press, not unlike a modern etching press.[19]

One drawback of copper engravings, however, was that they wore out fairly quickly; by the 1820s copper was being replaced by steel, which was harder and had a longer life.[20] The use of steel for engravers' plates was introduced in England, but it was the invention of an American, Jacob Perkins, who used it for banknotes.[21] It was quickly taken up in America. We know that the standard edition size for Benjamin's books, at least in the 1830s, was 1,000 copies.[22] Copper plates would be well worn after 1,000 impressions, yet the title pages of both the first (1830) and third (1832) editions state that the book was "illustrated with 64 large quarto copper plates." Subsequent editions refer simply to "engravings" and do not use the word "copper," or the word "quarto." To determine the extent to which Benjamin's plates were re-engraved, I have compared the editions or issues of 1830, 1832, 1844, 1845, 1848, 1851, and 1853. What I found was very interesting. I have been able to determine that for the 1830 and 1832 editions the plates were printed from the same engravings but that those of 1832 were retouched and had occasional additions, such as numbers. In fact, the same plates appear to have been used for the first ten editions, from 1830 all the way through 1845 (a total of 10,000 copies). I conclude that these were steel plates even though the title page in the first and third editions specifies "copper."[23] Still, not surprisingly, by 1845 the plates show wear. For the next edition, 1848, new engravings were made, also by Annan and Smith, and these were used for subsequent editions. But in the edition of 1853, something has happened: the plates are noticeably *darker*. It seems likely that the engravings (having now gone through three printings) were retouched with a graver and rule to deepen the lines, enabling them to hold more ink. Details were retouched and certain numbers also re-engraved. This fascinating sequence of printings and impressions tells a story and shows what can be learned from a close inspection of the book as object. It is yet another way to study the history of the book.

Downing's 1841 *Treatise*, by contrast, used a completely different kind of illustration: the wood engraving. Indeed, it was the first American architectural book to be fully illustrated in this medium.[24] The 1841 edition has nine historiated initials and eighty-eight wood engravings within the text. Reproductive wood engraving, one of the key developments in the nineteenth-century printing revolution, helped to make illus-trated books available for a mass market.[25] Its great advantage was that as a relief process—in contrast to line engraving, which was intaglio—it could be set in the same forms with the letterpress, making for a much more efficiently printed and harmoniously designed page (figure 11.5). Wood engravings were cheap and relatively quick to produce. The designs were cut with a graver into small blocks of end-grain boxwood, a very dense and extremely hard material. (G. B. Tatum has pointed out that A. J. Davis, the principal draftsman for Downing's illustrations, "seems to have drawn directly on the whitened wood blocks, not troubling to reverse the design.")[26] These blocks were then cut—in many instances by Alexander Anderson (1775–1870), the re-nowned American wood engraver; most of his blocks for Downing were signed.[27] Downing and his publishers cannot take credit for this technological innovation—it was fully developed long before 1841—but the fact remains that they were the first to use it to illustrate architectural books.

A comparison of the final elements, the bindings, is dramatic because we are dealing with two separate materials: leather and cloth. The Benjamin book of 1830–41 repre-sents a continuation of the tradition of hand bookbinding, whereas Downing's *Treatise* of 1841 is an early and fully developed example of so-called edition binding or casing-in. Moreover, the difference, is not just skin deep; it is structural, and one must literally look beneath the surface to understand it.

The traditional internal construction of a handbound book involved sewing the signatures together and fastening them inside the covers. For all the Benjamin books the signatures were sewn on hemp cords, which were sunk in shallow grooves made in the spine of the book with a saw. The finished binding thus had a flat back or spine, but it was still bound in the handcraft tradition with the covers attached by the cords. There were two ways to do this: one was by lacing them to the boards; an easier method was to fray the cord ends, paste them to the inside of the boards, and cover them over with the pasted-down endpapers. This process, which added strength, was called *boarding* and had to be done one volume at a time. This was how all of Asher Benjamin's books were bound, even his last one, *The Elements of Architecture*, first pub-lished in 1843. At this point the book was covered with leather, usually dyed sheepskin, and in the final stage—called finishing—the simple spine label was applied.[28] In an-other carryover from eighteenth-century tradition the spine label almost always said "Benjamin's Architect" or "Benjamin's Architecture," no matter what the actual title of the book was (figure 11.6).

Much of this is in contrast to the casing-in method. The preparatory work for the Benjamin and Downing books was essentially the same. It involved folding (done by hand until after the Civil War), collating, smashing (that is flattening the sets of folded sheets), sawing the grooves in the spine, and sewing the signatures together. The next step was a process called *rounding:* that is, tightly clamping the set of folded and sewn sheets in a vise and shaping the spine with a backing hammer. For both books this was hand work. In its cloth *case,* however, the Downing book began to take on its "modern" appearance (figure 11.7).

These cloth covers were prepared and decorated separately from the body or *block* of the book. They consisted of three parts—the front cover, the back cover, and the spine—all made from one piece of cloth. The cases were made by hand. The process required cutting the boards and cloth to proper size, gluing the boards to the cloth, and turning in the edges over the boards.[29] In 1841 cloth was a fairly new material for bookbinding. It was used first in England and by about 1830 had begun to appear in American bindings.[30] But initially the fabric was always English; not until the 1880s or 1890s did Americans begin to manufacture book cloth.[31] Cloth for edition bindings was a thin cotton muslin. For color, it was treated with dye (various shades of green were used for the case of the 1841 *Treatise*); for texture, it was treated with sizing. And the most important feature was added at the end: the gold stamping (and sometimes, on the covers, blind stamping: that is, an impression without the addition of color). The base of the spine of every copy of the *Treatise* I have ever seen still in its original binding bears a gilt stamp that was clearly designed for this specific title (figure 11.8). It is a vignette of a vine-covered arbor encircling a picturesque Gothic cottage, beneath which is a cartouche of gardening tools, including sickle, shovel, pick, spade, and rake. It is quite a clever device, perhaps designed by Downing himself or even by A. J. Davis.[32]

A broad comparison of the Benjamin and Downing bindings is revealing. In the nineteenth century the Benjamin books were still being produced by eighteenth-century methods and traditions. They looked plain and old-fashioned, whereas the Downing bindings were very modern in design, conception, and production. Still, one must keep all this in perspective: the new casing-in process, though producing a more modern-looking product, was in fact not a machine process but simply a modification and improvement of traditional methods, but using new materials.

The comparison I have been making is to a certain extent an artificial construct, but I think it does allow us to evaluate various aspects of these two books. We can continue this exercise by looking at their respective publishers. The 1841 edition of the *Practical House Carpenter* was published by the "obscure" Boston publisher Benjamin B. Mussey. A manuscript history of nineteenth-century Boston booksellers tells us that even though Mussey began his business as a bookseller in a small way with limited capital, about the year 1830, he left a "considerable estate" on his death in 1854 or 1855.[33] According to the *Dictionary of Literary Biography* (1978), Mussey published historical and

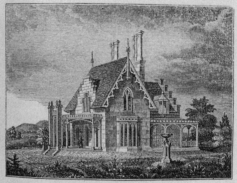

windows, by the introduction of mullions and tracery in the window openings, and indeed, by a multitude of interior and exterior enrichments generally applied to the Tudor mansions, a villa in the Rural Gothic style may be made a per-

[Fig. 36. Cottage of N. B. Warren, Esq., Troy, N. Y.]

fect gem of a country residence. Of all the styles hitherto enumerated, we consider this one of the most suitable for this country, as, while it comes within the reach of all persons of moderate means, it unites, as we before stated, so much of convenience and rural beauty.*

To the man of taste, there is no style which presents greater attractions, being at once rich in picturesque beau-

* The only objection that can be urged against this mode of building, is that which applies to all cottages with a low second story, viz: want of coolness in the sleeping chambers during mid-summer. An evil which may be remedied by constructing a false inner-roof — leaving a vacuity between the two roofs of six or eight inches, which being occupied with air, and ventilated at the top will almost entirely obviate the objection.

42

FIG 11.5 A page from Downing's *Treatise* showing how the wood-engraved illustrations were integrated on the same page with the text. Courtesy of the American Antiquarian Society, Worcester, Mass.

FIG 11.6 (*opposite, top*) Two copies of Benjamin's *Practical House Carpenter* showing original "binder's titles." Collection of the author.

FIG 11.7 (*opposite, bottom*) Downing's *Treatise* showing the original publisher's cloth casing. Courtesy of the American Antiquarian Society, Worcester, Mass.

literary works; the Boston booksellers manuscript mentions an algebra textbook and a book of church music. Neither the nineteenth- nor the twentieth-century source mentions anything at all about architectural books, much less Asher Benjamin. Yet of the forty-two entries in Hitchcock for Benjamin's seven books between 1797 and 1843, fully seventeen were published by Mussey and three more by his successor firm in the later

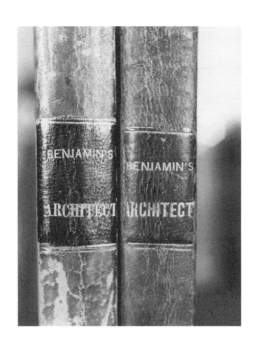

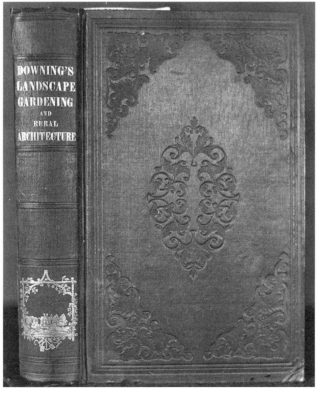

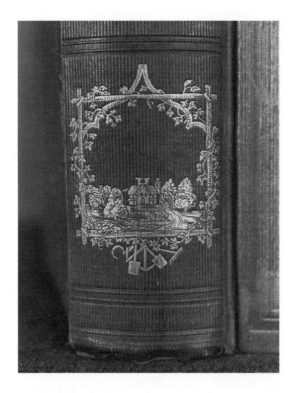

FIG 11.8 Detail of the gilt stamping on the cloth casing of Downing's *Treatise* showing the emblematic use of gardening tools, cottage, vines, and Gothic arch, all designed specifically for this book.

1850s. Thus one can conclude that Benjamin B. Mussey was both prolific and success-ful at his business, and part of his "considerable estate," presumably, was due to the profits he made from publishing the works of Asher Benjamin.

To turn the tables for a moment, we can try to see the publishing history of *The Practical House Carpenter* from the point of view of its author. Historians have tended to gloss over or ignore the economics of authorship and publishing, and with good reason: this area is almost impossible to research unless one has access to the author's papers and the publisher's archives—and except for prominent literary figures, these usually do not exist. This whole subject is one of the least understood aspects of book history. It would be extremely helpful to examine one of Benjamin's publishing con-tracts, but to my knowledge Asher Benjamin's literary estate has not survived. One small piece of information, however, sheds some light on the matter of his copyright and his share of the profits. The verso of the title page of the third (1832) edition of

The Practical House Carpenter bears the following printed notice: "The author claims, as proprietor, three eighths; Annan and Smith, as proprietors, two eighths, and R. P. and C. Williams, three eighths." This notation signifies that the copyright was divided among the author, the publisher, and the engravers. (One might have assumed that the engravers would do their work for a set fee to be paid by the publisher, but apparently they took their payment as part of the copyright: that is, a portion of the proceeds from the sale of the book.) So how much did Benjamin earn from his seven published books? We know only that when he died in 1845, he left a healthy (for the time) estate valued at over $17,000, and of this amount $2,000 was for the "copyright of three works on architecture."[34] Thus it is fair to say that his lifelong labors of writing seven architectural books did indeed generate him wealth.

We know more about Wiley & Putnam, publishers of Downing's 1841 *Treatise*. That firm was founded in 1840, but its antecedents went back to 1807.[35] Charles Wiley was interested in agricultural, technical, and architectural books; George Palmer Putnam was more interested in literature. Recall that the imprint read New York and London; the reason was that Putnam established a branch office and bookshop in London in 1841. It was the first agency for the sale of American books in Great Britain; it also allowed Wiley & Putnam to reprint English books in America. G. P. Putnam lived in London for seven years, until 1848, and upon his return to America he left the partnership and began his own publishing company.[36] Wiley's firm continues to publish architectural and technical books.

Under the imprint of Wiley & Putnam, Downing's 1841 *Treatise* became a successful and influential work. In 1853 the Philadelphia publisher Henry C. Carey, in an article titled "Best Sellers of the Fifties," stated that by that year—just twelve years after it had first appeared—it had sold 9,000 copies.[37] That Downing's book was also sold in London is of interest (as is the whole subject of early nineteenth-century American architectural books in England). In contrast, although I have seen many English architectural publishers' and booksellers' catalogues from before 1850, none of Asher Benjamin's books were offered there.

A final aspect for comparison is the matter of the authors' presentation copies that exist for both Benjamin and Downing. Since authors were unlikely to give copies of their books out indiscriminately, finding those they inscribed enables us to identify persons who were close to them and whom they held in high regard.[38]

I am indebted to Abbott Cummings for information about three Benjamin presentation copies. The first is an 1833 *Practice of Architecture* with the inscription "Presented to Charles Bulfinch Esq. with the regards of the author." This copy is now in the library at MIT. The second, the 1843 edition of *The Elements of Architecture,* is inscribed "A. J. Davis with the respects of the author." This is now in the Boston Athenaeum. The third, also the 1843 *Elements,* is inscribed "The Gift of the Author A. Benjamin Esq. of Boston, rec'd March 18, 1843"; it was given to Harvard and is still there. Such copies are very rare in the marketplace; in thirty-two years, of the more than one hundred Benjamin books that have passed through my hands, I have found not one presentation copy. For Downing too, only a few are known. Many years ago I owned a first edition of *Cottage Residences* which was inscribed "For N. P. Willis Esq. with the regards of A. J. Downing" (Nathaniel Parker Willis, a popular writer and essayist, lived the last seventeen years of his life at "Idlewild," near Newburgh on the Hudson).[39] I know of one other presentation copy, now in a private collection, of the 1841 *Treatise;* its inscription reads, "Presented to J. C. Loudon, Esq. F.R.S. with the esteem of the author."[40]

What conclusions may we draw from these two case studies? There are many distinctions between Benjamin and Downing as writers on architecture. First, the training in their respective professions: Benjamin was a house carpenter turned architect, and Downing a horticulturist. Second, their separate approaches to style: Benjamin was a proponent of the Greek Revival, and Downing an advocate of Gothic Revival forms and their variants.

Benjamin's approach to design was conservative, as was his approach to his book publishing. The emphasis in his *Practical House Carpenter* was on the technical over the aesthetic. In format, binding, illustration, and printing his books reflected a conservative tradition. Downing's books could hardly have been more different. In format, binding, illustration, and printing they reflected the latest innovations. Downing's approach to style was progressive, and the form and content of his books privileged aesthetic concerns over technical instruction.

Consequently, each author addressed a different readership, reflecting their divergent approaches to the discipline and practice of architecture. Benjamin was speaking to an audience within his profession. His readers were housewrights, carpenters, and architects. In contrast, Downing's readers were potential homeowners. They were not professional builders but modern consumers from a growing middle class concerned with taste—in much the same way that lay audiences today follow such style setters as *House and Garden* and the always tasteful Martha Stewart.

NOTES

I wish especially to thank Michael Winship of the University of Texas, Austin. Through his course "The American Book in the Industrial Era, 1820–1940," given at Rare Book School, University of Virginia (summer 1997), he brought much of the material in this essay into sharper focus.

1. See, e.g., Robert Darnton's "Scholarship and Readership: New Directions in the History of the Book," in *Books and Prints, Past and Future: Papers presented at the Grolier Club Centennial Convocation, 26–28 April 1984* (New York: Grolier Club, 1984), 33–51.

2. *A History of the Book in America* (New York: Cambridge University Press; Worcester, Mass.: American Antiquarian Society, 2000–). The first volume, *The Colonial Book in the Atlantic World*, was published in July 2000.

3. Dell Upton, "Pattern Books and Professionalism: Aspects of the Transformation of Domestic Architecture in America, 1800–1860," *Winterthur Portfolio* 16 (1984): 107–50.

4. Henry-Russell Hitchcock, *American Architectural Books* (Minneapolis: University of Minnesota Press, 1962), no. 124.

5. Ibid., no. 354.

6. Abbott Lowell Cummings, "Benjamin, Asher," in *The Macmillan Encyclopedia of Architects*, ed. Adolf K. Placzek (New York: Free Press, 1982), 1:178.

7. Abbott Lowell Cummings, "An Investigation of the Sources, Stylistic Evolution, and Influence of Asher Benjamin's Builders' Guides" (Ph.D. diss., Ohio State University, 1950); Jack Quinan, "The Architectural Style of Asher Benjamin" (Ph.D. diss., Brown University, 1973).

8. George B. Tatum and Elisabeth Blair MacDougall, eds., *Prophet with Honor: The Career of Andrew Jackson Downing, 1815–1852* (Philadelphia: Athenaeum of Philadelphia; Washington, D.C.: Dumbarton Oaks, 1989); David Schuyler, *Apostle of Taste: Andrew Jackson Downing, 1815–1852* (Baltimore: Johns Hopkins University Press, 1996).

9. Hitchcock, *American Architectural Books*, iii.

10. A. J. Davis, *Rural Residences*, intro. Jane B. Davies (New York: Da Capo Press, 1980), i–vi.

11. Jane B. Davies, "Davis, Alexander Jackson," in *Macmillan Encyclopedia of Architects*, 1:508.

12. A simplified but adequate explanation of format can be found in John Carter, *ABC for Book Collectors*, rev. 5th ed. (New York: Knopf, 1980), 100–101. For more thorough coverage, see Philip Gaskell, *A New Introduction to Bibliography* (New York: Oxford University Press, 1972).

13. Hellmut Lehmann-Haupt, Lawrence C. Wroth, and Rollo Silver, *The Book in America* (New York: R. R. Bowker, 1951), 85–90; Judith A. McGaw, *Most Wonderful Machine: Mechanization and Social Change in Berkshire Paper Making, 1801–1885* (Princeton, N.J.: Princeton University Press, 1987), esp. chap. 4, "Mechanical Paper Makers: The Evolution of Paper Machinery, 1799–1885."

14. Lehmann-Haupt, Wroth, and Silver, *The Book in America*, 90.

15. Ibid., 72–80.

16. W. T. Berry, "Printing and Allied Trades," in *A History of Technology*, ed. Charles Singer (London: Oxford University Press, 1958), 5:683.

17. Jacob Abbott, *The Harper Establishment; or, How the Story Books Are Made* (New York: Harper, 1855), 74–77.

18. Lehmann-Haupt, Wroth, and Silver, *The Book in America*, 73, 77.

19. Anthony Dyson, *Pictures to Print: The Nineteenth Century Engraving Trade* (London: Farrand Press, 1984), esp. chap. 4, "Plate-Printers' Workshops and Their Equipment."

20. Basil Hunnisett, *Steel-Engraved Book Illustration in England* (Boston: David R. Godine, 1980), esp. chap. 2, "Siderography and After," and chap. 4, "The Art of Steel-Engraving."

21. For Jacob Perkins, see *Dictionary of American Biography,* 14:472–73.

22. Hitchcock, *American Architectural Books,* no. 120.

23. It is possible, though, that they were *steel-faced* copper plates; see Hunnisett, *Steel-Engraved Book Illustration,* 33. I thank Georgia Barnhill of the American Antiquarian Society for sharing her thoughts on this matter of copper versus steel.

24. The one exception was the frontispiece, drawn by A. J. Davis and steel-engraved by H. Jordan.

25. There is a very extensive bibliography on the medium of wood engraving; a good guide is given in Georgia Bumgardner, "Graphic Arts: Seventeenth–Nineteenth Century," in *Arts in America: A Bibliography,* vol. 2 (Washington, D.C.: Smithsonian Institution Press, 1979), nos. K186–K246 (i.e., sixty entries). See also Gavin Bridson and Geoffrey Wakeman, *Printmaking and Picture Printing: A Bibliographical Guide to Artistic and Industrial Techniques in Britain, 1750–1900* (Oxford: Plough Press, 1984), 102–26.

26. George B. Tatum, introduction to *The Architecture of Country Houses* (1850; reprint, New York: Da Capo Press, 1968), xi.

27. There is a considerable bibliography on Anderson; Bumgardner, "Graphic Arts," lists twelve monographs or titles: nos. K762–K773.

28. Lehmann-Haupt, Wroth, and Silver, *The Book in America,* 149. See also Bernard Middleton, *A History of English Craft Bookbinding Technique* (London: Holland Press, 1978).

29. Lehmann-Haupt, Wroth, and Silver, *The Book in America,* 149–50.

30. Douglas Ball, *Victorian Publishers' Bindings* (Williamsburg, Va.: Book Press, 1985); Sue Allen and Charles Gullans, *Decorated Cloth in America: Publishers' Bindings, 1840–1910* (Los Angeles: Clark Memorial Library, 1994). See also Calvin P. Otto, *Only in Cloth: Publishers' Bookbindings, 1830–1910* (Charlottesville, Va.: Book Arts Press, 1998).

31. Lehmann-Haupt, Wroth, and Silver, *The Book in America,* 148: "The establishment of the Interlaken Mills in Rhode Island in 1883 was the first lastingly significant step towards independence [of English-made book cloth]."

32. These decorative gilt stampings have received much attention; see Allen and Gullans, *Decorated Cloth,* and Otto, *Only in Cloth.*

33. Melvin Lord, comp., "Boston Mass Booksellers Papers 1640–1860," 2:92, MS, American Antiquarian Society, Worcester, Mass.

34. The will and inventory of Asher Benjamin, Suffolk County Probate Court, no. 34426, Massachusetts State Archives at Columbia Point, Boston. I am very much indebted to Anne E. Macdonald for bringing this document to my attention.

35. *The First One Hundred and Fifty Years of John Wiley & Sons, Inc., 1807–1957* (New York: Wiley, 1957).

36. G. H. Putnam, *A Memoir of George Palmer Putnam* (N.p.: Putnam, 1903), 50.

37. See D.C. Seitz, "Best Sellers of the Fifties," *Publishers' Weekly,* 28 January 1922, 183–84.

38. There is much literature on the presentation copy. See Carter, *ABC for Book Collectors,* 155–56; John Winterich, *A Primer of Book Collecting* (New York: Crown, 1966), chap. 2, "Association Books"; S. J. Iacone, *The Pleasures of Book Collecting* (New York: Harper & Row, 1976), chap. 9, "Signed, Inscribed, and Presentation Copies"; Philippa Barnard, ed., *Antiquarian Books: A Comparison for Booksellers, Librarians, and Collectors* (London: Scolar Press, 1974), 30, 330–31; J. Sparrow, *Association Copies: An Essay with Examples Drawn from the Author's Own Collection* (Los Angeles, 1978).

39. This copy is now in the collections of the Humanities Research Center, University of Texas, Austin. For Willis, see *Dictionary of American Biography,* 20:306–9.

40. I am indebted to Bradford Gail Lyon, owner of Elizabeth Woodburn Books of Hopewell, N.J., for this information.

XII

LOUISA TUTHILL, ITHIEL TOWN, AND THE BEGINNINGS OF ARCHITECTURAL HISTORY WRITING IN AMERICA

Sarah Allaback

In 1841, Louisa Tuthill wrote a letter to the Philadelphia publishers Carey & Hart about a work that would both improve public taste in architecture and furnish "correct models for imitation." She added, "In preparing this work for publication, I have been allowed to avail myself of the invaluable library of Ithiel Town Esq. of New Haven, and have received from him and several other architects, plans and elevations for buildings of various kinds."[1] Seven years later, in 1848, Lindsay & Blakiston of Philadelphia brought out Tuthill's *History of Architecture from the Earliest Times,* the first history of architecture published in America.

Why would a widowed mother of four with a few children's books to her credit take on such a project? By the late 1830s, Louisa Tuthill was a successful writer of juvenile fiction and etiquette books, not a historian or even an intellectual. Though part of a literary circle, she seems to have been a fairly conventional Victorian lady. The circumstances surrounding her decision to write a history of architecture remain a mystery, but it is clear that writing for children caused her both to begin theorizing about the connections between moral development and architectural design and to realize that she, a mere woman writer, might actually make a difference. Tuthill had grown up watching the New Haven green become the setting for elegant new buildings that expressed urban progress in a variety of styles. By the late 1830s she lived within walking distance of the most extensive architectural library of the day. It is easy to see why,

FIG 12.1 Thomas Cole, *The Architect's Dream*, 1840. Courtesy of the Toledo Museum of Art.

as her belief in the importance of aesthetic education developed, architecture would take on a central role in her effort to improve American life. In Ithiel Town's library Louisa Tuthill found the "history of architecture from the earliest times" and, with it, a path to good taste and ethical living.

In 1840, when Tuthill was busy with her history, Thomas Cole painted *The Architect's Dream*, a tribute to Ithiel Town and his books (figure 12.1). The figure on the pedestal need not have been painted from life, but the books were based on actual volumes borrowed from Town's library, as were the images behind them. Although he commissioned the painting, correspondence from Cole to Asher B. Durand reveals that Town disliked it enough to demand another. He wanted a work of "rich and varied landscape, history, architecture of different styles and ages, etc. or ancient or modern Athens."[2] Despite Town's disappointment with the work, Cole had successfully illustrated the extraordinary importance of books to the development of nineteenth-century American architecture. This essay examines Town's equally significant contribution to the beginning of architectural history writing in America.

Born in Thomson, Connecticut, in 1784, Ithiel Town began his working life as a carpenter. In 1805 he was living in Boston and attending Asher Benjamin's drawing school. During his time in Boston, Town most likely had access to the library of his teacher's mentor, Charles Bulfinch, as well as to the reading room of the newly opened Boston Athenaeum. His first building in New Haven, Center Church, was based on a design by Benjamin. After the construction of this Federal-style church in 1814, Town designed Gothic Trinity Church next door. In 1817 his Greek Revival state house was added to the green, the trio forming a textbook illustration of early nineteenth-century revivalism.[3] If revivalist architecture depended on the distribution of books with designs and pictures, Asher Benjamin inspired the revivalist philosophy by example in his own writings, his buildings, and, one can imagine, his teachings (figure 12.2).

In 1820, Ithiel Town patented a bridge truss, the Town Lattice Truss, a revolutionary design that enabled bridge engineers to span much longer distances than ever before.[4] His invention was used across rivers from Massachusetts to South Carolina. Town's interest in books dated back to his Boston days, but it was the truss invention that provided him with the financial freedom to pursue his passion for collecting expensive volumes, engravings, and other treasures. In 1826, the year Town became a founding member of the National Academy of Design, he entered into a partnership with Martin Thompson, and they opened up shop in the Merchant Exchange building in New York City. Alexander Jackson Davis joined the firm in 1829, and James H. Dakin worked with them for about a year and a half. During the late 1820s and the 1830s, Town and his partners were arguably the country's greatest advocates of Greek Revival architecture in America.[5]

Town's architectural library was accessible not only to these architects and their friends in the profession but also to New York intellectuals, artists, and writers. Mention of the firm's fantastic "architectural rooms" in a popular guidebook published in 1828, *The Picture of New York,* suggests that the public was also welcome in Town's office and library at that early date.[6] Even before he joined Town's firm, Alexander Jackson Davis studied in the library, borrowed Stuart and Revett's *Antiquities of Athens* (1762), and recorded this life-changing experience in his diary: "1828 March 15 First study of Stuarts Athens, from which I date Professional Practice."[7] Later, he would document Town's achievements: the first store with granite piers, the first use of the Greek order in doorways of New York townhouses, the first church in Greek temple form, and so on. As Davis, Cole, and other contemporaries recognized, many of the firm's innovations could be traced back to historical sources, the volumes in Town's extensive library.

FIG 12.2 Portrait of Ithiel Town by Nathaniel Jocelyn. Courtesy of the National Academy of Design, New York.

In 1829, with profits from the truss as well as his successful architectural practice, Town traveled through Europe in the company of painters Samuel F. B. Morse and Nathaniel Jocelyn, searching for valuable prints, books, and art objects to add to his collection. Much of his business abroad was done through John Weale, an English publisher, who would ship the rare volumes Town requested. In correspondence with Weale, Town mentioned selling some of the new books he received to American architects; he had no use for "common practical books published for general circulation."[8]

Over the next decade Town's collection would total 10,000 to 11,000 volumes, thousands of engravings, and numerous antiquities. Before the New Haven library was even built, William Dunlap called the collection "truly magnificent and unrivaled by anything of its kind in America, perhaps no private library in Europe is its equal." Dunlap acknowledged Town for "information and opportunities" that contributed to his own pioneering history of American art and artists, *History of the Rise and Progress of the Arts of Design in the United States* (1834).[9]

Like his friend Samuel Morse, Town was an avid promoter of art and architectural education. His treatise *The Outlines of a Plan for Establishing in New-York an Academy and Institution of the Fine Arts* was published in 1835, about the time he began building himself a new house in New Haven, the second floor of which was custom designed for the growing library.[10] It seems likely that Town imagined his home library a contribution to the cultural life of New Haven, much as the office library was a resource for New York architects and intellectuals. The building was of fireproof construction with solid brick partitions, even in the closets, and interior plastering on brick without laths except in the ceiling (figures 12.3, 12.4). The two-inch-thick mortar floors were coated with "water-cement." The entire second floor was fashioned with shelves for books and cabinets for curiosities. A selection of architectural books remained in the New York office, but most of the collection was moved to New Haven.

The new library quickly became famous. In 1839, Lydia Sigourney, known as the Sweet Singer of Hartford and the American Hemens for her poetic verse, wrote an article about Town's New Haven library for the *Lady's Companion.* Along with a portion of Town's plan for the art academy, the article included an extensive physical description of the place Tuthill frequented while writing her history. Like the New York library, the New Haven collection had become a featured site for tourists, as well as for scholars and architects. Sigourney's article, written for a popular audience of women readers, provides the best contemporary description:

> In the second story [of Town's house] is a spacious apartment, forty-five feet in length, twenty-three in breadth, and twenty-two in height, with two sky-lights, six feet square,— three windows at one end, and three sash doors, opening upon the balcony. There, and in the lobbies, and study are arranged, in Egyptian, Grecian and Gothic cases, of fine symmetry, between nine and ten thousand volumes. Many of these are rare, expensive and valuable. More than three fourths of these are folios and quartos. A great proportion are adorned with engravings. It is not easy to compute the number of these embellishments— though the proprietor supposes them to exceed two hundred thousand. There are also some

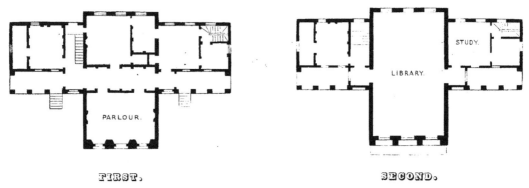

FIRST,   SECOND.

FIG 12.3 Ithiel Town's Library, New Haven, Conn. Courtesy of the Beineke Rare Book and Manuscript Library, Yale University, New Haven.

FIG 12.4 (*bottom*) Floor plan, Ithiel Town's Library, New Haven, Conn. Courtesy of the Beineke Rare Book and Manuscript Library, Yale University, New Haven.

twenty or twenty-five thousand separate engravings—some of them the splendid executions of the best masters, both ancient and modern. In these particulars, the library exceeds all others in our country.[11]

She concludes by encouraging the traveler to visit Town's library on Hillhouse Avenue.

After publication of the article, Town wrote to Sigourney, inviting her and her friends to use the library as often as convenient.[12] Louisa Tuthill was one of Sigourney's friends, but she might just as easily have been invited to Town's home through other acquaintances, such as Benjamin Silliman, the Yale professor and editor of the *American Journal of Science and the Arts,* or Mary Lucas Hillhouse, also known as the American Hannah More. Hillhouse Avenue had been designed by James Hillhouse (Mary's father) and laid out by his son, James Abraham, a poet who lined the street with elms and invited his intellectual friends to build houses set back from the broad, landscaped boulevard. Hillhouse's own estate, Sachem's Wood, stood at the head of the avenue, the houses of Professors Silliman and Kingsley nearby, and farther down the street the establishment of Aaron Skinner, proprietor of a boys' school, and Mrs. Apthorp's boarding school for young ladies. These were not only Town's neighbors; they were his clients.[13]

Louisa Caroline Huggins was born near this New Haven neighborhood in 1798, the seventh child of a merchant-class New Haven family (figure 12.5).[14] She was educated in local private schools and a female seminary. At age nineteen she married Cornelius Tuthill and became part of a literary circle centered on her husband's magazine, *The Microscope.*[15] She became close friends with poets James Gates Percival and John Greenleaf Whittier. When Cornelius died in 1825 and Tuthill was left with four young children, she began writing, ostensibly for comfort but also for additional income. Her first books, *James Somers: The Pilgrim's Son* (1827) and *Love of Admiration or Mary's Visit to Boston* (1828), were stories intended to promote the moral development of children. Tuthill's third book for young readers, *Architecture, Part I, Ancient Architecture* (1831), strove to cultivate youthful taste, a mission that would evolve over the course of her career. That small volume formed the basis for her *History of Architecture.*[16]

Town's collection must have seemed staggering, even to the most worldly members of his elite social circle. To a single parent of four, writing "for solace against affliction," the library offered untold possibilities and creative inspiration.[17] Like Town, Tuthill believed in the power of books to improve America's built environment. Whereas Town was a practicing architect, however, Tuthill could only write about architecture. Nevertheless, she had high aspirations. Her history of world architecture for the

FIG 12.5 Louisa Caroline Huggins Tuthill (1798–1879). From George Dudley Seymour, *New Haven* (1942).

common reader was intended to be part of an "every family library." The book's dedication, "to the Ladies of the United States of America, the Acknowledged Arbiters of Taste," implied that women were accepted aesthetic critics with the power to influence public artistic standards. Tuthill used her influence to address "the painter, the poet, the sculptor and the novelist," among other potential readers.[18]

The manuscript Tuthill sent to the publishers Cary & Hart in 1841 was tentatively titled "Architecture, Ancient and Modern: The past and present condition of the Art in the United States, with plans for its improvement." At that time, Tuthill described her book as "about 350 pages, octavo, illustrated in the letterpress, like Loudon's architectural works published in London." She had been working on the manuscript for several years, and it had been "highly approved" by the scientific and literary men who reviewed it. Tuthill explained that she chose a Philadelphia publisher in the belief that better woodcuts could be found there than in any other city.[19] Although Tuthill's early manuscript has never been found, the letter reveals that her work in Town's library took place before she moved to Hartford in 1838. After 1841, perhaps because the first manuscript was rejected, Tuthill added additional contemporary sources and illustrations.[20]

Although Town's library was filled with many of the European classics—Vitruvius, Alberti, Stuart and Revett, Piranesi, among others, and the work of more popular authors such as Loudon—Tuthill's sources for American architecture were hardly as numerous or comprehensive. America's architectural history had been briefly addressed in various editions of Asher Benjamin's carpenter's guides. In *The Rudiments of Architecture* (1814) described the first attempts to construct shelters in America, and in prefaces to his books of the 1830s he discussed the differences between revivals of two current fads—Roman and Grecian architecture. The history of architecture was mentioned in Dunlap's *History of the Rise and Progress of the Arts* (1834) and summarized by Benson Lossing in his *Outline History of the Fine Arts* (1842). Alexander Jackson Davis's *Rural Residences* (1837) and Andrew Jackson Downing's *Treatise on Landscape Gardening* (1841) offered the "common man" (though a relatively well-off one) plans for a range of house styles.

Tuthill's effort was something entirely new, however. Compared with Downing's domestic style book and its imitations, her book displays a variety of historical examples and building types. Like Downing, she borrowed from the work of John Claudius Loudon, whose *Encyclopedia of Cottage, Farm and Villa Architecture* included both detailed plans and short essays (figure 12.6). But whereas Downing imitated Loudon's production in style, format, and content, Tuthill merely incorporated him as one of

FIG 12.6 "Villa in the Swiss Style," from John Claudius Loudon, supplement to *Encyclopaedia of Cottage, Farm and Villa Architecture* (1842). This reappears as "Cottage in the Swiss Style" in Tuthill's *History of Architecture* (1848).

her authorities on taste. Town's library offered Tuthill an armchair Grand Tour. It was a window on the exotic adventures of the world traveler as well as legitimate entry into the exclusive field of architectural history writing. Since his library contained books on every subject—from hydraulics to fiction, ancient history to modern philosophy—it is not surprising that Tuthill ventured into unexplored territory, touching on the importance of city parks, architectural education, and construction techniques. Not even funereal architecture escaped her analysis. The book concludes with an engraving of Henry Austin's massive Egyptian gateway leading into Grove Street Cemetery, New Haven, where Tuthill herself would be laid to rest in 1879.[21]

Over four hundred pages, including appendixes, *The History of Architecture from the Earliest Times; Its Present Condition in Europe and the United States* was a serious attempt to document architecture from its ancient origins to its recent manifestation in America. The book offers biographies of eminent architects and a glossary of architectural terms. There are chapters on "principles of architecture," a discussion of "causes which retarded the progress of the art in the United States," and a list of "materials for building in the United States." Tuthill cites a variety of sources, including William Chambers's *Designs of Chinese Buildings* (1757), John Britton's *Architectural Antiquities of Great Britain* (1804–14), and Augustus Pugin's *Specimens of Gothic Architecture* (1822), all of which she would have found on the shelves of Town's library. The *History* contains some 150 wood and steel engravings, many illustrating contemporary buildings such as Glenn Cottage, a model home from William Lang's *Views of Cottages* (1845). After using historical sources to establish the context for her analysis of American architecture, Tuthill criticizes current buildings and offers suggestions for improvement.

Town's library was then no longer in existence, but the time she had spent there, surrounded by designers and patrons, not only gave her unusual exposure to the profession (especially for a woman) but also credibility with any other architect or institution she might approach for assistance with the book. And Tuthill's attitude toward architectural revivalism must have been influenced by Town's example, as well as the choice of literature on his bookshelves. Her chapter "Qualifications for an Architect" describes the importance of training the practitioner in design principles, arguing that such an education in taste would enable the architect to develop original combinations of past forms. On the basis of principles governing appropriateness to site, climate, and other conditions, Tuthill advocates Grecian villas for certain urban settings and Gothic for country estates. The mansion of James Dundas by Thomas Ustick Walter is a rare example of a convenient and elegant city house; the Italianate Athenaeum in Philadelphia, engraved from an original watercolor by John Notman, is praised for its adaptation to site and ornamentation (figure 12.7). The key to architectural success, she asserts, is choosing the appropriate historical sources and adapting them to both site conditions and the client's requirements—all in the name of that vague and much debated principle of judgment, Taste. Throughout her work, Tuthill shows how the exercise of good taste, the aspect of architecture arbitrated and cultivated by women, results in personal and societal improvement.

In *Success in Life: The Artist* (one of a series), written almost twenty years after publication of the *History*, Tuthill quoted Dunlap's 1834 description of Town's "truly magnificent library," which is "open to the inspection of the curious, and freely offered for the instruction of the student." In a footnote she brings the reader up to date on the

FIG 12.7 The Athenaeum at Philadelphia, engraving by Edward Robyn from Tuthill's *History*, plate 26.

melancholy state of the library, since "sold and dispersed." She asks, "Was there no institution to purchase it?"[22] Before leaving on a trip to Europe in 1843, Town had arranged for a portion of his library to be auctioned off by the New York firm of Royal, Gurley and Hill. After his death in 1844, this company and Cooley, Keise and Hall of New York sold the remainder of the collection over a four-year period, advertising it as "the largest Private Library, Collection of Engravings, etc., ever offered in this country."[23]

One 1844 inventory of the library conveys an idea of the extent and variety of Town's collection, as well as a sense of the place he designed for it. The appraisers listed page after page of general categories—"Chinese books," "Historic Gallery," "Aphorisms, Morals," "Epitaphs," "Emblems," "Emblems and Fables," "Ancient Armor," "Antique Gems"—alongside the identified architectural, historical, scientific, and fictional works. Portfolio prints numbering in the thousands were organized in lots and identified only as "portraits" or "lithography" or "architectural." Other lots included scrapbooks, maps, catalogues, boxes of seals, medals and minerals, various curiosities, woodcuts, "a drawer of coins, medals, seals and curiosities," copper plates, and cases of silver mathematical and drawing instruments. Finally, in despair, the appraiser listed "contents of bookcase" and "various curiosities in bookcases," boxes and cases of prints, and trunks of pamphlets. Besides its built-in shelves, the library was furnished with showcases, glass cases, wood pedestals, busts, two cupids, a Laocoön, and a model of the Parthenon. And this was only a partial catalogue of the fantastic rooms.[24]

Why Town chose to sell his library is unclear, but—as much as modern historians would benefit from the collection as a whole—its dispersal may have ultimately increased its influence over American culture. According to Town's biographer Roger Newton, the sale of the collection inspired James Lenox to begin his own library, which later became an important part of the New York Public Library.[25] It may have served as a similar motivating force for Augustus Street, who visited the library as a Yale art student and founded the Yale School of Fine Arts in 1864. Henry Austin, a student of Town's who remodeled the New Haven library after his death, assembled his own office library with books from his mentor's collection. The volumes of Pugin, probably those Tuthill consulted, are said to have been used in Austin's design for the Yale College Library, a building that Tuthill described and illustrated. It is impossible to know the extent of these influences. Most significant is the fact that the library was remembered for generations to come as both a useful reference collection and a marvelous place to visit.

That Tuthill did not see herself as the only woman writing about architecture may have been a result of working in Town's library. She cited "several valuable works in Europe" (perhaps by Anna Jameson, the English art historian) and the translation of Francesco Milizia's *Lives of the Architects* by Eliza Cresy as proof of women's contributions.[26] Madame de Staël's *Corrine,* which includes lengthy descriptions of ancient buildings and monuments accompanied by theoretical observations, was another influence. Tuthill included excerpts from both Jameson and de Staël in her *Young Lady's Reader,* published in 1839, when she was in the midst of her architectural research.[27]

Town had a personal reason to welcome women to his reading room. As the single father of a daughter, Etha, only eleven years younger than Tuthill, he realized the need to improve educational opportunities for women. He was listed as a patron in catalogues of the New Haven Female Seminary, the school Etha graduated from in 1825. The library inventory contains a reference to the "Lady's Dictionary" and "Lady's Portraits," volumes that may have been useless in Tuthill's research but indicate their owner's sensitivity to scholarly pursuits of the opposite sex. During his first European tour,

Town wrote to Etha of Robert Smirke's King's Library, with its "nearly 100,000 volumes in splendid bindings." He noted that the institution was "open to everybody three times a week and to artists every day," and even young ladies were welcome.[28]

Tuthill's *History* did not find space in "every family library"; although it was published simultaneously in England by John Chapman, there is no record of any contemporary reprintings.[29] The book was not heavily advertised before publication, noticed during the first year of issue, or purchased in quantities significant enough to require successive printings. Despite positive reviews in the *Princeton Review* and the *Literary World*, the *History* seems to have been ignored, even as many of Tuthill's other books went into multiple editions. Both reviewers admired Tuthill's effort, particularly as an American literary contribution, but neither was quite sure where to place the book in relation to the reading public.[30] Perhaps the novelty of subject, the author's gender, or the lack of practical purpose—except in its mission regarding taste—also affected the reviewers. Other books advertised in the *Literary World* included Downing's *Landscape Gardening* and *Cottage Residences,* George Wightwick's *Hints to Young Architects,* and *Gardening for Ladies* by Mrs. Loudon (John Claudius Loudon's wife)—all volumes with explicitly practical applications. Even though the *History* attempted to address the common American, it could not have seemed useful to the average man who might purchase Downing's *Residences* for building plans, and the typical lady may have considered the book a luxury beyond her means.[31]

Tuthill did find a broader market for her other work. She began her popular *Success in Life* series in the early 1850s and continued writing for young readers throughout the 1860s, producing such successes as *True Manliness or the Landscape Gardener* (1867). Meanwhile, she collected the work of the English art historian and critic John Ruskin. Tuthill had used selections from his writings in her *History,* and in 1859 she edited the first anthology of Ruskin published in America: *The True and the Beautiful in Nature, Arts, Morals and Religion,* which was reprinted twenty-three times. Two additional collections followed, the last published in 1878 when Tuthill was in her eightieth year.[32] As she explained in prefaces to her selections, she was most interested in making Ruskin's works available to the public in concise, inexpensive editions. Tuthill's lifework is a testament to her belief in the power of books to change people and the environment they build.[33]

In this day of revisionist history, when we find ourselves struggling to include women in our picture of the architectural profession, we benefit from a glance into Ithiel Town's library. Peer down through the six-foot-square skylight into the reading room: there's a woman studying architectural engravings, a Yale student reading in a corner, a reporter in a hoopskirt sizing up the place, and an art historian double-checking sources. Written records suggest that thanks to Ithiel Town, such a variety of people had access to the books and prints necessary to begin writing about the history of American architecture. Accounts of the library describe a place more like today's research libraries than that Victorian bastion of male privilege, the gentleman's smoke-filled study. It seems to have been a place where men *and* women shared the thoughts of the world's great philosophers and examined the artwork of the world's renowned artists. Certainly, the majority of New Haven was excluded from this privilege, but not white female bluestockings.

NOTES

1. Tuthill to Carey & Hart, 15 February 1841, Gratz Collection, Historical Society of Pennsylvania, Philadelphia.

2. Quoted in Louis Legrand Noble, *The Life and Works of Thomas Cole* (Cambridge, Mass.: Harvard University Press, 1964), 212–13.

3. N. P. Willis and W. H. Bartlett, *American Scenery* (London: George Virtue, 1840), includes a drawing by William Henry Bartlett of the famous group of buildings on New Haven green. On this phase of Town's architectural career, see William H. Pierson Jr., *American Buildings and Their Architects: Technology and the Picturesque* (Garden City, N.Y.: Anchor Books, 1980), 125–30.

4. Ithiel Town, *A Description of Ithiel Town's Improvement in the Construction of Wood and Iron Bridges* (New Haven, Conn.: S. Converse, 1821). An elevation and section of the bridge truss appeared on the cover of successive numbers of *Brother Jonathan* magazine in 1843. See "The Architects and Architecture of New York," *Brother Jonathan* 5, no. 9 (1843): 241–44, and no. 10 (1843): 271–74. The next article in the series featured domestic architecture and discussed "Mr. Town's method of rendering dwellings fire-proof, introducing a beautiful piece of architecture in the cut of his own house at New Haven, which contains his magnificent library, and which is perfectly fire-proof, without arched ceilings." See *Brother Jonathan* 5, no. 11 (1843): 1.

5. For further biographical details, see Roger H. Newton, *Town and Davis, Pioneers in Revivalist Architecture, 1812–1870* (New York: Columbia University Press, 1942); George Dudley Seymour, *New Haven* (New Haven, Conn.: By the Author, 1942); *Researches of an Antiquary: Five Essays on Early American Architects* (Boston: Houghton Mifflin, 1930); "Town, Ithiel," in *Dictionary of American Biography,* 19:610–11; Jane B. Davies, "Town, Ithiel," in *The Macmillian Encyclopedia of Architects,* ed. Adolf K. Placzek (New York: Free Press, 1982), 4:222.

6. See Talbot Hamlin, *Greek Revival Architecture in America* (New York: Oxford University Press, 1944).

7. Quoted in Jane B. Davies, "Alexander J. Davis, Creative American Architect," in *Alexander Jackson Davis, American Architect, 1803–1892,* ed. Amelia Peck (New York: Metropolitan Museum of Art, 1992), 18.

8. R. W. Liscombe, "A 'New Era in My Life': Ithiel Town Abroad," *Journal of the Society of Architectural Historians* 50 (March 1991): 12.

9. William Dunlap, *History of the Rise and Progress of the Arts of Design in the United States* (1834; reprint, New York: Benjamin Blom, 1965), 69.

10. Ithiel Town, *The Outlines of a Plan for Establishing in New-York, an Academy and Institution of the Fine Arts* (New York: George F. Hopkins, 1835). H. Allen Brooks has determined that the New Haven villa

was constructed in 1836–37; see his "Town's New Haven Villa," *Journal of the Society of Architectural Historians* 13 (March 1954): 27–28.

11. Lydia H. Sigourney, "Residence of Ithiel Town, Esq.," *Ladies Companion and Literary Expositor* 10 (1839): 123–27. Sigourney had visited the library at least once before deciding to "make it more known to the public." She asked Town for information on the number of volumes, engravings, and paintings, for a description of the rooms, and for a lithographic view of the library. She was also curious about "the incentives which first prompted to so great and meritorious a work." Sigourney to Town, 12 September 1838, manuscript collection, New Haven Colony Historical Society, New Haven, Conn.

12. Town to Sigourney, 21 January 1839, manuscript collection, Connecticut Historical Society, Hartford.

13. For more information about nineteenth-century New Haven, see Edward Atwater, ed., *History of the City of New Haven* (New York: Munsell, 1887); Elizabeth Mills Brown, *New Haven: A Guide to Architecture and Urban Design* (New Haven, Conn.: Yale University Press, 1976); Henrietta Silliman Dana, *Hillhouse Avenue from 1809–1900* (1900; reprint, New Haven, Conn.: Tuttle, Morehouse & Taylor, 1907); Ellen Strong Bartlett, *Historical Sketches of New Haven* (New Haven, Conn.: Tuttle, Morehouse & Taylor, 1897); Rollin G. Osterweis, *Three Centuries of New Haven, 1638–1938* (New Haven, Conn.: Yale University Press, 1953).

14. For further details of Tuthill's life and work, see Sarah Allaback, " 'To the Painter, the Poet, the Sculptor, and the Novelist': Louisa Tuthill's Architectural Writings," *Nineteenth Century* 12 (1993): 9–12; and Sarah Allaback, "Cultivating Architectural Taste in Nineteenth-Century America: The Architectural Writings of Louisa Caroline Tuthill" (Ph.D. diss., Massachusetts Institute of Technology, 1993).

15. Cornelius Tuthill was one of "a fraternity of gentlemen" who edited this short-lived biweekly journal. Several anonymous articles are attributed to Tuthill in the American Antiquarian Society's edition of *The Microscope* 1 (1820): "Although wit has . . . ," 37; "Perhaps you were . . . ," 85; "We have already . . . ," 109; the poem on 136; "Through the medium . . . ," 152; and "In the seventeenth . . . ," 189.

16. An engraving of the "Indra Subba, at Ellora" by Nathaniel and Simeon Jocelyn appeared on the title page of Tuthill's *Ancient Architecture* (and as plate 3 of her *History*). The authorship of this "small quarto of seventy-four pages beautifully illustrated" has been mistakenly attributed to its publisher, Hezekiah Howe of New Haven; see John Frelinghuysen Hageman, *History of Princeton and Its Institutions* (Philadelphia: Lippincott, 1879), 402. It is listed under Howe's name also in Hitchcock's *American Architectural Books* (1962) and the National Union Catalogue.

17. John S. Hart provided this description of the origins of Tuthill's literary career. His biographical sketch in John S. Hart, *Female Prose Writers of America* (Philadelphia: E. H. Butler, 1852), 100–104, was based on a letter from Tuthill in response to his inquiries about her work: Tuthill to John S. Hart, 1 February 1851, Rare Book Collection, Boston Public Library. A shortened version of Hart's Tuthill entry appeared twenty years later in John S. Hart, *A Manual of American Literature* (1872; reprint, New York: Johnson Reprint, 1969), 310.

18. Louisa Tuthill, *History of Architecture from the Earliest Times* (Philadelphia: Lindsay & Blakiston, 1848), viii.

19. Tuthill to Carey & Hart, 15 February 1841. Her comments regarding high-quality illustrations suggest the aspirations she held for the *History:* "There are no artists in this state whose woodcuts are sufficiently accurate and spirited to illustrate such a work. The facilities which you enjoy, for bringing out a Book of this kind, in a fine style, are superior, I am told, to those of most other publishers in the Union."

20. For example, Tuthill included plates of Bute and Glenn Cottages and wood engravings of small rustic buildings from William Bailey Lang's *Views, with Ground Plans, of the Highland Cottages at Roxbury, (Near Boston)* (Boston: L. H. Bridgham & H. E. Felch, 1845). These contemporary views were originally drawn by Hammatt Billings and may have been re-engraved by William Dreser of the Philadelphia firm Dreser and Edward Robyn. Dreser and Robyn completed the eight signed wood engravings of recent

American buildings that illustrate the *History*. The wood engravings of English domestic architecture were taken from an 1842 supplement to John Claudius Loudon, *An Encyclopaedia of Cottage, Farm, and Villa Architecture* (London: Longman, 1832). They are as follows: "A Villa in the Swiss Style," *Encyclopaedia*, 1185 (*History*, 280); "The Home Lodge at Chequers Court," *Encyclopaedia*, 1173 (*History*, 275 and 279, north and east elevations); "Cottage," *Encyclopaedia*, 1164 (*History*, 276).

21. Plate 32, "Entrance to the Cemetery at New Haven," engraved by William Dreser.

22. Tuthill, *Success in Life: The Artist* (Cincinnati: Derby, 1854), 86.

23. Liscombe, "New Era in My Life," 12.

24. "A True and Perfect Inventory of all the Goods . . . ," 1844, Ithiel Town Papers, New Haven Colony Historical Society, New Haven.

25. Newton, *Town and Davis*, 19–20.

26. Tuthill to Carey & Hart, referring to the translation by Mrs. Edward Cresy (Eliza) of Francesco Milizia, *The Lives of Celebrated Architects*, vol. 1 (London: J. Taylor Architectural Library, 1826).

27. "Corinne at the Capitol" and "Female Authorship" by Madame de Stael and "Semiramis" by Anna Jameson appeared in Tuthill, *The Young Lady's Reader: Arranged for Examples in Rhetoric for the Higher Classes in Seminaries* (New Haven: S. Babcock, 1839).

28. Liscombe, "New Era in My Life," 8.

29. See Sampson Low, ed., *The English Catalogue of Books Published from Jan. 1835, Jan. 1863* (1865; reprint, New York: Kraus Reprint, 1963), 787.

30. *Princeton Review* 20 (April 1848): 320–21; *Literary World* 2 (15 January 1848): 579.

31. In Orville Roorbach's *Bibliotheca Americana: Catalogue of American Publications, from 1820–1848* (New York: Orville A. Roorbach, 1849), 282, the *History* is listed as selling for $3.50. Many of Tuthill's juvenile books are listed at under fifty cents each and the *Success in Life* series at sixty-three cents each.

32. Sarah Josepha Hale considered her friend Mrs. Tuthill an expert on Ruskin and in a letter of 1 September 1866 requested her "written criticism" on "Ruskin's last work" (see "unidentified" letters in the Tuthill Family Papers, Bancroft Library, University of California at Berkeley). Hale was referring to Ruskin's *Ethics of the Dust: Ten Lectures to Little Housewives on the Elements of Crystallisation* (London: Smith, Elder, 1866).

33. Many of the excerpts from Loudon's *Architectural Magazine* included in the *History* were bylined "Kata Phusin," actually a young Oxford student named John Ruskin. See, e.g., Kata Phusin, "The Poetry of Architecture. No. 3. The Villa," *Architectural Magazine* 5 (June 1838): 241–42, in Tuthill, *History, 277*. Tuthill quoted Ruskin's *Seven Lamps of Architecture* in *Success in Life: The Artist, 73*. The first edition of *The True and the Beautiful* was followed by a second and third, published by John Wiley; the third was reprinted almost every year up to 1890. Another New York publishing house, H. M. Caldwell Company, issued an edition in 1886 and a reprint in 1896. Merrill & Baker of New York also introduced a second edition at this time. Tuthill's other Ruskin collections were *Precious Thoughts: Moral and Religious. Gathered from the Works of John Ruskin, A. M.* (first published by Wiley in 1866 and reprinted in 1867, 1868, 1869, 1872, 1877, 1879, 1881, and 1884; a second edition was issued in 1890, which both Merrill & Baker and H. M. Caldwell reprinted in the 1890s), and *Pearls for Young Ladies* (simultaneously published by Wiley, Caldwell, T. Y. Crowell, and Merrill & Baker in 1878; Wiley reprinted it the next year and introduced a second edition in 1890).

CONTRIBUTORS

SARAH ALLABACK is an independent scholar with a doctorate in architectural history from MIT. She has written about the life and writings of Louisa Tuthill and the development of architectural education for women. Allaback is currently a consultant for the National Park Service in Denver.

BENNIE BROWN holds a master's degree in Art History and Architecture from the University of Georgia. He was the curator-librarian at Gunston Hall from 1974 to 1985 and there established a research program and rare book and reference center for the study of the colonial period. He is currently working on a comprehensive catalogue of art, architectural, gardening, and farming books in Virginia before 1840.

JEFFREY A. COHEN is an architectural historian specializing in nineteenth-century American topics. He has published studies of Benjamin Latrobe, Frank Furness, early architectural drawings, and architectural schools. He teaches in the Growth and Structure of Cities Program at Bryn Mawr College.

ABBOTT LOWELL CUMMINGS is Charles F. Montgomery Professor Emeritus of American Decorative Arts at Yale University, whose faculty he joined after a distinguished career as director of the Society for the Preservation of New England Antiquities. He is the author of many works, including a standard study, *The Framed Houses of Massachusetts Bay, 1625–1725*.

ROBERT F. DALZELL JR. is Ephraim Williams Professor of History at Williams College. He is author of *Enterprising Elite: The Boston Associates and the World They Made; Daniel Webster and the Trial of American Nationalism, 1843–1852;* and, most recently, in collaboration with his wife, Lee B. Dalzell, *George Washington's Mount Vernon: At Home in Revolutionary America.*

KENNETH HAFERTEPE holds a doctorate in American Civilization from the University of Texas at Austin. The former director of academic programs at Historic Deerfield, Inc., he is now assistant professor of museum studies and director of academic programs at the Strecker Museum, Baylor University. Among his many publications are *America's Castle: The Evolution of the Smithsonian Building and Its Institution* (1984), and *Abner Cook: Master Builder on the Texas Frontier* (1992).

MICHAEL J. LEWIS teaches American art and architecture at Williams College. He studied at the University of Pennsylvania, where he received his doctorate in 1989, and at the University of Hannover. He is the author of *The Politics of the German Gothic Revival,* which won the Alice Davis Hitchcock Award of the Society of Architectural Historians.

MARTHA MCNAMARA, assistant professor of history at the University of Maine, received her Ph.D. in American Studies at Boston University in 1995. She is the author of *Courthouse Spaces: Architecture, Law, and Professionalism in Massachusetts, 1658–1860,* forthcoming from The Johns Hopkins University Press. She is coeditor of *Maine History,* and serves on the board of the Maine Historic Preservation Commission.

JAMES F. O'GORMAN is Grace Slack McNeil Professor of the History of American Art at Wellesley College and co-convener of the Deerfield-Wellesley Symposium on American Culture. He is the author of *ABC of Architecture* (1998), as well as numerous books and articles on nineteenth-century American architecture and architectural drawings.

DAMIE STILLMAN is John W. Shirley Professor of Art History Emeritus at the University of Delaware. The author of *English Neo-Classical Architecture* and *The Decorative Work of Robert Adam,* as well as articles on English and American Neoclassicism, he is currently at work on a book about the architecture of the Federal period, *Neo-Classicism in America: The Architecture of the Young Republic.* He is also editor in chief of Buildings of the United States, a series of volumes on the architecture of each state.

RICHARD GUY WILSON, Commonwealth Professor of Architectural History at the University of Virginia, has written widely on many aspects of American and modern architecture and art from Thomas Jefferson to postmodernism. Among his publications are contributions to *The American Renaissance, The Machine Age in America,* and various other publications dealing with the arts and crafts movement.

CHARLES B. WOOD III has been since 1967 an antiquarian bookseller with a special interest in early architectural books. Earlier, he was employed by the Winterthur Museum and the New Hampshire Historical Society. He was educated at Trinity College, Hartford, and the University of Pennsylvania.

INDEX